Language Narratives and Shifting Multilingual Pedagogies

Multilingualisms and Diversities in Education Series

Editors: Kathleen Heugh, Christopher Stroud and Piet Van Avermaet

Multilingualism and diversity are fast becoming defining characteristics of global education. This is because human mobility has increased exponentially over the past two decades, bringing about an increase in socioeconomic, cultural and faith-based diversity with consequences for citizenship, identity, education and practices of language and literacy (among others).
The Multilingualisms and Diversities in Education series takes a global perspective on twenty-first century societal diversities. It looks at the languages through which these diversities are conveyed, and how they are changing the theoretical foundations and practices of formal and non-formal education. Multilingualisms and diversities in this series are understood as dynamic and variable phenomena, processes and realities. They are viewed alongside classroom practices (including curriculum, assessment, methodologies), teacher development (pre- and in-service; and in non-formal education), theory-building, research and evaluation, and policy considerations.

Volumes in the series articulate the opportunities and challenges afforded by contemporary diversities and multilingualisms across global settings at local, national and international levels. A distinctive aim of the series is to provide a platform for reciprocal exchanges of expertise among stakeholders located in different southern and northern contexts.

Also Available in the Series:
Engaging with Linguistic Diversity, David Little and Déirdre Kirwan
Language and Decoloniality in Higher Education, edited by Zannie Bock and Christopher Stroud

Forthcoming in the Series:
Multilingual Pedagogies in Practice, Mei French

Front Cover: Student-painted mural at the Wits School of Education, which is the research site for this project. The mural captures the spirit of democracy and diversity in post-apartheid South Africa.

Language Narratives and Shifting Multilingual Pedagogies

English Teaching from the South

Belinda Mendelowitz, Ana Ferreira and Kerryn Dixon

BLOOMSBURY ACADEMIC
LONDON • NEW YORK • OXFORD • NEW DELHI • SYDNEY

BLOOMSBURY ACADEMIC
Bloomsbury Publishing Plc
50 Bedford Square, London, WC1B 3DP, UK
1385 Broadway, New York, NY 10018, USA
29 Earlsfort Terrace, Dublin 2, Ireland

BLOOMSBURY, BLOOMSBURY ACADEMIC and the Diana logo are trademarks of
Bloomsbury Publishing Plc

First published in Great Britain 2023

Cover design: Grace Ridge
Cover image © Chris Anderson

A catalogue record for this book is available from the British Library.

A catalog record for this book is available from the Library of Congress.

ISBN: HB: 978-1-3501-6591-5
ePDF: 978-1-3501-6592-2
eBook: 978-1-3501-6593-9

Series: Multilingualisms and Diversities in Education

Typeset by Deanta Global Publishing Services, Chennai, India

To find out more about our authors and books visit www.bloomsbury.com and sign up for
our newsletters.

To all our students who have shared their stories.

Contents

Illustrations

Figures

Tables

Foreword

Belinda Mendelowitz, Ana Ferreira and Kerryn Dixon's book, *Language Narratives and Shifting Multilingual Pedagogies: English Teaching from the South*, comes to us at a time when we are – and we need to face this – more than a little confused about the world in which we live. We are disorientated. Our confusion, however, takes acute expression here in this so-called southern part of the globe, this place called South Africa. It presents itself at multiple levels: the social, the personal and everything in-between. It is both existential and practical: how we comport ourselves, how we decide who is friend and who is foe, the daily choices we make in how we live and whether we shall go or stay. We do not trust our politicians. Our established institutions – religious, educational and juridical, from which, historically, we draw succour and guidance – stand in timid anxiety, almost mute. Civil society, long the place in which we were able to think and struggle against the apartheid machine, is in disarray organizationally. At stake is persistent and constantly evolving injustice. The injustice is physical and material – unconscionable privilege – perched on unimaginable misery. The inequality is searing. It is into this malaise, and how inadequate that word is, that Mendelowitz, Ferreira and Dixon boldly and with foresight step with this book.

But what is the malaise and what does *Language Narratives and Shifting Multilingual Pedagogies* do for our management of it?

Looking at ourselves from a distance, as we academics seek to do, we are transfixed by the complexity playing itself out in front of us. Transfixion, however, brings little relief. We are struggling. With many things. But particularly with the affordances and limitations of the languages we have at our disposal, their definitional and categorical uses and their accompanying framing and sense-making functions. This is our first take-away from *Language Narratives and Shifting Multilingual Pedagogies*. It seeks to foreground the creativity latent and active in the multilingual repertoires of the everyday and how they open up pathways for coming to look at ourselves in new and generative ways.

Looking at ourselves more closely and immediately, sitting as we do right inside South Africa's daily rhythms and routines, our moods swing from extreme nausea and paranoia to, now less so than perhaps twenty years ago, fleeting moments of euphoria. Reading South Africa's mind, the psychologist Wahbie

Long (2021) describes it as being in a generalized state of alienation. Alienation is best described for him as 'a relation of relationlessness'.

I prefer the simpler characterization of disorientation to Long's 'alienation'. Socially and psychologically. It is less disabling. We are never outside of relationships. They have within them, always, possibility, even in our states of disorientation. Pre-eminent about possibility, is what Gilles Deleuze (1994) suggested in *Difference and Repetition* – the condition of *becoming*, self-creation, the refusal of imitation. 'Alienation' as a framing device traps us in the categorical networks of our representational thought. Those of 'race' and gender in the main. There are others. 'Race' and gender, however, inhabit the cellular structure of the languages we have learnt for presenting ourselves to ourselves and to others in ways that occlude the endless modes, assemblages and forms our identities might and can take. They present themselves as the foundational ways through which, and against which all becoming – self-creation – issues and is possible. Against this fixity, against the idea that our destinies are stitched into our beings – forever racialized and gendered – I ask that we give ourselves the permission to think beyond our dominant representational repertoires. Beyond the singularities of our racial orders and gender compulsions which come to provide alienation with its 'empirical' foundations. Disorientation concedes the reality of positionality, including that of alienation. It requires, however, agency – the will to act. And we do act. Our actions are not all socially and psychologically positive. But they represent the possibility that is always with. We are required, however, to be deliberative about the possibilities that arise for us and that we will make for ourselves. This is the second important take-away that *Language Narratives* offers us. Our language differences move us to act and enter into new and uncomfortable positions. With the help of their lecturers we see in this text how the students manage their discomfort. It is not always political correctness which ensues but there is evidence of thinking.

How do these offerings come to us?

The book is, in the first instance, about the field of sociolinguistics. Second, it is about curriculum and pedagogy. It is also about sociology itself, psychology, cultural studies, history and politics. The history and politics it provides bears, of course, on South Africa, but has powerful resonance for the discussion of difference almost anywhere in the world. Its wider significance lies in how the field of sociolinguistics, and here narrative pedagogy is the medium, can be worked with to provide an educational experience which is generative for both the individual and the wider society in which he/she/they function. It is this on which I focus in this foreword.

The sociolinguistic concern of *Language Narratives* is essentially about the dominance of English in a landscape of lived multilingual diversity. It comes in the wake of a regular stream of writing on language and multilingualism in South Africa (see, for example, Hibbert 2016 and McKinney 2017). The sustained focus of this corpus is how power is mediated through language. It reflects the place linguistics has arrived at in South Africa. While there remains an interest in philology and comparative linguistics, many South African linguistic scholars are concentrating their attention on how languages of dominance, English largely, can be worked with, engaged and confronted to support the project of democracy. The point of arrival is decidedly an engagement with dominant western approaches to linguistics. The contribution of *Language Narratives* in this company is to work substantively and analytically with the voice and insights of a distinctive segment of South Africa's multilingual landscape – preservice teachers, many of whom are setting out to be teachers of English. They are the students in the introductory sociolinguistics course developed by Mendelowitz, Ferreira and Dixon at Wits University, which has been offered every year since 2005 and has had something around 5,000 students pass through its portals. The students are distinctive in that their lecturers engage in a scholarly discussion with them about learning to teach the very thing which they all come to understand is the cause of many of the difficulties through which they and members of the communities from which they come are going. They are all, including the authors themselves, required to think and offer comment about what they are learning and doing with this incendiary language in their mouths and heads. There is, as a result, a critical edge in their reflections. They are aware of how power works and is distributed in the social networks they inhabit.

We have a lot to learn from these reflections – both those of the authors and of their students. The students' reflections are presented four times in the text as stand-alone segments. The very first entry is memorable. It has a student named Thapang, a graduate of the very first offering of the course, reflect on the impact of the course and gives one a sense of how informed multilingual South African subjects are talking about the linguistic space in which they find themselves. He/she/they speaks of a ride in a taxi, squeezed next 'to a big mama', not daring to nag, because if you did, you wouldn't want to find out what her response might be. And so he/she/they say, '(t)hose kinds of expressions make it easier to pick the language because they give you experiences you'll never forget. So, just sit and enjoy the sound of the eleven languages in a 15-passenger taxi. Smelling the cocktail mixture of armpit stench is the price you pay to enter the club of the polyglots' (Mendelowitz, Ferreira and Dixon, p. 1). The objective of the lecturers was to help their students develop a political awareness of their teaching: 'our pedagogic aim . . . (was to) embed (. . .) this sociolinguistic knowledge in real life worlds by having students' own embodied worlds come into the classroom and take their place alongside those of their peers and others' (p. 37). This awareness is evident in Thapang's reflection. It is not uncritical. The stench offends. It is, however, marked by a sense of amazement. Thapang accepts the 'everywhereness' of this multilingual landscape and revels in its sensuous sonic wonder.

Important about the way the authors use the narratives they gather is to emphasize how much speakers of language 'know and be, think and feel in the same moments' (p. 50), making possible, and this is the value of working with socially aware subjects, inner conversations with themselves which 'enable new relations with the world, possibilities to imagine alternatives' (p. 53). The sociolinguistic here segues into critical sociological and psychological ways of seeing. It offers important frames through which the subjects come to think of themselves and their situations.

In these sociological and psychological framings, interestingly, new subjectivities present themselves. Representationally 'race' and gender mark their points of departure. They are not quite able to escape from their clutches, but they consciously resist the categorical identities towards which they are steered. And they do so in a number of ways. It is this multiplicity of orientations that is important to take heed of in this text. As the students respond to their lecturers they deliberately and repeatedly confound their own racial and gender emplacements. With respect to 'race' they regularly and predictably seize and affirm outright atavistic positions. A Zulu forever – bone and marrow. Their home languages stir them like nothing else can. In this they take position against the presumptuousness of English – only, however, to invert its logics. Ontologically they subsist in the compulsions of categorical centredness. Without it – centredness – they believe that they are nothing. But often, too, atavism with all of its claims to authenticity, mean little for them. Their worldliness, contained in the English which they have come to appropriate, is unapologetically what they are all about. A return to a different centredness happens here. It is, however, creative. It wants relief from the grip of dominance.

With respect to gender their resistance is equally innovative. It is evident in their storytelling styles. One is not able to tell whether the narrator of a story is male or female. Students who are designated female enter and occupy male personalities with flair and verve. They call out, however, the patriarchal ugliness which pervades the everyday and in the process offer an implicit counter-pedagogical approach to how learning about power works and how it might be challenged.

Evident in these two glosses on 'race' and gender is the central value I draw from the book. An invitation to join the process of *re-orientating* ourselves. We have in the students' voices powerful examples of how this can be done, affectively and rationally. Nonhlanhla, in the closing meta-voice final segment of the book, explains to us, eloquently, how this worked for her:

> I am always, always aware and conscious of how the kids that I teach relate to English, because . . . English is seen as a whip. . . . I say, 'Do you realise that you can actually own English and make English your own? You've always done that.' I give them examples that, for example, when you speak in a way . . . you actually change some English words to make them relevant to you . . . that is your own that you've made. But now once you do that, find out what the standard word is for that is so that you can know about your own creation and the standardised. And in that way they are able to get more excited about any English, they will throw those words around . . . we actually terrorise English, we take it down, we call it words, we give it names, and then we bring it up today and we make it our own. I say 'Okay, now English can be our friend.' That's what the sociolinguistics module made me more conscious about. (p. 187)

We are invited in *Language Narratives* to join these critical interlocutors, people like Nonhlanhla, primed to think about their situations, and to ask how we ourselves might contribute to this extraordinary civilizational challenge of finding our way out of the morass in which we find ourselves.

Crain Soudien

Series Editors' Foreword

We are delighted to be able to offer this volume as a key text in Bloomsbury's Multilingualisms and Diversities in Education. The intent of the series is to offer cutting-edge research on multilingualism, diversity and education that spans a broad range of readership, from practitioners to policy makers, from researchers and academics to students and learners in the North and the South. This volume succeeds in delivering a text of immense value to each of these audiences by bringing solid theory and meticulous methodology to bear on everyday practicalities of the classroom in turbulent (and troubled) multilingual contexts, while also addressing (more indirectly) questions of (educational) policy. It is a magnificent volume, carefully researched, accessibly written and with excellent materials. We particularly appreciate the volume being based in a long-term ethnography/action research engagement covering sixteen years. This is an exemplar of an unhurried, deeply reflective and reflexive process of praxis that Freire brought to education.

The text was designed to address the preparation of teachers of English in an avowedly multilingual country, in which most students have not come from homes or communities in which English is their primary or first language. The nature of this course, set in the field of sociolinguistics, is clearly essential in a programme for the preparation of teachers and is thus equally relevant in both educational linguistics and applied linguistics – where the teaching of language/s and teacher education are key concerns. The research is foregrounded with a careful laying out of the macro-historical context of South Africa and layered through many opportunities where the data offers voices of students reflecting on long-term engagements with social and racial language trauma. The authors extend an unparalleled, carefully reflective tracing of narratives in role plays and critical meta-commentaries throughout. These are narratives in which newly acquired linguistics' knowledge is constructively deployed by students and lecturers, jointly assisting or inducting them into critical awareness of language. In particular, we learn of ways in which multilingualism forms the subjectivities of the students over time, and how language in general is closely entwined with everyday socio-political and historical contingencies in which they live. The complexity of their languaging is made evident for the students through their role plays and own reflections on language use. There are many sharp and vital points made in the volume, but the authors finally decide to focus by way of conclusion on whether the module delivered to the students is what the team had hoped to accomplish. The final chapter approaches this question in an innovative way, by letting students' voices tell what they had gained from the module in lieu of a more prosaic and traditionally academic 'Discussion and Conclusion'.

The southern focus is clear in the references the authors make to the sociohistorical and materials context, as well as the heterogeneity of the SA school class. Although the module was designed and carried through before 'the decolonial turn' in applied and sociolinguistics, much of its ethos and intent resonates strongly with more recent decolonial work, and the authors attempt to reflect on how the assumptions of their study articulate a decolonial agenda. Despite the southern focus, readers will see how the work (a labour of love) relates to context in Europe and North America, as well as the postcolonial world. They will appreciate the links the authors make between a wider body of literature, including narratives, and approaches that explore implications for teacher education beyond the mainstream Anglosphere in Europe, and to the conversations that have been occurring between southern and northern scholars over the last few years.

Among its many merits, a particular value of the manuscript is that it has relevance for the teaching of and through English in higher education (EMI) with implications that are likely to resonate where other languages of wider communication serve a similar function in both higher and school education. Given the expansion of EMI to many postcolonial/southern contexts in recent years, this volume has particular significance and will resonate with many teacher educators in almost every part of the world.

To conclude: This is an excellent text, one that will be particularly useful in multiple courses and programmes in which a decolonizing stance has become both inevitable and necessary. We are delighted to have this in the series.

Acknowledgements

This book has been many years in the making. It would not be possible without the stories our students have shared with us over the years, and their generous permission to include their language narratives, as well as their participation in focus groups.

In the same way that it takes a village to raise a child, it takes an academic village to write a book. There are many people we would like to thank for their different roles in inspiring, supporting and encouraging us to write this book.

All three of us were graduates of the Applied English Language Studies Department's postgraduate programme. Our experiences in this environment have had a huge impact on our intellectual trajectories, particularly our thinking about language and social justice as social practices.

We have co-taught this course with many different colleagues over the years. We would like to express our gratitude to them for their contributions, their input and insightful conversations: Leketi Makalela, Harriet Davis, Vis Moodley, Toni Gennrich, Hilary Wilson, Alison Beynon, Rika van der Merwe, Kathy Mabin, Nhlanhla Maake, Jean Reid, Ilse Fouche and Fatima Vally Essa. In the early years of developing this course, it was enriched by the generous sharing of resources and ideas by our colleague Peter Plüddeman, who was at PRAESA (Project for the Study of Alternative Education in South Africa) at the time.

We have been incredibly fortunate to have generous colleagues and friends who made time amidst their own busy schedules to read and give critical feedback on draft chapters – thank you so much! You became the audience that we imagined as we revised our chapters. In particular we would like to thank the following people: Andrew Brouard, Andrea Parmegiani, Navan Govender, Karen Lazar, Pinky Makoe, Grant Andrews, Fatima Vally Essa, Talia Barbeli, Laura Dison, Dominic Griffiths, Maria Prozesky, Toni Gennrich, Werner Paetzold, Sarah Godsell, Jamie Martin, Nelson Sweetnam, Michelle Mendelowitz, Sean Ramsden and Mwenya Kabwe. We also want to thank the following people who assisted us with questions about language varieties, translations and appropriate usage: Grant Coltman, Mongezi Bolofo, Neo Ramoupi, Ntsoaki Mokala, Gertrude Phakati, Corin Mathews and the late Manono Mdluli. A special thanks to Ingrid Sapire for her assistance with statistical analysis in Chapter 1 and Lee Rusznyak who shared her extensive institutional knowledge with us. We express gratitude to our colleagues in the Literacies, Languages and Literatures department for their generous support and encouragement throughout this process, including their responses to various questions on the WhatsApp group at odd hours.

We thank the University of the Witwatersrand for granting Belinda and Ana sabbaticals to write this book and the Humanities Faculty book completion grant for their generous support.

We would like to thank the series editors and commissioning editor Maria Giovanna Brauzzi for their enthusiasm and belief in the project from the outset and all the way through.

A special thanks to Chris Anderson for the cover page photograph, Yvonne Reed for insightful editing, Fatima Vally Essa for her efficient and insightful contribution to organizing and coding the data and Sean Ramsden for helping us put the manuscript together. All errors in the book of course remain ours.

And our final thanks go to long-suffering family and friends for their support and their understanding of our absences.

The authors gratefully acknowledge the permission granted for the re-use of material from the following publications:

Mendelowitz, B. (2017), 'Conceptualising and Enacting the Critical Imagination Through a Critical Writing Pedagogy', *English Teaching: Practice & Critique*, 16 (2): 178–93.

Orlek, J. (1993), *Languages in South Africa*, Johannesburg: Hodder & Stoughton and Wits University Press (courtesy of the Orlek Estate).

Earlier versions of the work presented in Chapters 4 and 5 have appeared in the following open-source journals:

Mendelowitz, B. and Dixon, K. (2016), 'Risky Writing: Working with a Heteroglossic Pedagogy to Deepen Preservice Teachers' Learning', *Perspectives in Education*, 34 (1): 120–34.

Mendelowitz, B. and Ferreira, A. (2007), 'Engaging Narratives: Using Language Biographies to Facilitate Learning', *Southern African Linguistics and Applied Language Studies*, 25 (4): 487–504.

Every effort has been made to trace copyright holders and to obtain their permission for the use of copyright material. However, if any have been inadvertently overlooked, the publishers will be pleased, if notified of any omissions, to make the necessary arrangement at the first opportunity.

Voices I

Where I come from, it's inescapable. It's everywhere you turn. It's in your face. You run away, it runs with you. There is no use complaining really – you've got to live with it. In the morning taxi, while squeezed next to the big mama, looking at her stare, looking down at my lean body, I dare not nag. Those Zulu eyes were put there for a reason, and you wouldn't want to find out what. The mouth – you don't want it opened. If shouted at, the sound will stay with you the whole day. Those kinds of expressions make it easier to pick the language because they give you experiences you'll never forget. So, just sit and enjoy the sound of eleven languages in a 15-passenger taxi. Smelling the cocktail mixture of armpit stench is the price you pay to enter the club of the polyglots.

Thapang, 2005

I am a Zulu girl who lives in a multiracial society. I am a model made of spears, shields, clan names, rituals and, most importantly, the power that my tongue has. IsiZulu flows in my veins just like the Blood River in KwaZulu Natal. Language has once upon a time been cruel and excluded me; however, this has impacted on my linguistic identity.

Sibongile, 2018

Being coloured we are regarded as cultureless. I've believed that for a long time, but recently discovered that I have as much of a culture as the next person.

Shireen, 2006

My language, Setswana, was carefully molded like ships by our forefathers, to transport culture, heritage, knowledge and, most importantly, identity.

Modise, 2020

I was born in a very simple world: a world of tradition, Mandarin, and when I did wrong, Taiwanese. For six years I existed in this medium until without warning I was thrust into 'School'. This was a new place with a new language and at my inexperienced age it was something I could not handle. I did not understand what the frightening adults wanted me to do and I did not understand what my peers said. Looking back I realize that the words they threw at me, although nonsensical, were as sharp daggers in my heart, as I could understand their body language. I spoke no English. I was different. And thus, I was the enemy.

Jai Li, 2008

Arabic is a language that holds a lot of significance in the life of every Muslim just as it does in mine. It has from the day I was born and my cousin recited the Athan in my ear. I remember my mother teaching me the Arabic prayers and verses when I was a young girl. Before going to bed each night my mother would sit next to me and recite a verse of the prayers and I would follow her lead till we completed the full prayer.

Ameera, 2018

When I lingo with my family, it brings us closer together. We express our intense excitement over a tawwe *game or* rugga *with an* yskoue bier *in one hand and a piece of biltong in the other. We* gooi 'n braai *on the weekend and* langarm *the night away. And still, when I am alone with only my thoughts to converse with, I write in Afrikaans. Sometimes* properste *Afrikaans or often just* kombuistaal. *I find there to be no better way in which I can express myself but by reaching deep within my very essence of being. I am a love child of Afrikaans.*

Hanneli, 2008

Introduction

This book is the story of a sixteen-year longitudinal study of an English-language course at a university in the Global South. At its heart are the stories of the first-year education students who have journeyed through the course with us. It is a story in which the past, present and future are entangled.

This book is located in the past. It looks back over a sixteen-year process of teaching and researching a first-year course introducing sociolinguistics to Bachelor of Education (B.Ed.) students, many of whom were planning to be English teachers. It is the story of what happened with a germ of an idea about the potential of narrative as a pedagogical tool to navigate the educational landscape and realities of a post-apartheid world in South Africa. This idea was accompanied by a conviction that teachers of English needed greater awareness of the politics of language if they were to teach in multilingual contexts. Stories have narrators, and this book is partly shaped by our younger selves, who were excited about the prospect of designing a course with student narratives at its centre.

This book is also located in the present. It is written by our older selves, who realize that being able to write a book based on a sixteen-year-long story of a course is a privilege. In a world characterized by large-scale change at global and local levels, very little stays the same. This is true in the broader educational landscape in South Africa, in higher education and in our own institution, where curriculum reform feels incessant and worryingly normalized and research is bound up in performativity agendas. To be able to design, teach, develop, think about and refine a course over time, in collaboration with multiple colleagues – and to maintain the core principles of language teaching with which we began – is unusual. In this present moment we think it is important to tell the story of what we term 'a narrative heteroglossic pedagogy' – a pedagogy that has emerged from working in the Global South.

This book is an example of what Liebowitz and Bozalek (2018) refer to as Slow scholarship of the south. 'Slow' does not refer to speed or duration, although duration is a strength of this work, but staying with the work, in the now. Slow scholarship is about maintaining an open-ended and deliberate depth of engagement that works across disciplines and ideas, eschewing economic expedience. Its value in southern contexts, Liebowitz and Bozalek (2018: 984) argue, is about 'repoliticising and reinvigorating everyday practice in academia'. In this book we do this by countering a monoglossic ideology, which, Menezes de Sousa (2021) argues, comprises an 'unmarked' Eurocentric knowledge that erases experiences, histories, bodies and knowledges of the 'marked' other. Rather, in considering issues of language and pedagogy we work affirmatively with the rich everyday experiences in the multilingual contexts our students inhabit. This work is 'situated, affective and embodied' (Liebowitz and Bozalek 2018: 984) and it is important to unpack the pedagogical, demographic, political and theoretical shifts that have taken place over the life of the course; to acknowledge that decisions about the acquisition and production of knowledge were not static or linear and the ways in which working with narratives gives students voice and agency.

This book is also located in the future. Our past selves wished there had been a book to guide us when we were beginning to think about ways in which we could work productively with linguistic diversity. Sixteen years on from where we started, despite the research in sociolinguistics that challenges traditional views of languages as 'bounded', van Avermaet et al. (2018) argue that educational programmes remain aligned to this perspective. In addition, there is also insufficient work in the language education literature that considers the educational implications of valuing young people's complex linguistic repertoires and multilingual practices (see Little and Kirwan (2020) for a successful example). As teacher educators whose students will teach diverse multilingual cohorts, considering the ways in which multilingual pedagogies are enacted in higher education and can be taken up by teachers is critical. It concerns us that teacher education programmes across the world do not adequately prepare students to work with cultural and linguistic diversity or value the multilingual resources teachers themselves have (see for example Conteh's (2018) work in England, and Scaglioni and Caruana's (2018) review of practices in southern Europe). This is of greater concern considering the need for education systems to be responsive to unprecedented levels of global mobility and displacement due to conflict and climate change. One of our aims in writing this book has been to provide an example of what did not exist for us, by bringing theory and practice in teacher education together: to crack open the workings of course design, pedagogy, content, theory and student needs. The process of cracking things open is not about looking for finite answers or neat endings. It is about the ongoing process of new becomings as new ways of thinking, teaching and researching multilingualism in complex contexts of diversity. We hope that readers of this book will find ideas that are useful for their own practices, that provide ways of working against normalized monoglossic views of language, that encourage the telling of new stories about language in education and create ongoing conversations in the field. In a period when there is greater recognition of perspectives from the south, we hope that the student stories presented here are examples of the richness that come from engaging with all students.

It is important to state at the outset that we speak *from* the south, and not *for* the south. The place from which we speak, or the locus of enunciation, reflects both a 'geo-political location' and a 'body-political location' (Grosfoguel 2007). Geo-politically the history and politics of South Africa shape what it means to write from this southern location. We write from an urban space, that of Johannesburg, whose existence as a city was predicated on colonial greed for mineral resources. We write from a university whose colonial roots positioned it as a liberal, English-speaking academy famous for its anti-apartheid stance. But we also write from a space where histories of marginalization and privilege, poverty and wealth, and ways of knowing and being in the world continue to be written onto our bodies as well as onto the racialized bodies of students who sit next to each other in our classrooms. However, being located geographically in the south does not automatically signal a southern perspective. A southern perspective requires an awareness of the body-political locations that can be used to challenge dominant western and colonial discourses. Southern perspectives have much to offer those working with marginalized communities in the Global North. It also means that as white academics writing from the south, addressing the uncomfortable questions that Pennycook and Makoni (2020: 14) raise: 'Who can speak for whom? What gives one the position to speak on these matters? How are academic legitimacy and credibility to be bestowed?' We return to these questions later in this introduction. Fundamental to a southern perspective is its humanizing orientation, which acknowledges that 'the complexities of lives lived in contrary conditions' is not just about the perpetuation of colonial inequalities but also gives rise to the 'creativity and resilience of communities' (Heugh et al. 2022: 6–7). Language is central to this, which Heugh et al. (2022) refer to as southern multilingualisms. This is where

> a diversity of agencies and identities find voice; where boundaries are traversed, and borders crossed; where speakers resist or submit to regimentation; where public and intimate spheres are discursively populated and lives jostled; and where political subjectivities are made and/or unmade in political struggle and rhetoric. (2022: 7)

Teaching and researching the sociolinguistics course

This first-year university English course in a multilingual teacher education context has been taught every year since 2005. Over this time more than 5,000 students have journeyed through it. Its focus is on language, identity and power, and at its centre is students' writing about their own lived language experiences, most often in the form of personal language narratives but sometimes in the form of dialogues accompanied by critical commentaries. As language practitioners and classroom-based researchers, we view teaching and research areas as interwoven. Research has always accompanied our teaching of the sociolinguistics course and insights from the teaching and research have fed into each other as part of an iterative process.

From the outset, narrative has been pivotal theoretically and methodologically, pedagogically and analytically. Narrative is more than just a fluid and flexible genre. It facilitates different ways of knowing that value the personal and require a level of reflexivity. The power of narrative lies in its provisional nature that enables the fluid (re)telling and (re)configuring of knowledges and prioritizes the integration of knowing and being that is often absent from the academic writing required by universities. Our conceptualization of narrative is underpinned by a strong critical orientation influenced by a social justice agenda and an awareness of the ways in which language works to entrench inequality but, equally, how it can be used to challenge inequalities. Narratives have an important place within decolonial methodologies (see Armitage (2022) yarning with the Anangu community in Australia and Daniels et al.'s (2022) process of co-constructing narratives as part of a Cree language revitalization and First Nations knowledge regeneration project). In keeping with its focus on narrative ways of knowing, we have written parts of the book in a narrative style.

Pedagogically, narrative is the overarching frame of this work that we combine with creative, critical and heteroglossic pedagogies. We've been influenced by Bakhtin's (1981) work on heteroglossia. In the book we show how narrative is inherently heteroglossic, enabling students to produce multi-voiced stories across language varieties, capturing past, present and future selves, as well as voices of others encountered in their lives. In developing a multilingual pedagogy in a context of complex and diverse language practices, the course is layered with stories because we do not want 'the single story in a single language . . . to overwrite historical networks among people and their communities' (Stroud and Heugh 2022: 59).

This book also foregrounds student voices and the insights their writing provides into our shifting multilingual context. The course took on a life of its own as we began teaching it in 2005, generating an archive of student stories and voices in the form of their language narratives. These narratives, while capturing the students' journeys, also took us as lecturers on a journey into their worlds, their histories and their language repertoires. Hearing the students' voices has been, and continues to be, a powerful learning experience for us. A key reason for writing this book is to enable others to hear students' voices, their experiences around language and the attitudes of their communities and themselves to languages. Our work lies at the intersection between the scholarship of teaching and learning (SOTL) and teacher language education, and we hope the multiple voices in the book will resonate with colleagues doing related work across a broad range of disciplines and contexts.

We have become increasingly interested in the way in which the language narratives capture students' linguistic identities at given moments in time. The book tells the story of continuities and shifts in students' identities as they navigate their relationship to English as hegemonic language and its impact on their other languages; the different selves constructed through specific languages and the conscious choices students make to reposition themselves at the intersection of language and other significant social categories and experiences. The narratives show how language works as a significant element of an intersectional identity, and how students' identities are (re)shaped by the confluence of multiple experiences that include place, time and a shifting sociopolitical landscape.

While we share the discomfort of a number of scholars (Ndhlovu 2016; Soudien 2021) about the limitations of sociological categories such as race, class and gender, we ultimately chose to work flexibly with the identity categories with which students self-identified at the moment of writing the narrative, seeing them as moments of identity reconstruction for students as well as new ways of learning. We also acknowledge that some students may subsequently have shifted the ways in which they self-identified at that time. This contentious issue is discussed in more detail in Chapter 1.

A pedagogy of English language teaching in a multilingual context

Writing this story enables us to share our experimentation with other educators across the world who may be asking questions about how to engage students in the politics of language across difference and about how to find points of connection and difference while keeping the language classroom space open, inclusive and dialogic.

This is a story of lessons learnt as language educators, the affordances and constraints of course material, assessment practices, our beliefs about language, students and social justice. It is not a neat story with shiny edges – it has gaps and silences, but in telling it we seek to capture our entangled and responsive way of working. We hope this will be valuable for educators teaching in contexts of diversity, who may also need to work beyond their own linguistic repertoires, as we have.

The heteroglossic element of our pedagogy enables us to challenge monoglossic orientations to language in order to embrace the play of multiple voices, registers, dialects and varieties in the multilingual space we inhabit. However, as language teacher educators, we are constrained by school language policies and national curricula that are still very much entrenched in monoglossic views of language. While these policies are out of alignment with both the fluid sociolinguistic realities of learners' lives and with burgeoning research on language education which challenges the boundedness of named languages (e.g. Abdulatief et al. 2021; Bock and Stroud 2021; García and Wei 2014; Makalela 2015; McKinney 2016; Ndhlovu and Makalela 2021; van Avermaet et al. 2018), we still need to prepare our students to teach in schools that are subject to these policies. Thus, we work within and against monoglossic language practices. While we cannot manage without named languages, we can and do treat their boundaries as porous. For this reason, our preferred term for our students' varied and multiple languages is 'multilingual repertoires'. This term signals a view of languages as not unbounded but also not siloed, and available as a fluid set of resources which have legitimacy in the English classroom. This is particularly important for us as language teacher educators. We want students to emerge from the course with a critical and nuanced understanding of language. As preservice teachers, this is an important part of developing a professional identity that will enable them to engage with criticality, dialogism and diversity in their future classrooms. We want our students to become teachers who can take action and we attempt to model being agents of change through the pedagogic choices we make.

Unpacking the course archive, 2005–19

The term 'archive' suggests a carefully catalogued collection of documents and records. This belies the messy process of qualitative longitudinal research. Even the term 'dataset' is in some ways misleading, conjuring up visions of a neat pile of objects awaiting expert analysis. We see this data as stories that have long inspired us and continue to live with us. Teaching this course over a decade and a half has resulted in the accumulation of a course archive that needed a great deal of sorting in preparation for writing this book.

We draw on multiple datasets. Primarily, we present and analyse students' writing which takes one of two forms: language narratives or dialogues with commentaries, both of which students submitted for assessment. We also carried out four focus group interviews with students in 2020, in which we asked them to reflect on their experience of the course. In addition, because the course itself is presented and analysed, all existing course materials constitute usable data. We draw on reading packs, lecturer materials, lecturer reflective notes and some additional teaching materials in discussing the pedagogic aspects of the course. While the type of analysis varies across chapters, depending on the specific foci and the aims of each one, in general we employ thematic content analysis, which draws on elements of discourse analysis.

Although the focus on students' voices is central, we had to make decisions about how these would be presented. Writing an academic book about students' lived experiences of language, in particular holding in balance our voices as academic authors and the integrity of student voices, has its challenges. The texts presented here are inevitably mediated by us. We have selected some narratives from the archive and not others, and these narratives have been subjected to fine-grained analysis that is interpretative and provisional. We recognize that, given the critical discursive lens of the analysis, students and readers may not interpret their work in the ways we have. It is important to mention that we received ethics approval from the university for all the data we present here. All student names are pseudonyms and we have used the written work only of students from whom we have obtained permission to do so.

In attempting to maintain the integrity of the student voices, we made four decisions. The first was to include extended extracts of student texts to give space to their voices. The second was to only lightly edit their narratives for readability (e.g. correcting typographical and spelling errors) in order to ensure that the language varieties students use remain intact. The third decision was not to edit for content. The student narratives have not been censored – some address issues or use language that may be considered controversial. In this book there are examples of students' insights about language that are not progressive. Our decision to include these was made because such insights enable us to understand the kinds of challenges students face and the issues they are grappling with. Our decision is congruent with our belief that the classroom should be a space that welcomes and works productively with student experience. It was not made without careful thought and some trepidation. Finally, we have also included stand-alone examples of student voices interspersed across the book.

Asking difficult questions

Along the way, we have had to confront a number of big questions about the work we are doing – some of them uncomfortable and unable to be conclusively answered, and others that this book attempts to address.

South Africa is a multilingual, diverse, post-colonial society riddled with linguistic inequalities, including the linguistic hegemony of the English language. A question that must be asked of our work then is: Should energy not be devoted to developing indigenous African languages rather than to teaching English? The question itself sets up a false binary. This is not an either/or scenario. This is because *both* the development of African languages *and* the provision of access to English are social justice imperatives. So as a society, we need teachers, applied linguists, language educators, policy-makers, language activists and so on, who collectively address both of these imperatives by focusing their attention on where their expertise lies. Our expertise positions us as English educators working within a critical paradigm.

As Janks (2004: 40) warned us – teachers of English – almost twenty years ago, 'those of us who teach this language have an awesome responsibility'. Her subsequent argument around the access paradox continues, even now, to shape our approach to teaching English in the south. We are acutely aware of the paradox or double-bind within which we operate: the very act of teaching a language of power such as English further entrenches that power; yet not providing access to English does not undo its power, it simply marginalizes those who do not gain access to the extensive linguistic capital it provides. We agree with Heugh (2018: 358) that '[f]ailure to deliver access to academic varieties of language that open doors to future advancement is failure to deliver equity and social justice'. But widening access is not enough. What Janks proposed was a pedagogy that

> gives mastery of English together with a critical view of its status as a global language. Education needs to produce students who understand why linguistic diversity is a resource for creativity and cognition, who value all the languages they speak and who recognise the paucity of English only. (2004: 35)

This book is a response to that call, showing how we attempt to do this in English teacher education in the south, drawing on emerging decolonial thinking.

A related question is whether we – as white, privileged, middle-class, female academics – can do this work, in a post-colonial society that continues to battle historically entrenched inequalities, which include the linguistic hegemony of the language we are teaching. This is an uncomfortable question. Many would say, and we would agree, that we are complicit in the very 'colonial matrix of power' (Quijano 2007) that we are purportedly challenging. We can see how our work could be classified as 'settler moves to innocence' (Tuck and Yang 2012). In other words, as participating in 'those strategies and positionings that attempt to relieve the settler feelings of guilt or responsibility without giving up land or power or privilege, without having to change much at all' (2012: 10). Indeed, we cannot confidently refute this categorization. Our identities as white settlers, with linguistic privilege accrued and strengthened under apartheid, are undeniable. Baked into these identities we can discern, for example, our western epistemic frames and our English-centric lives. However, as Vice (2017: 448) argues in her exploration of racial identity in South Africa, 'we are importantly what our racial positions have made us, and [. . .] we are also importantly, more than this or, sometimes, not this.' So, like our students, we too occupy complex, contradictory, multilayered identity positions. While we need to be constantly vigilant and critically self-reflective with regard to our racial positionality, we do not want to recentre whiteness here. From the outset we need to acknowledge that our narrative will have blind spots and any number of other flaws. But we need to risk these because the alternative would be to be paralysed into silence lest we say or write something that has meanings or implications beyond those that might be immediately discernible to us. So, this is a flawed and somewhat precarious undertaking. And while this runs the risk of white saviourism, we believe this is how we are able to contribute to the difficult conversations that are needed in this and other southern contexts.

We have found it fruitful to see ourselves as occupying various insider and outsider positions. We are outsiders to the multilingual communities most of our students come from. But we are insiders to English, Englishness and English expertise. We strive to strategically find ways in which we can leverage this expertise in addressing some of the linguistic inequalities in our multilingual, diverse context, disrupting hegemony from within. One of the contributions this book hopes to make is to provide an example of how we as educators in a diverse, multilingual context worked beyond our own linguistic repertoires. Our decision to prioritize multilingual repertoires was an ideologically driven and a contextually responsive one. It was intended to facilitate access for marginalized students (and, it is important to point out that in the South African context it is the majority that is marginalized) and offer a challenge to the hegemony of English. But this ideological impetus is not matched by our own linguistic repertoires. We remain acutely aware that we have succeeded in living virtually our whole lives in South Africa and reaching doctoral-level education without acquiring proficiency in any of the indigenous South African languages. However, our own language histories are not uniform. English was the main language spoken around Belinda when she was a child and through it she entered the world of books, stories, words and imagination. Her parents were children of Jewish immigrants from Eastern Europe, and when she looks back, she becomes aware of a history of unspoken losses – of life before becoming refugees and immigrants, of conversations and secrets peppered with heritage languages such as Yiddish and Hebrew. Ana only started learning English when she started school, having emigrated from Mozambique as a young child with Portuguese as a home language. Within a few years, English had become her dominant language. It came to form the very marrow of who she is, and it is only as an adult that she has been able to critique this early uncritical assimilation into the hegemony of English. Kerryn, whose ancestors hail from England and Wales, was brought up in a middle-class, English-speaking South African home. She chose isiZulu as a third language at high school and was taught by a white man whose passion for the language was contagious. She went on to major in isiZulu at university but considers herself a failed isiZulu speaker as a result of being steeped in a grammar-translation approach that taught a formal, 'standard' variety of the language that is not spoken in Johannesburg.

So, our third and final question is: What does it mean to navigate the shift from epistemic access to epistemic disobedience? One of the many shifts that this study embodies is that wrought by the decolonial turn (Maldonado-Torres 2018). In the early years of teaching this course, we were concerned with epistemological access (see Ferreira and Mendelowitz 2009a). Now it is epistemic disobedience (Mignolo 2009) that challenges our onto-epistemic positions. What we attempt to show in Chapter 3 is the shift from transformative pedagogy to an entangled, emergent decolonial praxis. It is emergent because we are still exploring the contours and depths of decoloniality. We need time to develop 'dispositions for not yet contemplated ways of thinking' (Nakata et al. 2012: 130). It is entangled because we have been steeped in the western episteme all our lives, even in this southern setting. Even though we may locate ourselves in those critical, reflexive spaces that apply a critical orientation to Eurocentric knowledge production and dissemination, we still inevitably inhabit this episteme. We need to find ways of working within these contradictions while aiming for an imperfect decolonial praxis.

It is thus essential to engage seriously and in an exploratory way with decoloniality. We do not want to jump onto the 'decolonial bandwagon' (Moosavi 2020) as part of a performance of 'woke' academia. We have resisted publisher suggestions to include the term 'decolonial' in our book title because we don't believe its inclusion would be an accurate characterization of our work. But this does not mean that we are not engaging with decoloniality. As teacher educators in the Global South who firmly locate ourselves in a social justice paradigm, we have to take the decolonial turn seriously – even if it means needing to interrogate our social justice paradigm for its own potential to reinscribe coloniality. It was the student protests demanding free and decolonized education that took us to decolonial theory. However, as Morreira et al. (2020: 11) remark, 'it may prove easier to attack the racist culture and practices of coloniality in universities through manifestos and journal articles and pull down the statues of notorious racists than replace the modern episteme on which the very idea of the public Western university is founded.'

Navigating this book

In this book we do three things. (1) We theorize pedagogy and show how we have operationalized this theorization. (2) We present student language narratives and dialogues that are the products of our pedagogy. (3) We analyse these narratives and dialogues in order to understand more about how students are navigating their linguistic positions in our multilingual southern context.

The first three chapters provide a contextual, theoretical and pedagogical framework for the book. Chapter 1 is the story of the course, providing a detailed account of the shifting macro and micro contexts of the course over time. The institutional context, the broader sociopolitical, linguistic and historical South African contexts are presented together with an overview of the student cohorts and the course curriculum. In Chapter 2 we discuss why narrative ways of knowing have always played a central role in the sociolinguistics course. We present our conceptualization of narrative and outline its flexible pedagogic potential, as well as the ways in which it may be harnessed for decolonial ends. In Chapter 3 we explain the theoretical underpinnings of our pedagogy and its enactment through various activities, readings and other course materials.

The second part of the book focuses on our analysis of student narratives. Each data chapter uses different lenses through which to read and analyse the narratives. Taken together, these chapters capture the shifting voices and identities of students over a period of time. In Chapter 4 we illustrate how language works as a significant element of an intersectional identity, and how students' identities are (re)shaped by the confluence of multiple experiences. We offer a close reading of three narratives, drawn from the first three years of the course, to explore students' identity shifts in relation to the dynamic position of English, various African languages and Afrikaans. In Chapter 5 we focus on the dialogue and critical commentary assignment in order to concretely demonstrate the ways in which our heteroglossic pedagogy operates. We illustrate the value of combining creative and critical genres in the academic space. In Chapter 6 we work with the dialogue and critical commentary assignment in relation to our conceptualization of the critical imagination. In this chapter we show how the narrative dialogue task opens possibilities for students to use their multifaceted resources to make critical-creative moves and to critically re-imagine a range of social issues. In Chapter 7 we present an analysis of five narrative extracts to show how recent cohorts of students are (re)positioning themselves in relation to English in ways that are disruptive of – or indicate continuities with – the hegemony of English. We explore the extent to which the #FeesMustFall movement brought about discursive shifts in the South African higher education landscape and consider the impact of this movement on student narratives. We also explore the extent to which students take up critical or uncritical ownership of English and language and race in institutional spaces. The final chapter is written as a metalogue rather than a conventional academic conclusion. It is constructed from student focus groups and presents their reflections on the course and their learning. A reflexive return to past learnings opens up new pathways and possibilities for a multilingual pedagogy that is constantly in motion.

1

The Story of a Course

*Ana and I are sipping coffee outside the School of Education canteen. We
are discussing ideas for a new first-year course for 2005. This conversation
takes place in the time before massification and early in our careers when
there is time for leisurely conversations. The Bachelor of Education is a
new degree with many new challenges and little research to inform our
approach. So far, in our 2003/4 courses we have struggled to engage the
group in its entirety, to pitch the course at appropriate levels, to be inclusive
but sufficiently challenging, and to facilitate interaction among students
from diverse backgrounds. Our lectures and tutorials seem to comprise
students living in parallel worlds, with minimal points of connection. Many
of our previous attempts to address these challenges have inadvertently
turned the spotlight on disparities and disconnections within the group.
We have an intuition that sociolinguistics as disciplinary content, with
narrative as a key teaching and learning tool, could provide multiple entry
points for the engagement of this diverse student group – with us and with
one another. Every first-year student has a language history to draw on and
none of them would have studied sociolinguistics before, regardless of their
schooling background. This, we hope, could enable us to place students'
diverse lived experiences at the centre of the course.*

Extract from Belinda's reflective notes, October 2004

Where does a story begin? How far back do you go? And how wide do you cast
the net that encircles the telling? We began teaching the sociolinguistics course,
on which our study is based, in 2005 but to understand that story, it needs to be
embedded in a larger and more complex story that has the history and politics
of South Africa as its backdrop. The students who have journeyed through our
English course have histories, contexts and stories of their own. The language
narratives they write for us are snapshots of a moment in time. To enable an

understanding of these moments, our first aim in this chapter is to situate the course in time and place, beginning with a broad outline of the sociohistorical and political context and then moving to the specificities of our own institutional context and then looking at who our students are. Our second aim is to present the course curriculum, moving from its initial conceptualization, including the politics of knowledge selection, to the various phases through which the course has been, and finally to a discussion of the pivotal role of language narratives within it. However, telling the story of a course that has been offered for sixteen years is a challenge. Over this time, not only has its content and pedagogy shifted but so have the fields in which the course is located, most notably language education and sociolinguistics. And beyond this, we have shifted as academics, as have both our student body and the institutional and sociopolitical contexts in which we are all situated. It is precisely these shifts that have both challenged and fascinated us, and ultimately prompted our attempt to capture this story. But the devil is in the capturing. We have tried to avoid creating a narrative that focuses on the minutiae and follows multiple, interdependent threads in dizzying ways, and equally to avoid the creation of a seamless, totalizing course narrative that belies the messy reality.

We begin by looking at the broad linguistic landscape in South Africa before focusing on context and students.

Language and social context: The backstory

Language is always political. At the southern tip of Africa, waves of political oppression have had a distinct and irrevocable impact on societal language use, and '[l]anguage has played a central role in South Africa's transition from colonialism to apartheid to democracy' (Kamwangamalu 2003b: 235). During separate periods of colonization, first Dutch and later English became the language of officialdom and access to resources. Under British rule, a policy of Anglicization meant that schooling in English became widespread. When the white supremacist Afrikaner Nationalist Party came to power in 1948, in addition to formalizing the racist, segregationist policy of apartheid – which separated people according to racial classifications and officially entrenched white minority rule – it also aggressively pursued the development of Afrikaans. This was the language that had arisen from contact in the seventeenth century between the Dutch language and various indigenous and slave languages along the Cape coast (Alexander 2009). And thus it was that until 1994, English and

Afrikaans were the only two official languages in South Africa. Under apartheid the indigenous African languages were systematically marginalized, with the exception of their strategic use by the apartheid state in the Bantu Education Act (1953). Here the state sought to use education in indigenous African languages for black learners as a means of delaying their access to high-status languages (i.e. English and Afrikaans), thus limiting their access to higher education and their possibilities for social mobility (Kwamangamalu 2003a) while reserving well-paid jobs for the white English- or Afrikaans-speaking minority (Alexander 1997). (See Kwamangamalu 2003a for a more detailed discussion of social change and language shift in South Africa than is possible here.) The first non-racial democratic elections in 1994 ended white minority rule in South Africa and established a new democratic government led by President Nelson Mandela.

Under the new democratic dispensation, eleven official languages are recognized: Sepedi, Sesotho, Setswana, SiSwati, Tshivenda, Xitsonga, Afrikaans, English, isiNdebele, isiXhosa and isiZulu – in the order listed in the Constitution (SA 1996). This sought to redress some of the imbalances of the past as well as to promote linguistic inclusivity and racial reconciliation. While this move seemed radical at the time, the policy has 'remained largely at the symbolic level due to financial considerations as well as the lack of political will to implement it' (Hibbert 2016: 9). The Constitution also declared that all individuals have a right to be educated in their home language, and a policy of additive multilingualism was put in place at school level – in other words, learners were expected to acquire literacy in their respective mother tongues and then add other languages (or at least one) while continuing to develop the mother tongue. This too has, for various reasons, had limited impact and English remains the widespread de facto medium of instruction at schools. In public schools in 2007, 'approximately 65% [of learners] were *learning in* English, although English was the home language for only 7% of learners' (Posel and Zeller 2019: 291). The national school curriculum offers English (as well as all other official languages) at two levels, at Home Language (HL) level and at First Additional Language (FAL) level, the former assumes 'native speaker' English competence while the latter assumes that English is being learnt as an additional language (previously referred to as ESL). While this is intended to accommodate school learners at different levels of English proficiency and to enable black African learners to study their mother tongue at HL level throughout their schooling, its success is limited. With regard to the equitable provision of access to English, for example, the teaching of English FAL is frequently associated with low levels of cognitive demand which is a cause for concern given the fact that most English FAL learners are learning all their other subjects through the medium of English from grade 4 onwards. Additionally, since schools that offer English at HL level are largely historically white or Indian schools located in middle-class areas, and those that offer it at FAL level are historically black schools located in poorer socioeconomic areas, the distinction between English HL and English FAL intersects with both class and race in complex ways.

The question of whether there has been a post-1994 language shift towards English, with a corresponding loss in the African indigenous languages, remains an open one. As early as 2003, Kamangwamalu identified a trend towards societal unilingualism in English – particularly among urban black communities – and warned against the demise of indigenous African languages. He maintained that 'if anything had changed at all . . . it is that English has gained far more political clout than Afrikaans' (Kamangwamalu 2003a: 232) and famously wrote about the recognition of eleven official languages as an example of 'when $2 + 9 = 1$' (Kamangwamalu 2003b). Later scholarship has suggested that the situation is more nuanced, however. Deumert (2010) argues that while English 'has established itself as the unquestioned *lingua franca*' (2010: 15), it is not *replacing* indigenous languages but being taken up in ways that suggest 'a widening of linguistic repertoires' (2010: 17). In other words, growing bi- and multilingualism is being incorrectly interpreted as indicative of a shift in the dominant language of individuals or groups. This position is reinforced by Posel and colleagues (Posel and Zeller 2016, 2019; Posel, Hunter and Rudwick 2020), who use census data to show that an increase in the use of English as a *second-home* language is being reported but that its overall increase as a first language has been minimal, a position supported by others (e.g. Hibbert 2016). African languages, they maintain, remain at the centre of everyday communication for the majority of South Africans. They also make the point that despite the official indigenous African languages having roots in colonial and apartheid linguistics (Makoni and Pennycook 2012), they continue to function as 'markers of identity and resistance to the importance of English in domains of power' (Posel, Hunter and Rudwick 2020: 1). Ironically, they identify the apartheid state's segregationist policies, especially enduring apartheid spatial geographies, as one of the reasons for what they see as the continued vitality of African languages, indicating that 'many South Africans remain within their own ethno-linguistic communities for much of the day, especially beyond the urban centres' (Posel, Hunter and Rudwick 2020: 11).

It is against this broad linguistic landscape that we present the stories of language that our university student cohorts have been writing over the years. Our qualitative study has two aims: to provide insights into students' lived language experiences as captured in their rich and textured narratives; and to describe and discuss critically a narrative heteroglossic pedagogy that seeks to provide access to the disciplinary knowledge of English as subject in a teacher education curriculum, while validating and using students' multilingual repertoires.

Institutional context and student diversities

Within the macro-level South African sociohistorical, sociopolitical and linguistic context outlined earlier, the School of Education at the University of the Witwatersrand constitutes a micro-site. Wits University, as it is commonly known, is a public, English-speaking university with a 'reputation as a liberal, white university with a strong anti-apartheid public image' (Odendaal 2019: 32). It is located in the city of Johannesburg, the economic hub of Southern Africa. Mbembe and Nuttall (2004: 365–6) have described Johannesburg as 'the premier metropolis in Africa in terms of technology, wealth and racial complexity . . . a thoroughly polyglot urban formation whose influence, connections, and identifications extend beyond its locality and well beyond South Africa' – although more recently, it has also been described as an 'anxious' and 'troublesome metropolis' (Falkof and Van Staden 2020). Gauteng, the province in which Johannesburg is located, is the smallest, wealthiest and most linguistically diverse province in the country.

This racial complexity and polyglot formation was evident in our student body from the early 2000s, as captured in the challenges we identified in this chapter's introductory vignette. At the inception of the course in 2005 – then titled 'Language and Identity' – our overriding impression of the students in our lecture theatres was of extensive diversity across multiple levels – linguistic, cultural, racial, ethnic and socioeconomic backgrounds, as well as varying experiences of schooling. A version of the sociolinguistics course has been taught every year since 2005, presented to over 5,000 first-year Bachelor of Education students. Demographic data obtained from the university data base confirms the degree of diversity among our students; however, it is necessary to introduce this data with a caveat. University admissions data is a blunt instrument. Additionally, self-reporting on language practices is known to have limitations as a method of gathering data, particularly when data gathering instruments have unexamined monoglossic assumptions built into them, thereby undermining their ability to capture a heteroglossic reality. For example, students may not be able to indicate more than one 'home language'; and those who do not speak a standard dialect of a language may not have the option to explain this. Nevertheless, this information provides a broad indication of how things stood when the course began and shows a number of interesting trends over a period of sixteen years, as we discuss later. Table 1.1 presents the student demographic data for the first student cohort, in 2005. We present comparable data for the period spanning from 2005 to 2020 later in the chapter.

It can be seen in Table 1.1 that in 2005, all eleven official languages were represented as languages spoken in the home. English, however, was by far the dominant language spoken at home, with isiZulu coming in at a distant second. One of the university admission criteria is for students to have taken English as a language subject at school either at HL level or at FAL level. As we discussed earlier, these two curricula represent quite different levels of preparation for university study *through* the medium of English, as well as university study *of* English. The one-third of the student cohort in 2005 that had matriculated with English FAL would have had to work much harder to attain the levels expected of first-year students working in English by virtue of the kind of curriculum they had been exposed to at school.

In order to construct a representation of student identity that moves beyond the linguistic and is multifaceted and intersectional, Table 1.1 also provides information on gender, race and class. The predominance of female students (71.5 per cent, Table 1.1) is unsurprising given the feminization of the teaching profession. The continuing classification of students according to apartheid race categories is a contentious issue; however, arguments have been made for the ongoing use of these racial categories under certain circumstances. While race is a social construct, apartheid race categories continue to have both symbolic value and material consequences, remaining 'a key marker of inequality – political, economic and social' (Bentley and Habib 2008, 9). Thus one of the primary reasons why universities continue to collect data in this way is to monitor the redress of historical inequalities and to measure change. What the data in Table 1.1 shows is that in 2005 there were almost equal numbers of black students and white students (41.8 per cent and 37.6 per cent, respectively), while the remaining 20 per cent consisted of Indian and coloured students. Lastly, we use the national school quintile system to derive some information on socioeconomic status. All South African state schools are categorized into five groups termed 'quintiles', largely for the purpose of allocation of state funding. Quintile 1 is the 'poorest' category, while quintile 5 is the 'least poor'. Learners attending quintile 1, 2 or 3 schools do not pay school fees. This system has limitations and has been criticized

Table 1.1 Demographic information for the first student cohort, 2005

Language spoken at home:			
English	153	63.9%	
isiZulu	30	12.6%	
isiXhosa	16	6.7%	
Sepedi	11	4.6%	
Sesotho	7	2.9%	Linguistic diversity
Setswana	6	2.5%	
SiSwati	5	2.1%	
Xitsonga	4	1.6%	
Tshivenda/Afrikaans/isiNdebele	2 each	<1% each	
Foreign	1	<1%	
School English:			Diverse access to English
Home Language (HL)	162	67.5%	
First Additional Language (FAL)	77	32.5%	
Gender:			
Female	171	71.5%	Gender diversity
Male	68	28.5%	
Race:[a]			
White	100	41.8%	
African	90	37.6%	Racial diversity
Indian	36	15.0%	
Coloured[b]	13	5.4%	
School quintile:[c]			
1	17	7.1%	
2	14	5.7%	
3	22	9.2%	
4	16	6.7%	Socioeconomic diversity
5	126	52.7%	
6	31	12.9%	
QI	4	1.6%	
Other	9	3.7%	
Total number of students	239		

[a]Racial categories constructed and imposed under apartheid rule are used because they continue to function as indicators of social inequality. Apart from the term Indian, we use all the lower case for all race labels . The scare quotes conventionally used around race terms to question their validity and highlight their status as social constructs have been omitted for ease of reading.

[b]The term 'coloured' has its own history of usage in South Africa. As Adhikari (2005, 1) explains, in South Africa it does not refer to black people in general, as it does in some contexts. Instead it refers to 'a phenotypically varied social group of highly diverse social and geographical origins . . . [who] have held an intermediate status in the South African racial hierarchy'. For more insight into the complexities, ambiguities and contestations of the term see, for example, Adhikari (2006), Petrus and Isaacs-Martin (2012) and Erasmus (2017).

[c]A state-run measurement of school resources from least resourced schools (1) to most resourced (5/6).

for allocating quintiles to schools on the basis of their geographic location rather than on their learner demographic. For example, schools in historically white, middle-class suburbs no longer always cater to the surrounding community and are often less resourced than their locations would suggest. The university has added a sixth quintile to use for capturing private schools. As shown in Table 1.1, only 22 per cent of students in 2005 came from no-fee paying schools while schools in middle-class areas were the most represented accounting for just over 50 per cent of the students. Nevertheless what we have is, once again, representation across the broad socioeconomic spectrum as captured by the quintiles.

We have presented this 2005 student data in this way because it speaks to the 'complex diversities' (Heugh 2018: 342) of our context in a number of ways. First, it is precisely these diversities in our student body that have enabled us to do significant work with/across diversity. As we show in Chapter 3, working with diversity is central to our pedagogy. Second, it demonstrates that from the start we have been engaging with diversity at multiple levels: linguistic, cultural, racial, gender and socioeconomic. Third, these diversities are not only multiple but internal to South Africa. In our teacher education context in the Global South, our diversities – especially cultural, ethnic and linguistic diversity – are not externally derived diversities that are a consequence of transnational global flows. They are internally existing diversities, borne of centuries of colonial oppression, separationist policies and political liberation alongside white settler colonialism. Fourth, it is important to note that race is implicated in many of these diversities. Language and class often function as proxies for race. For example, when we talk of students who speak indigenous African languages at home, we are almost certainly talking about black students. In Table 1.1, the 100 students who self-identified as white are likely to be completely subsumed into the 162 students who have indicated that they speak English at home. When we talk of students who attended no-fee paying schools, we are also almost certainly talking about black students. And therefore, while the students in our lecture theatres were diverse in 2005, the faultlines among them were clear and they were racialized.

One section of the cohort consisted of middle to upper-middle class students who had been to historically white schools; they were either mother tongue English speakers or had acquired 'native speaker' competence of English through having experienced all or most of their schooling through the medium of English. In the early phase of the course, this group was almost wholly made up of white and Indian students. Another section of the cohort came from lower-middle class, working-class or impoverished backgrounds and had attended poorly resourced schools with uneven access to English. This group has always consisted wholly of students of colour. At that point we were operating on our own impressions, but subsequently much has been written about the two-tier education system, or bimodal model of distribution (Fleisch 2008), that the racially segregated apartheid schooling system spawned, generating these faultlines. And these faultlines persist. A report released by Amnesty International in February 2020 states that 'owing to the deep roots of the legacy of apartheid, a child's experience of education still very much depends on where they are born, how wealthy they are, and the colour of their skin' (Amnesty International 2020). In 2004, under these conditions, it felt particularly challenging to attempt to design a course that aimed to generate a 'level playing field' for the full cohort of students. Their diversity – or, put differently, their historically constructed inequalities – positioned them differently in relation to language, knowledge and pedagogy. Attempting to design a course – an English course, moreover – that would position them equitably and enable all students to access university English knowledge seemed almost an impossibility.

Epistemological access and curriculum responsiveness

Our social justice orientation has always meant that epistemological access for all students is critical, particularly because language and language policies have been used in such divisive ways in South Africa. When we wrote about access in the early days of the course (Ferreira and Mendelowitz 2009a), we were primarily concerned about facilitating student access to academic and disciplinary knowledge, and assisting students to make the move from everyday knowledge to academic knowledge. We acknowledged the many different levels on which the battle for formal access to the university took place. We quoted the Wits Admissions Policy (2003, 2006), which spoke about formal and epistemological access to the university and which pointed out the negative impact of unequal schooling opportunities on student achievement. We also emphasized the importance of academic depth; and we flagged the fact that language was an access issue. Sixteen years later, all of these access points remain relevant but the issue itself has become far more complex. The national student protests that rocked the higher education sector from 2015 to 2017 not only brought to the fore ongoing issues of financial access to university but also reminded us that knowledge is not neutral and that it is racialized. The pandemic which gripped the globe in 2020 and forced us all online has shown that digital access too is a massive equity issue, reliant as it is on devices, connectivity and data which – in our context – are not a given for all students. And, over and above this, the knowledge debate has shifted significantly as a result of what has come to be known as the decolonial turn (Grosfoguel 2007).

When decolonial theorists writing in the fields of philosophy, politics and law, among others, begin to dismantle western theories of knowledge and question how they have been constructed, teacher educators like us need to pay attention. Knowledge is 'the goods' we deal with on a daily basis. We need to understand our knowledge 'goods', interrogate their provenance and critically reflect on the positions we are taking up by dealing in the knowledge we have selected to teach. Mignolo (2009: 2) writes:

> Sure, all knowledges are situated and every knowledge is constructed. But that is just the beginning. The question is: who, when, why is constructing knowledges?

This exposes the hubris of the zero point, that is the extreme arrogance of believing that 'you' can speak from a neutral position that is neither geo-politically located nor physically embodied. Western epistemology, Mignolo and other decolonial scholars believe, speaks from that hubristic position, positing its knowledge as abstract and universalist, while condemning other knowledges to speak from the mouths of others, locally and particularly. Those of us who have been steeped in the western episteme cannot now un-see it. But our orientation to it becomes irrevocably altered and this changes everything. This brings us to one of our difficult questions: How then do we move from facilitating epistemic access to facilitating epistemic disobedience (Mignolo 2009)? We readily concede that in the early years of our course, epistemological access was at least in part about enculturation into white western forms of knowledge. But even then, we were also working in ways that were anti-deficit and anti-assimilationist both linguistically and epistemically. Even before the disruptive potential of the language narratives became clear to us, we were consciously challenging hegemonic knowledge practices by repositioning multilingual students who were speakers of African languages as carriers of valued knowledge in the (English) classroom. Using the decolonial discourse that has since emerged, we can now talk of epistemic injustice – when students' capacities as knowers are occluded and their voices are not recognized (Fricker 2007, 2017) – and can identify the moves that we have made and are continuing to make in an attempt to reverse this injustice at the pedagogic level. Thus while we are not presuming to construct this course as preemptive decolonial practice, we do find ourselves now, as we write this book in 2021, precariously positioned within overlapping western epistemic frames and decolonial counter-frames.

In those early days, one of our aims was to facilitate epistemological access through developing a responsive curriculum. From the start we set out to design a course that responded positively to the student needs in a transforming society (Ferreira and Mendelowitz 2009a), drawing on emerging research that sought to enact curricular responsiveness in both cultural and epistemic ways (Moll 2004; Slonimsky and Shalem 2006). This kind of responsiveness implicitly acknowledges the primacy of context. In our ongoing engagement with curriculum and pedagogy in higher education, this book seeks to make a contribution to the scholarship of teaching and learning (SOTL). But, as others have done (Looker 2018), we contest SOTL's narrow focus on 'the classroom' and its implied universally applicable processes. Instead we insist upon a socioculturally embedded course that is responsive to context. The place in which this work is located – the Global South, South Africa, Johannesburg, Wits University – is not merely a 'container' in which teaching and learning occurs. We see it as an active ingredient in the teaching and learning process. As we will show, many of our curriculum choices have been informed by place – in particular, the focus on multilingualism and South African linguistic repertoires – and much of our pedagogic practice too is responsive to place. Therefore, following Leibowitz (2017: 1), we want to draw attention to what it might mean *for* the south to locate the scholarship of teaching *in* the south, thereby opening up the 'geopolitics of knowledge . . . for questioning'. We return to this discussion in chapter 3 on pedagogy.

The curriculum

Knowledge selection

From the start, we have been attuned to the politics of knowledge selection. Our choice of sociolinguistics as subject matter for the course was both ideologically and pedagogically motivated. In view of the disparate schooling experiences of our students and our attempts to lessen these disparities, we selected a slice of disciplinary knowledge that would, first, be unfamiliar to all of them – since sociolinguistics per se was not part of the school curriculum at either HL or FAL level – and, second, be equally accessible to all via their own lived language experiences. And, importantly, with a key focus being on language varieties, linguistic diversity and multilingualism, we were not only capitalizing on the diversity of the student cohort but also working against the systemic advantage afforded to English monolingualism. However, this could not only be an abstract knowledge move where we simply *told* students about linguistic diversity and its value. This move needed to be *enacted* in the curriculum and through the pedagogy of the course.

Our decisions were also informed by the professional nature of the B.Ed. degree: we believed that all future teachers needed the kind of sociolinguistic knowledge that we were working with. Not only those who would be teaching English, or any language, but teachers of all subjects would benefit from developing an awareness of the relationship between language and identity, and the impact of English as a hegemonic language on teaching and learning. Thus we asked, 'what counts as knowledge within the discipline of sociolinguistics' and then 'what knowledge from sociolinguistics is useful for *all* education students?' Later, when the composition of the student cohort shifted, we had to ask anew, 'what knowledge from sociolinguistics is useful for education students who will be *English teachers*?'. In addition, we had to remember that this was only a six-week introductory course at first-year level and that our students were studying to become English teachers and not sociolinguists.

With this in mind, we began by explicitly rejecting the usual language-as-grammar-and-lexis approach found in schools and encouraging students to think deeply and critically about what language really *is,* what it *does* and how it *works*? We wanted students to begin to see language as constructed, and to pick apart some of these constructs. And we wanted them – as language users – to begin asking how language impacts on who we are. In thinking through what a first-year sociolinguistics course in South Africa might look like in the mid-2000s, we foregrounded examination of language through a critical social justice lens and we made a point of drawing on renowned local scholars – such as Raj Mesthrie, Kathleen Heugh and Russell Kaschula, among others.

The topics and themes we selected were in many ways similar to those one would find in an introductory sociolinguistics textbook for undergraduate-level teaching. In fact, we included chapters from such books as reading materials for our students, again selecting South African textbooks so as to locate the course in our own context. A key text was a volume by Kaschula and Anthonissen (1995) titled *Communicating across Cultures in South Africa: Towards a Critical Language Awareness,* updated as *Languages, Identities and Intercultural Communication in South Africa and Beyond* (Kaschula 2022). The original volume was particularly valuable because, like us, the authors believe that 'we cannot learn language in a vacuum' (Kaschula and Anthonissen 1995: v) and embed their discussions of language in our multicultural environment, moving between English and isiXhosa linguistic and cultural practices. We also drew on existing teaching materials that had their origins in apartheid-era language activism. Prior to 1994, there were already movements to teach English in ways that valorized the linguistic variety in South African society; that recognized the power of English to either reinforce or challenge oppressive relations of power; and that worked outside the usual Anglonormative (McKinney 2017) tendencies of English teaching. These included materials from NGOs and other alternative education organizations (e.g. the National Language Project, BUA! Magazine, ELTIC and TELIP) which promoted multilingual education not only because of the social justice imperative to do so but because of the social reality of multilingual practices in South African society. We note that many of the resources that we drew on at the start of the course map on to Heugh and Stroud's (2019) historical overview of multilingual work in education in South Africa, which, they emphasize, both predates and exceeds conceptions of multilingualism in the Global North. In our discussion of pedagogy in Chapter 3, we demonstrate how some of these now-classic materials continue to be of value precisely because of the ways in which they engage with diverse linguistic identities and everyday multilingualism.

The theoretical frames and academic texts we selected have always been, and continue to be, used in the service of the narrative frame of lived language experience. We are working against ivory tower conceptions of university knowledge that are unrelated to student experience. We have aimed to challenge the false boundary between academic and everyday knowledges and to work with the relationship between the two. This can be seen as an onto-epistemological move which foregrounds the relationship between who we are and what we know. And in the context of teacher education, this move needs to be extended to who we teach and what they know. Thus taking up the conceptual lenses of the discipline (of sociolinguistics) enables students to think about identity and the politics of embodied knowledge in critical, living ways, and in a double student–teacher move, provides them with tools for thinking about their own future language pedagogies.

In its first phase the course was framed by critical sociolinguistics and drew strongly on discourses of democracy and linguistic human rights which have subsequently been critiqued for operating within a western epistemic universalist tradition. In some ways we found ourselves engaging in what Pennycook and Makoni (2020: 97) refer to as 'old-school critical work' in which we critiqued western epistemology from within western critical frames. Like others before them (see Comaroff and Comaroff 2012; de Sousa Santos 2012), Pennycook and Makoni are careful to point out the complexity of what constitutes the Global South, especially 'once it is acknowledged that the South may also be in the North, and that the geographical south [such as us our current location] by no means guarantees a southern viewpoint' (2020: 5). So, once again, we found ourselves straddling Global North and Global South knowledge frames. Our ways of handling sociolinguistic knowledge by working with narrative and embodied heteroglossic language experiences can arguably be seen as an emergent decolonial move which resulted from our determination to produce a responsive curriculum that took cognizance of the students we had before us. But the disciplinary knowledge, to which we were striving to give students access, was firmly rooted in the northern canon.

Shifts

The three phases: Shifting curriculum

As we have worked with the course archive, it has become clear to us that shifts in the curriculum and in the assessment tasks have shaped different phases of the course. In addition, shifts in the broader sociopolitical context and in dominant social discourses over the years have played a role in shaping these phases. It stands to reason that a course that draws on student identities, lived experience and issues of power and marginalization would itself need to be understood in a critical and socially embedded manner, hence the need to consider relevant aspects of the changing social and political terrain. The process of discerning the different phases of the course led us to view curriculum, institutional factors and the sociopolitical landscape as inextricably interwoven. Our analysis has revealed that the course falls into the three fairly distinct phases summarized in Table 1.2 with a ★ indicating the placement of the assessment tasks for reasons that are discussed later.

Phase 1: 2005–9

- Students: In the first five years of the course, English I was compulsory for all first-year BEd students, regardless of their phase specialization (i.e. whether they were qualifying to teach in primary or secondary school) or subject specialization (i.e. whether they were qualifying to teach English or other subjects).
- Course length/focus: (1) In 2005 and 2006, it was a cohesive six-week course titled 'Language, Identity and Education'. The first three weeks focused on language and identity and worked with reflective language narratives. The next three dealt with language and education and worked with language policies and practices, multilingualism and language learning, and teaching multilingual classes. (2) From 2007 to 2009, the course was split into two three-week units, the first of which was titled 'Language and Identity'.[1]

Table 1.2 The shifting contours of the course curriculum

Phases	Phase 1: 2005–2009	Phase 2: 2010–2015	Phase 3: 2016–2019
Week 1:	The self and language ★ *2005–7: Short language narrative here*	The self, identity and language attitudes	Self, identity and language attitudes
Week 2:	Language narratives	Language, context and culture	Language, context and identity
Week 3:	Language in social contexts ★ *2008–9: Long language narrative here*	Language variation	Language variation
Week 4:		Language practices, race and youth identities	Language narratives
Week 5:	*In this phase, the course was only three weeks in length*	Language profiling and prejudice	Language practices, race and youth identities
Week 6:		Language in diverse classrooms ★ *Dialogue & commentary OR Language narrative here*	Language profiling and prejudice ★ *Language narrative here*

- Assessment: (1) In the first two years, the reflexive language narrative was positioned near the start of the course, thus using students' lived experiences as a stepping stone or as a site of 'interim literacies' (Paxton 2007) that function as a bridge to academic knowledge. It was the first of three assessments, it was short (600–700 words) and counted the least (just 20 per cent of the overall mark for the six-week course). (2) In the next three years, having glimpsed its massive potential, we shifted the language narrative assignment to the end of the course and made it longer (1,200–1,500 words) and more cognitively demanding. In Figure 1.1 the two assessment rubrics are placed side by side to show the increased level of demand required of the language narrative task.
- Materials: We began using more voices of young South Africans drawn from published memoirs, new fiction and media texts. With the permission of their authors, we also began including selected student language narrative assignments as readings in the course materials of the subsequent year.

ENGLISH IN EDUCATION A: Language, identity and education

<u>EVALUATION & FEEDBACK FORM</u> for **Assignment 1: Language Biography**

NAME OF STUDENT: _____

Genre:　　**Personal reflective narrative**

CRITERIA	SUCCESSFUL		UNSUCCESSFUL	COMMENT
	4	3	2	1	
Selection & handling of CONTENT	Content well chosen and creatively handled; key course ideas are personalized and integrated into narrative; insightful analysis and thoughtful reflection	Content is well chosen and some links are made to key course ideas; narrative description is extended through some effective analysis and reflection	Content selected is suitable; narrative is predominantly descriptive with limited analysis or reflection	Content selected is inappropriate and irrelevant	
Language & style	Language is correct; style is fluent, confident and conveys a clear personal voice	Language is generally fluent and accurate; some evidence of a personal style	Language needs attention but overall does not inhibit the communication of ideas; paragraphing satisfactory	Language use is poor; errors interfere with the communication of ideas; inadequate paragraphing	

MARKER'S SIGNATURE:　　　　　　　　　　DATE:

/40

EVALUATION & FEEDBACK FORM: <u>Language Biography</u>

March 2009

NAME OF STUDENT: _____

CRITERIA	SUCCESSFUL			UNSUCCESSFUL	
	5	4	3	2	1
SELECTION	Content is well selected and ideas are exceptionally well developed throughout	Content is well selected and ideas are well developed throughout	Content is well selected and ideas are developed	Content selected is suitable and idea development is adequate.	Content selected is inappropriate and irrelevant
DESCRIPTION	Exceptionally vivid and evocative description of key incidents; creative use of language in ways that enable the reader to 're–live' the experiences.	Vivid description of key incidents; creative use of language in ways that enable the reader to understand and visualize the experiences.	Key incidents are clearly described, enabling the reader to understand the essence of the experience.	Key incidents are described adequately but there is limited elaboration.	Key incidents are listed with little or no elaboration.
REFLECTION	Narrative description contains exceptionally insightful reflection; significant re-evaluation of experiences.	Narrative description contains thoughtful reflection and re-evaluation of experiences.	Narrative description is extended through some effective reflection on and re-evaluation of experiences.	Narrative is predominantly descriptive with limited reflection on or re-evaluation of experiences.	Narrative is entirely descriptive with no reflective component.
ANALYSIS	Key course ideas are personalized and integrated into narrative; excellent links made to relevant course readings; attitudes are thoroughly questioned.	Key course ideas are personalized and integrated into narrative; good links made to relevant course readings; attitudes are questioned.	Links are made to key course ideas and relevant readings; attitudes are beginning to be questioned.	Limited links are made to key course ideas and course readings; attitudes are left unquestioned.	No links are made to key course ideas and course readings.
Language& style	Language style is fluent, confident and articulate, conveying a distinctive personal voice.	Language is correct; style is fluent, confident and conveys a clear personal voice.	Language is generally fluent and accurate; some evidence of a personal style.	Language needs attention but overall does not inhibit the communication of ideas; paragraphing is satisfactory.	Language use is poor; errors interfere with the communication of ideas; inadequate paragraphing.

/100

MARKERS'S SIGNATURE:

DATE:

MARK:

Figure 1.1 Comparison of assessment criteria for the two different language narrative tasks.

Sociopolitical landscape

The students in our lecture theatres during this period would have been born in the 1980s. They would have been old enough to understand the significance of 1994 when, for many of them, their family members would have voted for the first time. This was also the first generation of students to experience racially desegregated schooling. When schools opened up, patterns of migration showed movement of black, coloured and Indian students from middle-class families into historically white schools where better-resourced schooling was to be found (Soudien 2004). Tusini (2016a: n.p.) refers to these students as the 'first guinea pig black bodies' to move into historically white spaces. She describes the complex dynamic between the disruptive potential of these black students having access to – and being able to succeed in – these 'previously forbidden spaces', and the countervailing assimilationist mode in which this process occurred, which maintained the status quo and left whiteness unchallenged. In this first phase of the course many of our students' narratives described the move from township schools to these historically white schools – a shift that for students always went hand in hand with stepping into an English world and leaving their multilingual repertoires at the door.

    Chapter 4 in this book analyses student language narratives from this phase. Three published articles have also focused on this phase of work: namely, Mendelowitz and Ferreira (2007), Ferreira and Mendelowitz (2009a) and Ferreira and Mendelowitz (2009b).

Phase 2: 2010–15

- Students: In this phase, macro changes at national policy level trickled down to the BEd programme and changed it to cater *only* to those students who were either qualifying to be secondary school English teachers or who wanted an academic major in English.
- Course length/focus: The course was extended to six weeks, providing greater scope for in-depth engagement with disciplinary knowledge but remained embedded in lived language experiences as this was central to our preferred approach to language teaching. It was renamed 'An Introduction to Sociolinguistics'.
- Assessment: This phase was characterized by experimentation with a new kind of narrative assignment which was used in two of the six years. It had two parts: (1) students wrote a dialogue in a youth variety they were familiar with and (2) they then wrote an analysis of their dialogue. See Figure 1.2. This

was done with a view to assisting students to gain some critical distance from their own writing and to give them an opportunity to problematize certain discourses. Language narratives continued to be used in the other years.

- Materials: More academic texts were added to readings, including one which modelled the form of dialogue writing required for performative assessment purposes (Cook 2009).

ASSIGNMENT BRIEF & ASSESSMENT CRITERIA: April 2010

Dialogue with commentary

Section 1: Dialogue

Write a dialogue between two or more participants which illustrates the use of your own youth variety. Your dialogue must be situated in a specific context, and the audience and purpose of the dialogue must be made explicit at the outset.

The dialogue may be written in any language or dialect of your choice (e.g. Tsotsitaal, Afrikaans). However, you must provide translations. If the entire dialogue is written in a language or dialect other than Standard English, the entire text must be translated. If the text is written in Standard English with specific slang words, then a glossary must be provided. Follow the format of Cook's dialogue transcript on page 58 in the reading pack.

[50 marks]

Section 2: Commentary

Analyse the role of your youth variety in this dialogue in relation to the following categories:

Intended audience

Context and purpose

Group membership and expression of specific identities (e.g. gender and cultural identities)

[50 marks]

Assessment criteria

Dialogue:

1. Interesting use of language in a specific context.
2. Dialogue generates substantial content that is suitable for sociolinguistic analysis.
3. Dialogue is vivid, convincing and feels like a slice of real life dialogue.

Commentary:

1. Key categories are developed and used effectively for analysis.
2. Insightful analysis of the event and related language practices are evident.
3. The analysis explores the relationship between the key categories, e.g. the relationship between language and gender, group membership, language and race/class.

Figure 1.2 Assessment brief and criteria for the dialogue and commentary.

Sociopolitical landscape

This cohort consisted mostly of students born after 1994 who became known as the born-free generation. Like the term 'rainbow nation', the term 'born-free' is problematic, suggesting that the baggage of the apartheid past can be left behind whereas 'the recurring echoes of the past are often alarmingly resonant' (Bradbury and Clark 2012: 176). This complex entanglement of past and present is well expressed by Bundy (2014) who argues that the born-free generation aspire to be liberated from the past yet are themselves shaped by and positioned within its legacy. Expectations of change and of a better life than that of their parents are juxtaposed with disappointment and frustration with corruption, unemployment and poverty (Mattes 2012). Chikane describes the born-frees as 'a generation of South Africans who are indentured to the rainbow nation motif' (2018: 6) since they are trapped in the system without agency or power to change it.

Chapters 5 and 6 in this book analyse the student dialogues and commentaries from this phase. Three other publications have also focused on this phase of work: namely, Dixon and Mendelowitz (2016), Mendelowitz and Dixon (2016) and Mendelowitz (2017).

Phase 3: 2016–20

- Students: In this phase, the course continued to cater for specialist English teachers at high-school level. English I also became a compulsory course for generalist teachers aiming to teach in primary school.
- Course length/focus: Continued as a six-week course with the title 'An Introduction to Sociolinguistics'. Courses in 2016, 2017 and 2019 were disrupted by student protests resulting in a loss of teaching time. The course in 2020 was disrupted by Covid-19 and was delivered asynchronously online via the Wits e-Learning platform.
- Assessment: Due to the disrupted academic programme, take-home assessments were submitted online for some years. However, the extended language narrative – or a version of it – remained the dominant task in most years.
- Materials: These kept being updated, particularly the everyday texts that supported key sociolinguistic concepts. Increasingly, digital texts such as TED talks and YouTube videos were included in materials to be read/watched by students. We also developed a more explicit focus on language and race.

Sociopolitical landscape

The first #FeesMustFall protests started after the 2015 iteration of the course and before the 2016 iteration. These nationwide student protests were initially triggered by student anger about fee increases but as the protests unfolded it became clear that the fees were a symptom of widespread anger about racialized economic and educational inequalities and the lack of systemic change since 1994. These protests radically changed the discourses in universities, and the power relations between students and lecturers as well as in society at large. On the whole, the course was enriched by the raised political awareness of students, their engagement with new discourses and stronger student voices. Issues that had sometimes lain beneath the surface of previous iterations of the course were explored in more explicit ways and our positionality as white, middle-class academics steeped in the western episteme needed critical and creative reflection.

Chapter 7 in this book analyses student language narratives from this phase.

The shifting student cohorts

The demographic data we obtained on students is intended to provide supporting information for understanding some of the dynamics that emerge in their narratives. While we have not carried out an exhaustive analysis of this data, there are a number of clear trends that can be pointed out. In Table 1.1, we presented the data for the 2005 student cohort – the first group to whom we presented the sociolinguistics course. Here we present full data sets from 2005 to 2020 in Figures 1.3–1.5.

Figure 1.3 shows that every year all eleven official languages have been represented in the student cohort. (The single exception is in 2010 when there were no isiNdebele speakers.) Also noticeable is the decrease in English home-language speakers from 63.9 per cent in 2005 to 18.8 per cent in 2020. Conversely isiZulu home-language speakers – who have always been the second-largest home-language group – show an upswing from 12.6 per cent in 2005 to 31.1 per cent in 2020.[2]

When we compare the number of students who self-report speaking English as a home language with the number of students who take English as a subject at Home Language[3] level at school, we see that there is a significant increase in non-English home-language speakers taking English at Home-Language level. While in 2005 these two cohorts were similar proportions (49 per cent spoke English at home, and 51 per cent were studying English at school at Home Language level). However, by 2020, we see that while 38 per cent of students

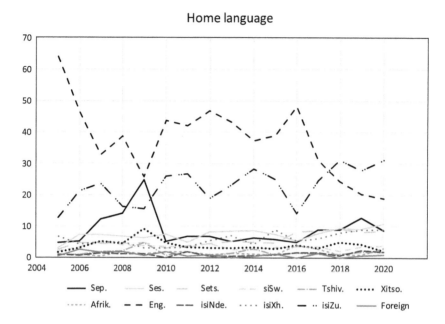

Figure 1.3 Students' reported home language, 2005–20.

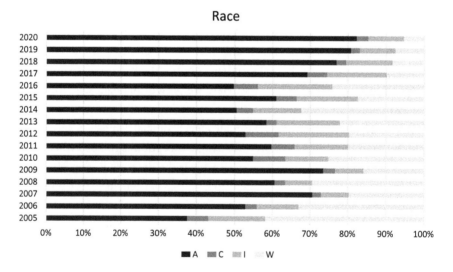

Figure 1.4 The racial demographics of the students, 2005–2020.

are reporting that English is their home language, 62 per cent of students are taking it at home-language level. In other words, English is steadily becoming the dominant school language of our students across the board, lending support to hypothesis that there is growing bilingualism in English (Deumert 2010; Posel and Zeller 2019; Posel, Hunter and Rudwick 2020).

School Quintile

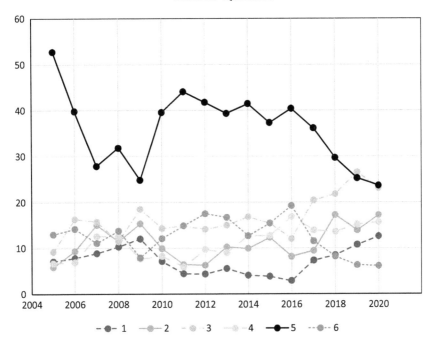

Figure 1.5 Quintiles of the schools in which our students completed their schooling.

Figure 1.4 shows the shifting race demographic. Indian and coloured students remain in the minority.

Throughout, Indian students represent between 7 and 9 per cent of the cohort, while coloured students represent between 2 and 8 per cent of the cohort. White students, however, have decreased from 41 per cent in 2005 to 5 per cent in 2020; black students have increased from 37 per cent in 2005 to 82 per cent in 2020. This correlates with the comparable English/isiZulu home language trend in Figure 1.3 and is indicative of the relationship between home language and race.

Lastly, Figure 1.5 represents the quintiles (i.e. socioeconomic indicators) of the schools from which students matriculated.

As can be seen in Figure 1.5, the full economic spectrum of schools is present. Students who attended no-fee paying schools (52 per cent in 2020) are to be found alongside students who attended top government schools and private schools (39 per cent and 6 per cent, respectively, in 2020).

Thus in 2005 our typical student would have been an English-speaking white female attending a historically white government school in the suburbs and taking English at Home-Language level at school. In 2020, our typical student is now an isiZulu-speaking black female taking English at FAL level at school and she would either be from a historically white suburban government school or from a no-fee paying school (each representing 23 per cent of the cohort). A more in-depth analysis of this data would need to, for example, compare some of these shifts against those of the broader university student population. It would also need to take into account how the changing university admission points may have impacted on student intake and would need to investigate whether the increased availability of bursaries and funding has widened access to previously excluded portions of the population. For our purposes, this data helps us to understand more about who our students are and how their language narratives speak from their positions in the shifting social terrain.

Texts selected

Selecting texts for the purpose of teaching this course has been, and continues to be, a central and dynamic aspect of our work. This is because text selection is aligned not only with curriculum but also with pedagogy. In other words, our text selection is not merely governed by what disciplinary knowledge we want students to engage with. It is informed by our pedagogic aims of embedding this sociolinguistic knowledge in real-life worlds by having students' own embodied worlds come into the classroom and take their place alongside those of their peers and others. In order to bring this about, when we collate the course reading pack we draw on a broader range of text types than those conventionally associated with university studies and/or academic knowledge. While individual texts may vary from year to year, they tend to fall into four broad and overlapping categories: academic texts, published language narratives, previous students' language narratives and everyday texts. Each category of text has a particular purpose in the overarching design of the course. Academic texts (e.g. academic articles or book chapters) introduce and explain the disciplinary knowledge of sociolinguistics and provide the analytical tools and metalanguage needed. Published language narratives (e.g. extracts from memoirs and essays) are used to illustrate how sociolinguistic concepts can be seen at play in lived, contextualized language experiences. They also serve to familiarize students with the written genre (i.e. reflective narratives) that they themselves need to produce. Student language narratives produced by students from previous cohorts provide highly relatable, contemporary, locally situated language narratives. Everyday texts (e.g. newspaper, magazine or online media articles; cartoons or memes; and YouTube videos and TED talks) serve to illustrate how language practices are embedded in society and provide additional entry points to complex sociolinguistic concepts and issues.

While categorizing texts can be useful for delineating their different roles, there are two important caveats to be made. First, from a pedagogic perspective, the role or purpose of a text is not inherent in the text itself but is enacted through the framing, activities and questions asked of that text in the process of pedagogizing it. To truly understand the role of texts in the classroom, it is necessary to investigate how they are put to use. To this end there is more detailed discussion in Chapter 3 on how we work pedagogically with texts.

Second, these four categories are not mutually exclusive. They separate knowledge into fairly random categories which themselves are shot through with the workings of genres, modalities, registers, contexts and other features. Indeed, some of the pedagogic work that we do is an attempt to challenge these very categories and to facilitate movement *across* categories as well as to generate hybrid modes or genres *within* categories. A recent example of this level of textual diversity is to be found in the 2020 online iteration of the course, around the work of well-known linguist David Crystal. Students are introduced to his ideas via three different types of texts: one of his academic articles (Crystal 1994), a newspaper article about Crystal (Baudot Morcillo 2016) and a YouTube video (Crystal 2013) where he gives a talk about the same issues. Thus the shifts across genre and modality are a way of providing multiple entry points to academic knowledge. We contend that attempting to use texts that use as broad a range of semiotic resources as possible plays an important role in facilitating epistemological access. This is particularly important because, as we have experienced over the years, students are always highly engaged in the first few weeks of the course when their own and their peers' language histories and experiences are at the centre of the discussion, but they often struggle with the texts that provide a more academic orientation to sociolinguistics.

A key contribution our study seeks to make is in relation to narrative pedagogy/narrative ways of knowing. We elaborate later on the theorized choice of language narratives and consider their role in the learning process.

Role of language narratives

It is summer holidays clear blue skies, hot, sticky days and late afternoon thundershowers. The university has emptied out, no students in sight. But Ana and I are on a mission – to find rich, vivid narratives that we can use for our evolving course that is starting to take on a life of its own. We are digging through the

library shelves and finding plenty of American compilations of the sorts of stories
we are looking for but no South African language narratives. We are frustrated by
this gap. Still, we leave the library each with piles of books full of promise and we
manage to get some local student language/literacy narratives from a colleague
who teaches a distance learning course for teachers.

Extract from Belinda's reflective notes, December 2004

Selecting resonant language narrative texts was a crucial part of our initial course development and it continues to be a significant part of our course design. As the previous vignette suggests, one of our early challenges was sourcing South African material that spoke to local multilingual practices, using local varieties.

Since those early days two factors have played a role in enabling us to more easily place local narratives front and centre. In the mid-2000s, the local publishing industry seemed to awaken to the richness of the South African experience, and there was a proliferation of compelling memoirs or memoir-like narratives written by young and old. Some of these offer valuable insights into how issues around language, identity and power were navigated by the writer, and they have thus found their way into different iterations of the course. Over the years, however, it has become clear to us that it is our students' own language narratives that have played the most significant role in addressing the gap in local language narratives. The dynamics of this process – both epistemological and ontological – are discussed in more detail later.

Published language narratives

We have used a variety of published narratives that explore language and identity issues in many different contexts. These narratives have come from different geographic and cultural contexts and have taken different forms. (See Appendix 1 for full details.) Narratives – sometimes embodying a single personalized voice and perspective, at other times containing multiple personalized micro-stories – are drawn from memoirs and autobiographies, from novels and poems, from lectures and testimonials and from newspaper and magazine articles. While around half of these narratives are South African or African, also represented are Chicanx writers, African American writers, an Aboriginal testimonial and others. We make no attempt to cover all possible positions and perspectives but we aim to signal that all voices are welcome. Exposure to this level of cultural and linguistic diversity is at least partly for the purpose of assisting students to imagine themselves and their stories into being alongside these published narratives. We want our students to see themselves –

even if just in glimpses initially – in the curriculum, and then write themselves into this curriculum.

Some narratives have come and gone over the years, but a handful have been retained over time. Although varying in style and focus, all have one thing in common: each writer has been part of a minority and/or marginalized group at some point and has experienced language at formative stages in her/his life in coercive and difficult contexts. Each writer takes a strong position on the issue raised and sometimes different writers provide opposing views on the same issue.

Table 1.3 provides an overview of what we consider to be our core narratives at the moment and is followed by some discussion about why they have become core to the course.

These narratives emanate from Kenya, the United States and various South African contexts. The quotations in the first column are intended to give a sense of the voice of each writer while alluding to some of the issues raised – such as naming and labelling; language and ethnic identity; and language, education and power. All these issues have profound emotional and educational significance and are strongly located in individual and social contexts. We believe that it is crucial to present these issues in the context of particular individual experiences rather than as decontextualized abstract concepts.

Gloria Anzaldúa's text, for example, provides a vivid illustration of movement between personal and broader social issues. Anzaldúa's essay 'How to Tame a Wild Tongue' (2000b) explores the theme of linguistic terrorism and marginalization from her position as a multilingual, Chicana writer. Her text exemplifies 'genre border crossing' and blurs traditional boundaries on a range of levels, containing 'a blend of poetry, memoir and historical analysis' (McQuade and Atwan 2000: 311) as well as fierce argument, polemic and reflection. She also blurs linguistic boundaries by switching between English and varieties of Spanish and makes a conscious choice not to translate her use of Spanish. In so doing she challenges monolingual English-speaking readers to put themselves in her shoes and to experience what it is like not to be accommodated linguistically.

Crossing the Atlantic, Ngũgĩ wa Thiong'o's (1986) narrative extract raises the issue of linguistic oppression in a colonial African context and his experiences, despite the 1950s setting, are painfully familiar for many of our students. While it is valuable to draw on a narrative located in a relatively familiar context, there are also benefits to using global narratives that raise familiar issues in unfamiliar contexts. These texts invite identification at a safe distance, generating debate about painful issues within a contained space. For example, Naylor's text (2000)

Table 1.3 Core published language narratives

Key quotation	Author and title	Context	Language issues emerging
So, if you really want to hurt me, talk badly about my language. Ethnic identity is twin skin to linguistic identity – I am my language.	Gloria Anzaldúa / *How to Tame a Wild Tongue*	1980s Texas, USA / Mexican/Chicana	The connection between home language, dialects and identity; linguistic persecution and linguistic terrorism
In Kenya, English became more than a language; it was the language, and all the others had to bow down before it in deference.	Ngũgĩ wa Thiong'o / *Decolonising the Mind*	1950s Kenya / Rural African peasant family/community	Language and colonization; the problems caused by studying in an alien language; language, identity and culture
So there must have been dozens of times that the word 'n–' was spoken in front of me before I reached the third grade. But I didn't hear it until it was said by a small pair of lips that had already learnt it could be a way to humiliate me.	Gloria Naylor / *A Question of Language*	1950s Harlem, New York, USA / Working-class African American community	The shifting meaning of language and naming in different contexts
My parents' ethnic origins are not enough to make me honestly say that I belong to the same community. Speaking a language or having a name that suggests a certain ethnic lineage is just not enough for one to become a member.	Fikile-Ntsikelelo Moya / *Ekasi Is My Roots*	2006 Johannesburg, South Africa / Urban black	Challenging assumptions about language heritage and identity
How can you expect anyone to respect you when you turn your back on your own culture so easily, when you are so quick to adopt the dominant culture?	Nicole Johnston / *A Cocktail of Cultures*	2006 Johannesburg, South Africa / Minority ethnic communities	Explores different perspectives on identities among South African youth from minority ethnic communities
There is a sense of loss, because at some point I started dreaming and thinking in English. . . . But also, this language has given me access to so many things – my career, for one.	Nolwazi Tusini / *Language Matters*	1990s and 2016, South Africa / Urban black	Explores attitudes to English through interviews with black students who attended historically white schools in the 1990s

about being labelled a 'n--' by a white child in an American 1950s' context generates robust debate about naming, and inevitably students make connections between the text and their own experiences of derogatory naming in the South African context.

The three final narratives draw on the voices of contemporary, young South Africans. Moya's text (2006), since its inclusion into the pack in 2006, continues to generate particularly significant and engaging debates about the role of language in urban identity construction and the possibility of conscious choice in constructing a new or hybrid identity. It has resonated for many of our students who often use extracts from it to frame their own language narratives. In the same vein, Tusini's (2016b) text draws on multiple perspectives of young black South Africans regarding the losses and affordances of taking ownership of English and its implications for their identities. Johnston's (2006) text provides a range of perspectives from young South Africans from ethnic minority communities.

Having provided an overview of the kinds of narratives used, in terms of themes and shifting genres, we now turn to a discussion of the role of the students' own language narratives in the learning process.

Students' own language narratives

The formal inclusion of selected student narratives in course reading materials has become a central pedagogic strategy. It is these student language narratives that have become representative of local language experiences, and they have taken their place alongside published narratives such as those of Ngũgĩ wa Thiong'o, Gloria Anzaldúa and Barak Obama (2007). Since 2006, the course reading pack has always contained approximately five to eight language narratives from previous years' students. But, when moving online in 2020, there were no longer any printing constraints operating and students were given access to weekly folders with multiple student narratives as optional extension work. Each week a new folder of such narratives was made available and students were encouraged to read them, as shown in Figure 1.6, a screenshot of the weekly reading task in 2020.

We regard it as crucial that the students write their own language biographies and 'bec[o]me authors alongside the authors they read' (Zamel 1998: 195), not just passive consumers of other people's narratives, but active producers of their own histories. This encourages them to make direct links between what they are reading and what they are writing, and to think about their own histories in relation to those of others.

Week 1 Reading: Past students' language narratives

Every week we will provide a folder in RESOURCES that contains rich and interesting language narratives written by past students. Go to the **Sociolinguistics folder** in resources. Then click on **the student language narratives folder.** Make sure that you read at least one a week. This will give you a sense of the kinds of issues students have written about in previous courses, extend your understanding of the issues and help prepare you for writing your own language narrative.

Read 'O *Nascimento do futuro*' (the birth of the future) by Thapang and '*My story of language: adaptation, transition and integration*' by Shanaya.

Sneak preview of this week's narratives....

THAPANG

Are you haunted by the ghosts of your past? They seem to follow Thapang everywhere he goes! The melody of languages and tongues clicking over the sound of the hustle and bustle of city traffic. Have you ever experienced this kind of music to your ears? But be wary, sometimes opening your mouth may turn into a violent encounter. Continue reading '**O Nascimento do futuro**' by Thapang to find out what happens next.

SHANAYA

Do you sometimes feel like you don't fit in the moment you open your mouth? The way you speak can sometimes make you feel different from others. This is because we carry traces of who we are and where we come from which are reflected in the way we speak. Read '**My story of language: adaptation, transition and integration**' by Shanaya to explore her journey of being 'different'.

Figure 1.6 Weekly reading task from the 2020 online course.

Finally, it needs to be said that there seems to be a 'magic factor' associated with using students' language narratives that is as difficult to express as it is easy to discern. Over the years, we have found students particularly drawn to the narratives of their predecessors in the course. They have derived inspiration, it would seem, not just from the fact that they have access to potentially relatable language histories but because these were written by students who – one year, two, three, five years ago – had been here, doing this course, sitting in the very seats that they were sitting. And here were their stories in print, being drawn into our collective pool of language knowledge and experience. And because we began each course by letting students know that they would be producing their own language narratives and that, with their permission, their narratives might find their way into future course reading packs, they were aware that their own soon-to-be-written stories could be read by future students. On a surface level, there was the alluring possibility of a certain 'fame' being accorded to them, leaving their mark on the course, as it were, before moving on. But on a deeper level it was, from our side, a concrete manifestation of how profoundly their own knowledges and experiences were being valued: they were not only being taken seriously in the here and now of the course, but their stories might live on beyond it. This was the effect of the onto-epistemological move we sought to generate through the course design.

The purpose of this chapter has been to provide an overview of the historical, political and institutional contexts from which the course emerged, and to explain how these shaped both its initial conceptualization and various changes over time. Three phases of the course have been identified and described in order to enable the data analysis chapters (Chapters 4–7) to be read against this backdrop, thus deepening the relationship between the students' work, the course pedagogy and the broader sociopolitical context. Chapter 2 unpacks the narrative frame which holds the course together.

2

Narrative Ways of Knowing

We are stories. Stories stitched with scars of history and language. Draped into breadths of fabric. Coloured, pressed and starched cloths of moments we are forced to wear, quoted into human identity.

Extract from Pumla's narrative, 2017

I started engaging more with other people in class. I feel as if, before this, I would have been a person who would have stuck to themselves, attend and leave, attend and leave, but all of a sudden, I was interested in other people, because now I had my story, and this was my story, and I want to know, 'What's your story?'

Extract from Thulisile's focus group discussion, 2020

From the early stages of conceptualizing the sociolinguistics course, we envisaged that narrative would play a key role in framing course content and engaging the students through reading and writing processes. The central role of narrative began as an intuition, as often happens in course development. Over the sixteen years that we have taught and researched the course, this intuition has been strengthened and has become a strong conviction, validated by our experience of teaching the course and by the research and readings we have done.

More than ever, we are convinced that narrative as a way of knowing has a critical role to play in teacher language education. Although much has changed in the composition of our student cohorts, the higher education landscape and the broader sociopolitical terrain in South Africa, the elasticity of narrative as a pedagogical tool enables us to make ongoing culturally responsive shifts to meet the needs of our students.

This chapter provides the framework for this book by discussing why narrative has always played a central role in the sociolinguistics course. We will discuss our conceptualization of narrative and what we understand by narrative ways of knowing. We draw on interdisciplinary and shifting theoretical frames, readings, our conversations and insights that have emerged from our practice. Our thinking about narrative has been influenced by scholars from a range of disciplines: Bruner (1986) in cognitive psychology, McEwan and Egan (1995) in educational philosophy, Busch (2014) in sociolinguistics, Goodson and Gill (2014) in critical educational narrative studies and Bradbury (2020) in critical psychology.

As already discussed, our work is underpinned by a critical orientation. Following Freire (1996), we are interested in teaching and learning that is dialogic, that foregrounds connections between self and other, the individual and the world. We are particularly interested in language and literacy as tools for social change. Reading and writing are powerful processes that can facilitate new ways of seeing, particularly when one works with a critical orientation. However, we do not limit ourselves to scholarship with a critical orientation. Rather, over the years we have drawn on ideas about narrative that we find inspiring and put them to work for critical purposes. Despite disciplinary and underlying ideological differences between, for example, Bruner's focus on the individual's inner worlds and our focus on the self in sociocultural contexts, we find it productive to extend Bruner's ways of knowing into multiple ways of knowing that include exploration of the relationship between language and power, social identities and critical lenses.

Furthermore, as teacher educators in the Global South, it is critically important for us to grapple with decoloniality in relation to our conceptualization of narrative. The second part of this chapter is an exploration of the connections between narrative as a way of knowing and decoloniality. This provides us with an opportunity to further explore the elasticity of narrative and the extent to which it can work as an emerging decolonial praxis.

What is narrative?

Gill (2014b: 71) defines narrative as encompassing 'a sequence or sequences of events which take place within particular historical, social, cultural, political and individual personal situations'. While it is common to think about chronological order as a feature of narratives, the reality is much more fluid, often entailing moves between past and present. Furthermore, narratives are never about linear progression as the process of telling a story draws on multiple selves and perspectives. For example, one might be telling a story about a past self but with the perspectives and insights of one's present self.

Narrative is also a fluid and flexible genre that can take multiple forms and can include oral, visual and written modes. Stories are everywhere. They can be found in social interactions, fictional and autobiographical texts, everyday texts and objects, to mention but a few. For audiences there are multiple ways to access stories including reading, viewing and listening across modes and digital platforms.

The narratives that interest us are frequently at the cusp of narration, reflection and argumentation. This element of genre boundary crossing is one example of what we mean by the elasticity of narrative as it challenges artificial boundaries between academic and everyday knowledge, enabling students to integrate knowing and being in their writing. We are particularly interested in narratives that draw on all three elements – telling a story, reflecting on its meaning and making an argument based on the issues that emerge. The focus of our course and research are two kinds of personal written narratives: a language narrative and a dialogue with a critical, reflective commentary. These two narrative genres have different but complementary affordances as we will illustrate in Chapters 4–7.

Having defined narrative, we move to a discussion of how narratives (re) shape identities. We conceptualize narrative as a fundamental marker of being human that has always been an integral part of human activities across time, space and cultures. We make sense of our lives through stories and construct our identities through the stories we tell ourselves and others, as well as the stories we hear from others. As readers of stories, we always make stories our own, rewriting and re-imagining them and assimilating them into the emotional landscape of our own lives (Bruner 1986: 37).

Hence, storytelling is an important part of identity construction. Storytelling enables us to explore both our inner and outer landscapes, external events and experiences and the landscape of consciousness, our inner worlds of thoughts, feelings and knowing (Bruner 1986: 14). As Pumla's opening extract of the chapter suggests, we carry around a mix of positive and negative stories, with power and coercion playing a role in the storied identities we take up. Narratives, as cultural texts, are never neutral and some narratives are more valued than others. But there are always gaps and spaces for resistance and scarring stories can be unstitched and restitched as we retell a story from a different perspective in ways that reshape present and future selves.

Language and identity are central to this process. Drawing on Weedon (1987) and Norton (1997), we work with a poststructuralist view of identity as multiple, fluid and constructed in/across broader sociocultural contexts. While language enables multiple activities, we are particularly interested in language as tool for 'conceptualizing the world' (Bradbury 2020), (re)constructing selves and critical reflection. Equally, we are interested in students' narratives about their multilingual language histories and identities. Hence, we have a dual fascination with language as cultural tool and as subject matter.

Elements of narrative

This section outlines what we consider to be the key elements of narrative. We begin with a description of a significant narrative encounter and move between vignettes throughout this section in order to enact and apply narrative ways of knowing.

The first two drafts of this section were written using a traditional academic style and process. Both were somewhat decontextualized, silencing our histories and voices. The (re)writing of this chapter using narrative as a springboard generated a different web of ideas, enabling us to bring the different parts of ourselves together into an embodied scholarly performance that merges knowing and being. However, this blending of narrative and academic discourse leads to complicated use of pronouns as there are multiple voices. There is the 'we' of the voice of the three authors but there is also the 'we' of the literacy history group members in the narrative. And then there is the 'I' of Belinda's personal reflective memories.

A significant narrative encounter (the Applied English Language Studies Seminar Room)

I have always loved stories and as an English teacher, stories always played an important role in my work. However, one significant experience made me realize how powerful students' stories can be as an educational tool.

> *After ten years of teaching, I have taken a year off to do a postgraduate degree in Applied Linguistics. It is both exciting and terrifying to be a student again. The lecturers' emphasis on collaboration, linking theory to practice and active learning are helping me to overcome my fear and find an academic voice. The seminar room space, with its moveable tables, reinforces the sense that this is a space for collaborating and sharing ideas with peers and lecturers.*
>
> *Now, in the second term we are doing a course with Professor Pippa Stein on literacy as social practice. In 1996 this is a new wave of ideas and with each new seminar my ideas about literacy are being reconfigured and my sense of what is*

possible is expanding. Pippa is writing some of the key concepts on the blackboard as she talks with conviction about how reading and writing and oral storytelling are social practices located in multiple socio-cultural settings. We journey to case studies at taxi ranks, in living rooms, and prayer gatherings. We are introduced to ideas of Brian Street, Shirley Brice Heath, David Barton and Mastin Prinsloo.

My mind is already bursting with these new ideas, excited and overwhelmed that the idea I grew up with – of literacy as an individual, decontextualized activity – has flown out the window of the seminar room.

And then Pippa drops a bombshell!

She tells us that our main project for the course is a group literacy histories performance project. She allocates us into groups that she has carefully chosen to facilitate cross-cultural interactions. We move hesitantly across the seminar room to sit at a table with our newly formed group and begin to read through the project briefing in detail. I am feeling a mix of intrigue, enthusiasm and discomfort. The slow realization dawns that we will need to dig deep into ourselves and excavate memories, making them vivid and engaging for an audience. And so it begins, my introduction to narrative ways of knowing that upend old ways of knowing, taking me in an entirely new direction as student and educator. (Belinda's Reflection 1)

Narrative ways of knowing

The literacy histories project provides a vivid example of narrative ways of knowing. By this we mean, coming to know – and be – through stories of lived experiences. Unlike the dominant western, scientific academic mode, narrative ways of knowing are provisional and value personal experience. In addition, narrative ways of knowing incorporate affect and emotion. Belinda's memory continues in the next vignette and provides more details about the ways of knowing that were facilitated by the project process.

A whole new way of knowing opens up to me in relation to lived experience, and one that is collaborative. We are required to share stories about our literacy histories with group members and make connections to the theories. This is an entirely different starting point to what I expected having come through a traditional undergraduate degree that seldom privileged the self and lived experiences.

My participation in this project is a powerful learning experience, making me realise that personal and everyday stories can be the focus of learning and can help students to explore meaningful connections between lived experience and conventional academic knowledge. Instead of writing a conventional essay about theories of multiliteracies, we enact our literacy histories within the theoretical frames of the course. As a group we debate which theoretical lenses we should use to frame our stories and whether we would gain more theoretical insights by writing a formal essay. We find it exciting when theory overlaps with specific scenes of our presentation, but mostly integrating theory and practice is difficult. (Belinda's Reflection 2)

The project enabled the participants to bring their own personal, social, cultural and linguistic resources and identities into the classroom and to use these resources to construct knowledge. It was an embodied learning experience in the sense that it enabled the participants to know and be, think and feel in the same moments. The usual ordering of knowledge construction was reversed, as participants moved recursively and fluidly between personal experience and memories and readings and theory. It opened up narrative ways of knowing in productive ways. This included a broadening of the process of knowing to include fellow students as resources, challenging the notion of academic learning as individualized and solitary. The final presentation was a performance, which made it an even more strongly embodied experience for presenters and audience. Across the various groups, stories traversed cities, countries and continents and included dances and songs as elements of performance.

Bruner (1986: 12–13) refers to this process as 'narrative modes of thought' and contrasts it with 'paradigmatic thought', which emphasizes logic, argument and general cases (i.e. knowledge that takes the form of generalizations). He acknowledges that different kinds of imagination play an important role in both ways of knowing, an important insight that is all too often overlooked. Bruner argues that these are two distinct but complementary modes of thinking and that both are necessary 'to capture the richness and diversity of thought' (1986: 11). However, paradigmatic thought has been privileged in western culture at the expense of narrative modes of thought.

In 1986, Bruner's challenge to western epistemologies was significant, opening a path for educators like us to approach language teacher education with a more flexible view of knowledge construction. However, we find his binarization of narrative/paradigmatic ways of knowing limiting and we move beyond these binaries. We agree with arguments made by Mayher (1990: 100) and Huberman (1995: 129) that narrative and paradigmatic thought are not necessarily as distinct as Bruner claims and that the formulation of thought and knowledge can shift between the two modes in a single text, spoken or written.

Locatedness (temporality and spatiality)

During the literacy history project, we meet at each other's houses to exchange stories in different parts of Johannesburg. These informal, personal spaces are more conducive to getting to know each other than the formal academic space of the university. We begin to know each other not only as fellow students but as individuals with our own specific histories and stories. As we share stories, we journey across multiple time periods, memories and emotions, places and spaces with each other as far apart as Cape Town, Johannesburg, KwaZulu Natal and Lagos. Learning happens in unexpected, informal ways, in-between rehearsals.

One evening after discussing teenage love letters, we get onto the topic of courtship and flirtation in different cultures. David and Sizwe exchange stories about acceptable practices for expressing interest in women in each of their cultures. I speak about my association of flowers with love, while Sizwe says that he has never given or received flowers in his life. Gender seems to play a significant role in shaping our literacy histories, in some ways overriding our cultural differences. As teenage boys David and Sizwe both recalled retreating into a world of books while Joslin and I shared similar memories of letter-writing playing a big role in our teenage literacy practices, amidst a flurry of social activities. These included letters to and from friends and love letters. (Belinda's Reflection 3)

This vignette illustrates the locatedness of narrative in time and space. There are multiple moves facilitated by the process of sharing stories. These include the moves between different locations of group rehearsals and how these constitute different spaces for storytelling. While place is a geographical location with long-term stability, spaces are made through the interactions of people who occupy them and their social and cultural practices (Horner and Dailey-O'Cain 2019). The home rehearsal space was generative for the sharing of stories across difference and facilitated imaginative moves across time and spaces, facilitating the construction of participants' narrative identities in relation to each other.

McEwan and Egan (1995) argue that narrative always locates its content, whether it is facts, theories or dreams, in the context of someone's emotion and from the perspective of someone's life. Hence, the locatedness of narratives in time and space facilitates the telling and retelling of individual stories in relation to broader sociopolitical, cultural and emotional contexts. It creates space for embodied identity work and engagement with emotion in knowledge construction, something that is frequently erased by academic discourse.

Telling, retelling and selection

The literacy histories project facilitated the process of telling and retelling stories for various audiences: the audience of group members, selves as audience and the postgraduate class for the final presentation. Participants had to decide which stories from a lifetime of literacy experiences to select, what details to exclude and how to tell the stories. These choices were shaped both by what each group member considered significant and by which stories they felt comfortable sharing. Inevitably, there were some gaps and silences around memories that were too difficult to share in this particular space. However, these silences were not only about individual, personal choices but also about the dominant discourses which always influence what is considered sayable and shareable in public domains.

> *We are a diverse group – one Nigerian woman (Joslin), one white South African female (me), one black South African male (Sizwe), one white South African male (David). We have productive opportunities to hear about experiences that were both similar and different to our own in terms of gender, race, ethnicity and culture.*
>
> *I still have the photographs of the final performance. Looking at those photographs, what strikes me is Joslin's strong presence as she enacts in visceral ways the telling of a traditional Nigerian story. She is dressed in full traditional garb, a red and black outfit with a matching headscarf. She takes centre stage, using all the physical and semiotic resources available to her – movement, gestures, dramatic voice. She alternates between sitting on a chair and leaping around the room, while we as her audience sit on the floor, enraptured by her story. In contrast, my portrayal of early literacy is more sedentary – about escape into other words in solitary ways and sitting on my father's lap as he reads to me. (Belinda's Reflection 4)*

Narrative is an embodied process and always entails elements of performance and imagination. As literacy history stories were shared, participants tried to engage the various audiences through vivid storytelling. This aspect of the encounter highlights another feature of narrative that we consider important. The storyteller has the dual role of narrator and main protagonist while the people, places and events of her life are transformed into characters, setting and plot. The storyteller often makes the characters more convincing by capturing their distinct voices through effective use of dialogue. Hence, narrative is an imaginative process that enables the teller to construct a narrative self. The vignette also illustrates the power of narrative to facilitate (re)imagining and dialogue across difference, self and other.

Narrative as dialogic process

The discussion of dialogues across difference brings us to the dialogic aspect of narrative, a central part of our conceptualization. Dialogism extends way beyond a conversation between two or more people. It refers to multiple dynamic interactions with the self, with others and with texts and cultural resources. We would agree with Chadwick (2017: 12) that narrative is 'radically dialogical' and we argue that it operates in three different ways. The first and the most self-evident is that narratives are told to an audience (listener/reader), and the shape and selection of the story and the way it is told will be affected by the context of telling and the relationship between the narrator and audience.

The second aspect of the dialogic process entails a dialogue with the self. We find the work of Bradbury (2020) particularly insightful for this discussion. Following Vygotsky (1997), she argues that inner conversations and dialogues with the self are a critically important aspect of the narrative process. The narrating self becomes both subject of the story and object of reflection and analysis, enabling one to see the self as other, through one's own eyes and the eyes of others. Bradbury (2020: 23) concludes that these inner conversations 'enable new relations with the world, possibilities to imagine alternatives and transform the present parameters of our situation'.

The third and related aspect of the dialogic process is that it is multi-voiced (Bakhtin 1981). In the process of creating a narrative we draw on voices of our past, present and future selves as well as voices of others we have encountered throughout our lives. We are social selves. 'We cannot escape history or stand outside culture' (Bradbury 2020: 10). Throughout our lives we internalize the voices of others and as a result narrative is infused with multiple voices. Although as humans we are constrained by these internalized voices, there are gaps and spaces for the development of resistant voices (Bradbury 2020).

Narrative as an educational tool

In their conceptualization of narrative, Goodson and Gill (2014) foreground the transformative, humanizing and reconciliatory potential of critical narrative in both formal and informal educational contexts. We share their belief that narrative has the potential to be transformative in the context of teaching and learning. In this section, we present three tools that we use to deepen our students' critical and creative engagement with narrative: critical reflexivity, creativity and criticality.

Critical reflexivity

Critical reflexivity is a fundamental element of our conceptualization of narrative as educational tool. It is what enables us to take students on a journey into and beyond their individual stories. Gill (2014b: 75) defines critical reflexivity as 'one's ability to deconstruct certain assumptions and to construct and reconstruct meaning'. Depending on the writer's level of engagement, it can facilitate the production of a counter-story – a story that resists dominant narratives (Morrel 2008) and reconstructs meanings, which can enable new ways of seeing. From a critical literacy perspective this entails challenging the ideological assumptions embedded in dominant narratives.

Gill and Goodson's (2014) theory of context provides valuable insights into the relationship between contexts, dialogic processes and critical reflexivity. They argue that in order to engage critically with stories we need to consider the particularity of individual experience in broader social contexts. It is the dialogic relationship between the individual and the social that enables the development of a 'critical narrative gaze' and critical reflexivity (Gill 2014b: 76). Developing such a gaze involves exploring how one's individual identity is located within larger sociocultural, historical and political narratives and how one is positioned by the power dynamics of these narratives. An important aspect of such exploration is engagement in critical conversation and self-reflection that ultimately enables one to challenge identity positionings and imposed discourses.

Inner conversations enable the distancing and perspective shifts that are necessary for critical reflections on stories. However, in an educational context, inner conversations need to be facilitated alongside the use of disciplinary concepts that have the potential to generate new insights. Without the disciplinary concepts, it is possible that some students will simply retell their stories with insufficient reflection, reproducing internalized voices uncritically. Even with the scaffolding of disciplinary concepts, we have found that first-year students sometimes struggle to keep critical distance and emotions in balance when writing their language narratives, and we have needed to try out various interventions to help students with this. We elaborate on these in Chapter 3.

In the context of this book, students' narratives surface a range of Anglonormative ideological assumptions, in other words, 'the expectation that people will be and should be proficient in English and are deficient, even deviant, if they are not' (McKinney 2017: 80). These include the following assumptions: that white, South African English accents are the norm, and any other accent is a deviation; that there is only one acceptable variety of South African English, and varieties that do not fit are not 'proper English'; that in order for students to master English the dominant language of teaching and learning in South Africa, they should not speak their home languages at school. When students use sociolinguistic disciplinary concepts to reinterpret these experiences with a 'critical narrative gaze' they are potentially empowered to problematize these assumptions and to begin writing counter-narratives. We encourage students to compare how they interpreted an incident at the time and how they interpret it differently now through the disciplinary lens. This comparison enables the juxtaposition of different version of memories, experiences, voices and lenses.

Creativity and Criticality

While our conceptualization of narrative is underpinned by a strong critical orientation we are equally interested in the narrative imagination and the ways in which narrative can generate both criticality and creativity.

Writing a personal story is a creative act which shares many of the features of fictional writing. We share countless stories with friends, colleagues and family. Each time we do so, we have already made a selection from our memory archive. Think of the memory archive as 'a sort of slide projector flashing images on the wall of the mind' (Hampl 1999: 34). Some of these are dim, distant fragments – others are bright, loud and insistent. The process of memory selection is never simply about memory retrieval or reproduction. Rather it entails the selective reconstruction of specific memories that are frequently reinvented in the telling.

Hence, a storyteller makes the selection and then begins to narrate one version of the story rather than other possible versions. As she tells the story she naturally tries to make it engaging and vivid for an audience, drawing on literary strategies such as plot, setting, character and dialogue. It is not surprising that Hampl (1999) refers to the process of remembering and narrating a story as an imaginative process, one that draws on both memory and imagination.

So where does narrative fit in with this imaginative process? Gill (2014b) argues that re-storying – the process of looking for deeper meanings of stories and making connections to other stories – is the key to the development of the social imagination and collective transformative action. We prefer to use the term 'counter-storying' because of its explicit focus on writing back to dominant ideologies. Furthermore, we work with the concept of the critical imagination (Mendelowitz 2017), which brings together imagination and criticality in the context of narrative. We argue that when students engage in tasks that facilitate the critical imagination, both the poetic and social imagination can be developed. The poetic imagination mobilizes empathy (Kearney 1988), while the social imagination is about inventing alternative realities (Greene 1995). In Chapter 6 we elaborate on this concept and illustrate how it works in practice.

A central thread running through our conceptualization of narrative, which intersects with all its key elements, is fluid narrative identities. We construct and reconstruct our identities through the stories we tell. This is both a creative process and a process that facilitates criticality as we select versions of experiences and reinterpret them with a 'critical narrative gaze'. These include moves between past, present and future selves and identities and explorations of how specific cultural and social spaces have shaped the formation of different selves. An important aspect of these moves is the dialogic nature of narrative, including dialogue with the self and with others. All of these elements of narrative enable the integration of knowing and being.

While we have always worked with notions of narrative, language and power, it is only recently that we have turned to theories of decoloniality to deepen our thinking about the relationship between narrative ways of knowing, coloniality and power in educational contexts. This aspect of narrative is explored in the next section. We draw on many of the key elements discussed so far but with the double elasticity of a decolonial gaze: What else does this gaze enable us to see and know?

Narrative and decolonial ways of knowing

This section explores how our work can contribute to an emerging decolonial praxis, particularly in relation to institutional power, reconfiguring knowledge and embodied identity work. We build on other work being done in the area of narrative and decoloniality, some of which is located in teacher education (Martin and Pirbhai-Illich 2016), multilingualism in higher education (Bock and Stroud 2019, 2021; De Souza 2019) and in community projects (Shell-Weiss 2020). We are particularly interested in Maldonado-Torres's argument (2007: 243) that coloniality persists in the knowledge production process and 'criteria for academic performance'. We explore what this means for a narrative approach that seeks to reconfigure what counts as knowledge and who counts as a knower in institutional spaces, and also the potential contribution of a narrative approach to the broader project of transforming teaching and learning.

Narrative ways of knowing have the potential to be a tool for reconfiguring knowledge construction and for providing access to powerful knowledge in the language education classroom. Our conceptualization of powerful knowledge resonates with the work of Luckett (2019: 54), who argues for the importance of broadening 'the concept of "epistemological access" to include socio-cultural and ontological access and taking into account the effects of our own positionality and institutional roles', while being careful not to reduce 'knowledge to power relations' (2019: 55). We are interested in knowledge that is powerful for its critical and imaginative potential, embodied and situated knowledge that opens up a 'critical narrative gaze' (Gill 2014b: 76) and knowledge produced or reconfigured by students. Our view of powerful knowledge is aligned with decolonial thinking where the narrative imagination occupies a pivotal role as the link between knowledge and lived experience, challenging personal/academic boundaries and ultimately delinking from western hegemony (Luckett 2019). Disciplinary knowledge plays a role in this process of knowledge construction in a recursive way – as a tool that students can apply critically to their analysis of their language histories but not as an end in itself. Both the western episteme and the hegemony of English are challenged through the course content and pedagogy. There is significant resonance between the locatedness of narrative, the decolonial concept of the locus of enunciation and our conceptualization of powerful knowledge.

The locus of enunciation

Grosfoguel's (2007) argument that all knowledge is situated within a body-politic/s of knowledge provides a significant link between narrative, decoloniality and our work with reconfiguring knowledge. We speak from specific locations in the power structure – the locus of enunciation. While there are many different ways of defining this concept, we find De Souza's definition (2019: 10) of 'the space from which we speak', a valuable starting point for thinking about it in relation to all that has been discussed so far. De Souza elaborates as follows:

> To speak from a space means you are speaking from a body located in space and time. When a body is located in space and time, a body has experience, a body has been exposed to history and the various conflicts of history. (2019: 10)

This concept enables us to deepen our understanding of the importance of the locatedness of narrative. It moves us beyond literary takes on perspective and spatiality/temporality towards a much more intricate web of power relations between the embodied speaking subject and the institutional and political locus. The locus of enunciation is not limited to geopolitical locations but includes where we are situated in discourse and colonial knowledge/power relations. It is part of a broader set of decolonial ideas that challenge the way the speaking subject is rendered invisible in western philosophy and science (Grosfoguel 2007) and has important implications for our thinking about narrative identities in the work we do, and the possibilities for our students of writing stories and constructing knowledge from an African locus of enunciation.

This embodied notion of knowledge is in striking contrast to western philosophy where the speaking subject is concealed by the myth of universal western knowledge. This myth of neutrality and objectivity is perpetuated at universities when, for example, students are told to write academic essays in the third person, to remove traces of themselves from academic discourse. While this is a very elementary example it is highly significant in the ideological message it conveys.

Narrative as disruptor of knowledge hierarchies

Narrative creates multiple opportunities to work in embodied, located ways with students. From a pedagogical perspective, working with narrative has as its starting point the assumption that knowledge is provisional and subjective. Yet this on its own is not enough to make convincing claims for narrative to be a productive decolonial pedagogy. The key links to decoloniality are the way knowledge is constructed within a narrative pedagogical framework and the broadening of who counts as knowers, whose resources are valued. Grosfoguel (2007) makes direct connections between the disembodied western idea of epistemic neutrality and the western construction of a hierarchy of superior and inferior knowledge. Western epistemic claims to objectivity and universality position other knowledges as inferior. He concludes that 'a broader canon of thought than simply the western canon' (2007: 212) is required for the epistemic decolonial turn.

In our course, students share stories about their language histories and identities in large groups, in small groups and in their written assignments. As described in Chapter 1, each year the course materials include a selection of language narratives of previous cohorts of students alongside published language narratives. Hence, the knowledge and experiences that students bring to the course are an integral part of the learning process, both for the student and the lecturers. Students become co-constructers of local knowledges about multilingualism. This is a powerful example of how narrative disrupts the existing hierarchies of knowledge, repositioning students as knowers and reconfiguring what counts as knowledge. This co-construction of knowledge also enables the creation of a multi-voiced space where students can engage with a diverse range of stories written by current and past students.

For the purposes of this chapter, we focus on a linguistic hierarchy that positions European languages as the languages of knowledge building while positioning non-European languages as producers of folklore and culture (Mignolo 2000 cited in Grosfoguel 2007). In the course, the assumptions underpinning this linguistic hierarchy of knowledge are subjected to a critical gaze both in relation to English (top of the global hierarchy) but also in relation to isiZulu, the most dominant African language in South Africa. De Souza (2019), drawing on Santos, discusses ignorance in the context of multilingualism in extremely productive ways. He argues that 'ignorance is always somebody's knowledge' (2019: 12). Looking at knowledge in this way challenges the colonial hierarchy of knowledge where we move towards a position of solidarity by making an effort to understand another person's knowledge in a collaborative and inclusive manner. In our course, one of our challenges is to get students to see language varieties as systems with their own set of rules and sociocultural purposes rather than substandard or deviant. The challenge to established western linguistic hierarchies has implications for the students' rethinking of their identities.

Narrative, decoloniality and dialogic contexts

However, from a pedagogic perspective creating spaces for sharing stories and personal experiences does not guarantee critical engagement, nor does it necessarily link to decolonial methodologies unless the stories are critically contextualized in broader socioeconomic historical contexts. Context is key in enabling moves between the individual and broader issues. This argument is underlined by Chadwick (2017), who cautions against narrative approaches that focus on the individual at the expense of broader structural and societal issues. Instead, Chadwick (2017: 12) focuses on the multiplicity of narrative analysis, the discontinuities and silences rather than seamless coherence, arguing that

> Stories are constructed in the cracks between multiple and at times contradictory collective voices, and identity/narrative is thus radically dialogical.

We find this emphasis on 'cracks, absences and discontinuities in stories' (2017: 11) valuable for both our conceptualization of narrative and for pedagogy. This is the key to effectively using a 'critical narrative gaze' and moving beyond the individual towards a more systemic analysis of experience that takes account of power and the writer's positioning in multiple spaces.

An integral part of finding cracks and contradictions in stories is conceptualizing voice as multiple in a Bakhtinian sense (1981). Each individual's voice draws on other voices from her past, present or imagined future. The word, according to Bakhtin (1981), belongs to the individual and the other, frequently consisting of contradictory discourses. The speaker/writer needs to appropriate the discourse and take ownership of it. But in order to do that effectively the writer needs the tools to critically interrogate discourses and how they work to position one. The need for such tools is evident in the dataset as students grapple with new disciplinary concepts to analyse their narratives but retain traces of other voices and discourses from home, school, the media or various other domains.

Disciplinary knowledge and key concepts play a significant role in providing students with new lenses that enable them to begin to reread their experiences from new perspectives and to denaturalize common-sense assumptions. The pedagogical point here is an important one; it is not enough to do feel-good work that validates the students' experiences and identities. There must be epistemological access to different knowledges alongside the construction of new knowledge. At the same time, we need to acknowledge the contradictions of working critically and reflexively with predominantly western lenses. We elaborate on this issue in Chapter 3.

Narrative as challenge to institutional genres of power

Despite recent calls to decolonize curriculums, universities in the Global South reproduce western knowledge systems and valorize English. Furthermore, pedagogical choices frequently privilege white, middle-class students and marginalize black, working-class students (Mgqwashu 2019). One of the key elements of this replication of western epistemologies in universities is the genre of the academic essay.

While there are aspects of the academic essay that are valuable – the problem is its dominance and the way it marginalizes other genres, which could open up alternative possibilities for learning. It renders the self invisible, marginalizes lived experience and valorizes an academic style that assumes objectivity. Hence, in its conventional form, the academic essay hides the locus of enunciation (De Souza 2019). In the context of teacher language education specifically, we problematize academic writing and raise questions about the extent to which academic courses teach students to minimize risk-taking in essays, to bury their creativity and to comply with perceived expectations in order to pass.

Mgqwashu (2019) proposes that teaching methods from school through to tertiary level need to be flexibly responsive to the cultural and educational needs of African learners. He concludes that we need to engage critically with all forms of knowledge (be it western or African) and that we should be opening the space of the academy to different forms and genres of knowledge construction and different kinds of learning and pedagogy. We agree with Mgqwashu (2019) that this debate about the coloniality of knowledge and higher education should not become reductionist and that student epistemological access must be foregrounded.

In an earlier section of this chapter, we defined narrative ways of knowing as coming to know and be through drawing on reflexive narratives of the self and other. In the same way that there are many ways to tell a story; there are multiple ways to tell, write and think about academic knowledge. We are straitjacketed by the academic essay genre in terms of both possibilities for thinking and the convention of capturing ideas in writing. As illustrated in the discussion of the vignettes, the shift in style also surfaces epistemological and ontological shifts.

Narrative and other non-traditional creative genres and pedagogies have an important role to play in challenging western epistemologies, particularly the artificial mind–body divide that is dominant in universities. Knowledge is embodied; it rewires the mind and identities of students. More specifically, neural pathways are reconfigured by what we read and write (Wolf 2008). De Souza (2019: 10) argues that bodies have been rendered invisible in academia because 'we inherited the idea of modernity: the separation between the mind and the body where it's only the mind that is important, not bodies'.

In contrast, narrative foregrounds the body and the self in time and space, drawing on memory, reflexivity, experience, history, emotion, affect and sensation. When students are invited to bring all of these elements into the classroom, identities and bodies that have been rendered invisible become visible, present and in dialogue with others. This invitation creates opportunities to break silences and open spaces for multiple voices. It is particularly important as our southern positioning requires a consideration of a range of factors when selecting genres and pedagogies.

The use of alternative genres such as the language narrative and the dialogue assignment can challenge institutional genres of power and their underlying discourses and epistemological assumptions, facilitating embodied learning, challenging the artificial mind–body divide and making the self and emotions visible. Furthermore, these alternative genres encourage students to engage more holistically with different elements of the learning process – bringing together creativity, affect, cognition and criticality. These are all important elements of an evolving decolonized curriculum and have significant implications for (re)configuring knowledge and transforming teaching and learning.

Narrative, identities and decoloniality

Ndlovu-Gatsheni (2013: 178) argues that we need African higher education institutions that do not alienate African students from their communities and that will 'produce African graduates who do not suffer from identity crises'. How does narrative facilitate productive decolonial work with students' identities in an English course that focuses on the relationship between students' languages and their identities? And how might the course respond to Ndlovu-Gatsheni's call for institutions that are inclusive of a range of identities?

As discussed earlier in this chapter, the process of writing a narrative is an act of reshaping identity. But which aspects of this process relate to decoloniality? Narrative foregrounds the locus of enunciation which is usually rendered invisible in undergraduate academic writing. In the course and assignments students are invited to talk and write about key experiences that have shaped their linguistic identities. These experiences and identities take centre stage, written in a genre that prioritize the personal, creative and reflexive. Therefore, what emerges are the complexities of an African locus of enunciation (Ndlovu-Gatsheni 2013) as students share contrasting localized stories of relevance, rooted in their society and social practices. This creates a collective history that comprises the memories, experiences and, particularly, 'conflicts of history' (De Souza 2019) that shape being and knowing. One key area for us in a language course is the complex relationship between English and African languages as a result of the colonial past.

Ngũgĩ wa Thiong'o (1986) has written seminal texts about the devastating impact of colonialism on colonized nations in terms of language, culture and identity – but most importantly how it annihilated a people's belief in their heritage and themselves. He describes the impact of linguistic and cultural imperialism as follows:

It makes them want to identify with that which is furthest removed from themselves; for instance, with other people's languages rather than their own. (1986: 3)

His work helps to contextualize the linguistic conflicts of history that many students bring to the course and potential identity conflicts. However, it should be noted that the position of English in Africa is contentious. For example, Jefiyo (2020) argues that English is an African language. Obviously, each student negotiates these identities differently, partially depending on their conditions of possibility. For some, there may not be a conflict. Others may have taken ownership of English and made it their own. This has become increasingly common in the more recent language narratives and is discussed in relation to the hegemony of English in Chapter 7. Nevertheless, it is a history that is difficult to escape entirely in the context of the complex histories of universities in Africa which are still rooted in western, colonial epistemologies.

Conclusion

This chapter has highlighted the elasticity of narrative as a way of knowing and as a powerful tool for transformative teaching and learning. As teacher educators in the Global South, we have found narrative to be a particularly flexible educational tool in contexts of diversity for making visible the multiple voices and identities of students on our courses.

We have argued that a narrative approach has potential for reconfiguring and re-imagining the way we think about knowledge, for creating a more inclusive classroom environment and for creating possibilities for students to take up different identity positions in relation to language issues. In particular, our narrative approach enables students to position themselves as constructers of knowledge from an African locus of enunciation and to engage critically with this evolving knowledge in relation to self and other. One can never predict what students will take away from a course. Some students emerge from the course feeling validated and empowered about their linguistic identities, while others emerge with greater awareness of their linguistic privilege. In all cases, we want students to emerge from the course with new tools to navigate their identities which they can utilize in their personal lives and in their professional roles as future language teachers.

But the work cannot stop there. Narrative work needs to move beyond validation and facilitate access to knowledge, and in time transform what counts as powerful knowledge. Disciplinary knowledge and key course concepts play a vital role in providing students with new lenses and tools for re-reading their experiences from new perspectives and for denaturalizing common-sense assumptions about language and identity. While this chapter focuses on the conceptualization of narrative ways of knowing, in Chapter 3 we show how narrative ways of knowing lie at the centre of our praxis.

3

Pedagogy in Motion

*In our first class we spoke about our language history. I felt a strange
sensation in my stomach. All this time I had been wrong, most people did
not communicate the same way that I did. A vast majority of my fellow
learners began telling their stories of how they speak different languages
when talking to different people, whether it be family members, friends or
teachers. Some mentioned that their families felt disappointed and betrayed
when they don't speak their home language. Some speak more than one
language for pleasure whereby others do it just to get through an average
day. There was a particular student that felt as if Standard English was
taking over the African languages and it was her responsibility to keep her
family language safe, a language that shaped her identity, a language that if
not spoken will be lost. A learner pointed out that often when people don't
pronounce her name properly they are in actual fact changing the meaning
of her name. I pondered about all the times I've been called the wrong name,
a Hebrew name which in English means gentile, by people changing my
name, it loses the meaning. This is a concept that hit home, it encouraged me
to learn the names of my peers and to learn about their essence.*

Extract from Ariela's language narrative, 2017

Introduction

Pedagogy doesn't stand still, nor should it. If pedagogy is 'the situated practice of
teaching and learning' and its 'proper focus . . . is the classroom together with the
class itself, or cohort' (Green and Reid 2008: 25), then pedagogy needs to adapt
to changing contexts and changing student cohorts. In the previous chapter
we presented our conceptualization of narrative and outlined its pedagogic
potential as well as the ways in which it could be harnessed for decolonial ends.
In this chapter, we present the narrative heteroglossic pedagogy we have refined

over the many years of teaching the course. We begin by outlining the ways in which an English course can be multilingual (and the ways in which it can't be). We then argue for the importance of using the classroom space to set up a language regime that values multilingualism and thereby undoes some of the monoglossic logic that is typical of English classrooms, positioning students for whom English is an additional language as knowers. We also foreground the importance of a pedagogy that enables one to teach beyond one's own linguistic repertoire, a valuable asset to an educator in contexts of complex diversity. In the second half of the chapter, we focus on the enactment of such a pedagogy. First, we discuss how, by setting the classroom up as a linguistic contact zone, students learn dialogically across difference through various pedagogic interactions. Then we present teaching materials and activities which focus on using carefully selected, multi-voiced texts in a range of semiotic modes in critical and creative ways. Where possible, we offer examples of students' responses to activities. By including such things as 'classroom activities' for university students, we are deliberately pushing back against narrow ideas of what counts as academic engagement in a higher education context. We are practitioners and the classroom, or lecture theatre, is the place where students, teachers, texts and talk come together. In this chapter, we hope to convey some of what can happen in this discursive space. We conclude by considering what our course may have to offer by way of decolonial praxis. For example, what does it mean to bring this course into the decolonial era? And how might it contribute to the development of a decolonial orientation to the teaching of English in a teacher education context of the Global South? Thus the overall focus of this chapter is on the elements that comprise the processes and pedagogy of the course. In the chapters that follow, we *show what this pedagogy enabled*, in the form of language narratives, or language dialogues and commentaries. The students' work – and the voices that speak through the work – are, in effect, material evidence of what the pedagogy generated. Here our aim is to enable the reader to understand where the language narratives and dialogues came from.

Flipping the script

Over the years we have taught many pre- and in-service teachers who have expressed scepticism at the possibility of drawing on their learners' multilingual resources in the English classroom where their focus should be, they say, on teaching and developing English skills. It might be doable, they feel, in classrooms of relative homogeneity, where the learners all speak English as an additional language and share a mother tongue in which the teacher is conversant. But it would surely be impossible in classrooms with learners from multiple linguistic backgrounds, such as those likely to be found in and around a 'thoroughly polyglot urban formation' (Mbembe and Nuttal 2004: 366), such as Johannesburg. The way they see it, the teacher would be unlikely to speak all the various mother tongues represented in the class, and in any case, any codes switching by the teacher would automatically exclude learners who don't speak that language. Logically, it is a small step from this way of thinking to imposing an 'English only' policy in the classroom. First, because English is the target language and there is a mistaken sense that an 'immersive' English experience can be created through the outlawing of all other languages; and, second, because English is also seen as a lingua franca, which it may well be, depending on the context, but that shouldn't imply that this is a neutral, value-free decision. Nevertheless imposing such a classroom policy, although misguided, can be intended as a well-meaning gesture where it is perceived as being 'fairer' and more inclusive to speak only English than it would be to draw in other languages.

This is not the kind of multilingual pedagogy we have in mind.

This view, we believe, is underpinned by a teacher-centred approach to teaching, one in which the teacher is positioned as powerful, all-knowing and as the *only* legitimate source of knowledge in the classroom. More specifically, it represents a monoglossic, prescriptivist approach to language teaching. However, this is the default script of the English classroom. It prioritizes ever-increasing proficiency in spoken and written English, standard English is normative, and in many environments 'English only' policies do indeed prevail. In the higher education context, the focus would be on acquiring academic discourse in English. The lack of fit between this default script and our multilingual southern context is staggering. As critically conscious English educators, we believe that widening access to English is imperative. We agree that failure to provide access to academic English limits life chances and compromises social justice (Heugh 2018). While we take seriously our responsibility to provide access to English, we do not believe this has to be done at the expense of students' rich multilingual repertoires and multicultural identities.

So we flipped the script.

We did this by centring our students' multilingual repertoires, positioning these as valued resources. This challenges the deficit position in which multilingual students are placed by the Anglonormative ideologies (McKinney 2017) that reign in English classrooms. African learners' vast linguistic resources are not recognized; they are regarded as a barrier or problem, or are rendered invisible when the only linguistic capital in English classrooms is standard English. By flipping the script, we sought to construct a more socially just, culturally, linguistically and pedagogically responsive curriculum.

A key way of operationalizing students' linguistic diversity as a resource is to conceive of the classroom space as a linguistic 'contact zone', that is a 'social space where cultures [we would say *languages*] meet, clash, and grapple with each other, often in contexts of highly asymmetrical relations of power' (Pratt 1991: 34). As we have previously discussed (Ferreira and Mendelowitz 2009b), whether and which linguistic resources are able to be deployed in a particular environment depends on the regime of language (Blommaert et al. 2005) which structures that environment, that is the hierarchy of symbolic values ascribed to the various languages present. An individual entering a particular space would be actively positioned by the regime of language operating in that space. In the pedagogic space of our course, we consciously construct a regime of language that values multilingualism and languages other than English in order to position students for whom English is an additional language as knowers. The very act of asking students to write a language narrative that can draw on their full linguistic repertoires or to write a dialogue in a youth variety of their choice (accompanied by an English translation) is a demonstration of this language regime. In inviting all students' languages into the classroom space in a number of pedagogic ways, we actively seek to structure an inclusive, multilingual regime of language.

In this way, we are contributing to the growing body of work exploring the different ways in which curriculum and/or pedagogy can work with multilingualism. Indeed, we are encouraged by some of the innovative, even ground-breaking work being done in the higher education context to shift official and unofficial language regimes.

A case in point is Ramani and Joseph's (2002) long-standing work at the University of Limpopo in developing a bilingual/dual-medium BA degree taught in English and Sepedi (Sesotho sa Leboa). This was underpinned by double imperative to use African languages as mediums of instruction, while also guaranteeing access to English. At the University of the Western Cape, Antia and Dyers (2016, 2019), while continuing to use English as a medium of instruction, have diversified the modes and languages available for epistemological access in a third-year linguistics course. Course materials are provided in English, and in formal and informal versions of isiXhosa and Afrikaans, including – in the case of the latter – Kaaps, a regional and often highly stigmatized, colloquial variety of Afrikaans. In addition, they have moved beyond the written mode by providing podcasts of English PowerPoint lecture materials in varieties of isiXhosa and Afrikaans; and they have provided for assessment to be multilingual, enabling students to write their answers in their chosen available language (Antia, Weldemichael and Dyers 2021). Additionally, there is a growing body of work on translanguaging being done in South Africa. Makalela's work on *ubuntu* translanguaging (2017, 2018b), for example, has been credited for reappropriating 'new' ideas about multilingualism from the North and repositioning them in the complex multilingual southern contexts where they have always circulated, and simultaneously disrupting the stigmatization of language mixing that attaches to a monoglossic logic (Heugh 2018; Pennycook and Makoni 2020). McKinney and colleagues are working on developing translanguaging as a pedagogy that disrupts Anglonormative ideologies while enhancing learners' meaning-making resources (Guzula, McKinney and Tyler 2016), arguing for the value of creating a third space in the classroom in order to achieve this (Abdulatief, Guzula and McKinney 2021).

While the foregoing work resonates with ours in relation to reconfiguring language regimes through curriculum and/or pedagogy, it differs from ours in terms of setting and conditions of possibility. Much of this work is being done in content subjects where the focus tends to be on knowledge and conceptual understanding. In our case, sociolinguistic knowledge is contained within an English curriculum intended also to develop English language skills. Some of the work done by McKinney and colleagues (Guzula, McKinney and Tyler 2016; Abdulatief, Guzula and McKinney 2021) foregrounds the value of having lecturers who share the multilingual repertoires of their students. This is an issue of concern for us given our own deficit positions in relation to indigenous African languages. One of our difficult questions was whether we could teach an English course that positioned multilingualism as a resource without having the contextually relevant multilingual repertoires ourselves. Could we do this if we, as lecturers, shared none of the languages of the marginalized students we wanted to include?

In our pedagogic vision, we frequently invite students to take centre stage, bringing with them the stories of their multiple and diverse languages. Stories that collectively paint a vivid picture of the multilingual landscape that they inhabit and how they negotiate their own linguistic repertoires. Students themselves tell their own stories – initially in bite-sized chunks but ultimately written as fully developed narratives or dialogues. While English remains the medium of instruction, this is a porous and pliable English, functioning, to borrow Chinua Achebe's well-known words, as an English 'able to carry the weight of [our] African experience' (1976: 84). It is a heteroglossic English, used to tell stories of students' own languages, drawing in words and phrases from across their linguistic repertoires, and interwoven with everyday experiences of language. In this way, standard academic English is disrupted and compelled to make way for new ways of saying, writing, knowing and being. Thus while we are working within the usual constraints of a neoliberal university, students' ways of knowing and being occupy, in a substantial way, the course curriculum. And since marks are currency in the neoliberal university, we confer further value and legitimacy on these ways of knowing and being by assessing them. The student narratives often form the bulk, or all, of the marks of the course.

Despite the careful planning, teaching this course each year always feels a little like a journey into the unknown: we open up our carefully designed space, and then we step back and wait. We wait for students to populate the space with their ideas, their stories and their relationships with language. We never know exactly what will happen. Technically we do not know what languages students bring with them but it doesn't matter because the space can accommodate any language – and thus it is a radically inclusive language pedagogy. Obviously official South African languages are strongly represented, especially those that are regionally dominant in Gauteng and the surrounding provinces from where many of our students are drawn. And there are always a considerable number of foreign languages present through immigration, sometimes several generations ago. Therefore, while we acknowledge that if we as lecturers shared our students' varied multilingual repertoires, undoubtedly 'more [could] be done' (Guzula et al. 2016: 223), we are also aware that we are modelling for future teachers of English how they themselves may be able to work in multilingual ways when they do not necessarily share their learners' linguistic repertoires. Given the linguistic diversity of the broader Johannesburg area, the disposition to teach beyond one's own linguistic comfort zone is a valuable asset for an educator. Thus part of the contribution that this book seeks to make is to demonstrate, first, that English can be taught in ways that engage and value multilingual repertoires and, second, that it is possible for educators to set up a language regime that goes beyond their own linguistic repertoires. This is a pedagogy that attempts to compensate for our limitations. We are still teaching English – but an English that is positioned as one language among many, as a powerful language in need of critique and a language that can be used to articulate and explore experiences of other languages. So when Heugh (2018) says that there are many multilingualisms, we add that there are also many multilingual pedagogies – this is one such pedagogy and it has been shaped by a combination of factors, including student identity, context and lecturer identity.

Pedagogy in motion

As a longitudinal study of a course that has been designed, taught and reworked over sixteen years, we believe our work is well placed to make a contribution to understanding how pedagogy shifts over time. This then is a longitudinal study of a *responsive* higher education pedagogy in a teacher education context. Along the way, after each iteration of the pedagogy, we instinctively apply a retrospective gaze that enables us to redesign the subsequent iteration of the course that takes place the following year for a new student cohort. There is the advance top-down pedagogy that comes from translating pedagogic theories into action; and there is the pedagogy from below (or bottom-up pedagogy) that comes from practices that develop more spontaneously and can then be theorized. Considered in this way, our study could be viewed as an extended action research project. It is possible to map the shifts in our pedagogic thinking and enactment over time. Over the years we have researched aspects of the course thus combining a teacher gaze with a researcher gaze in ways that are further reminiscent of the action research paradigm. Some of the shifts in our pedagogic thinking can be gleaned from the articles in which we have theorized our practice at various points along the journey of the course, between 2007 and 2017 (Mendelowitz and Ferreira 2007; Ferreira and Mendelowitz 2009a, 2009b; Mendelowitz and Davies 2011; Dixon and Mendelowitz 2016; Mendelowitz and Dixon 2016; Mendelowitz 2017).

In her work on narrative psychology, Bradbury (2020: 106) borrows from the quantum theory lexicon to coin the term 'wormhole narrative', using it to describe a narrative that is framed by present-day knowledge but 'stretches in both directions'. It stretches into the past, from where much of present-day knowledge is derived, and simultaneously contains 'the possibilities of yet-to-be future worlds' (2020: 106). This captures some of what we try to do in this chapter with regard to our pedagogic knowledge of the course. In our present-day writing moment, at the forefront of our minds is the current shape of the pedagogy of the course. But that shape has been distilled from the many previous iterations of the course and in our discussion we occasionally escape into the past to mention some of the things we attempted and the insights derived from those moments. Similarly, stretching in the other direction, we are beginning to discern possibilities for developing a more decolonial praxis. In the section that follows, we describe and explicate what we are calling a narrative heteroglossic pedagogy, identifying the key principles of the pedagogy and their interrelationship. We then discuss in some detail some of the most significant ways in which these principles have been enacted.

A narrative heteroglossic pedagogy

At its most basic level, the pedagogy we have developed is an approach to teaching in which reading and writing narratives about personal language histories and practices are central to the learning process (Mendelowitz and Davies 2011). It is a pedagogy that operationalizes narrative as a tool for learning about language, the self and others in critical and socially contextualized ways. Putting it to work in an English course in the linguistically diverse South African context enables us to productively hold in tension the need to provide access to a language of power with the imperative to work in critical, counter-hegemonic ways with that language.

In the previous chapter, the narrative component of the pedagogy has been extensively discussed so the focus here is on the heteroglossic component. By drawing in multiple and varied storied and storying voices covering a broad spectrum of linguistic repertoires, the conditions are created for a heteroglossic pedagogy. This is a pedagogy 'where the polyphony of voices, discourses and ways of speaking – all linked to different social-ideological worlds – is not kept out, but seen as a constitutive feature' (Busch 2014: 38). There are two interdependent ways in which a heteroglossic pedagogy is operationalized in our course. The first is through multi-voicedness or the diversity of individual voices and social worlds – an aspect that is heightened by our context of high diversity. The second is through the 'the social diversity of speech types' (Bailey 2012: 499) – the view of language that resists a monoglossic orientation to languages and includes linguistic phenomena like registers, dialects, voices and varieties in addition to named languages. If heteroglossia (Bakhtin 1981) is the coming together of opposing centripetal and centrifugal forces – where the former pulls towards a central, unitary, standard form of language while the latter pushes outwards towards marginal, non-standard forms of linguistic expression – perhaps our course could be seen as a symbolic space in which these two forces co-exist in continual tension. Within the constraints of an English course in a neoliberal English-medium university, standard, academic English is our centripetal force. But by seeking to create spaces within the curriculum where students can position themselves – however momentarily – beyond official, normative English discourses and draw on their full linguistic repertoires in either written or spoken modes, we are tapping into the potential of the centrifugal to function in counter-hegemonic ways.

This pedagogy is thus also critical. We are aware that working with diversity in socially contextualized ways does not automatically entail working *critically*. However, valuing linguistic diversity can be seen as a critical or counter-hegemonic move in a context where English occupies a hegemonic position. It should thus not be dismissed as a trivial, celebratory move. It sets up the inclusive language regime (Blommaert et al. 2005) of the course and thus we argue that it constitutes the first step towards a heteroglossic pedagogy – and that this is a necessary but not sufficient step towards criticality.

Busch writes about how a critical heteroglossic pedagogy would 'aim at developing among all participants . . . a high degree of linguistic awareness' (2014: 25). However, we believe that a truly critical pedagogy needs to go beyond linguistic awareness to language conscientization (Freire 1972). We agree with Blackledge and Creese (2014: 10) that 'celebrating diversity does not account for the ways in which linguistic difference often constitutes social inequality' – and it is these social inequalities that must be the focus of the next step towards criticality. And therefore we return to the pivotal role of the language narratives: these inequalities and power struggles are rendered visible in the real-life contexts of the personal language stories students read and tell and the dialogues they create, reinforcing the fact that the personal is political. Thus the second step is the critical pedagogy move, where we move beyond the narrowly personal to the social context in which the narrative is embedded – it is the narratives themselves, individually and collectively, that enable us to look beyond the individual to the system, rendering geopolitical structural relations visible. Thus in our students' narratives we encounter identity struggles in relation to powerful and marginalized languages (Chapter 4); we find them coming to understand the relationship between language and power (Chapter 5); we encounter how language can be used to police gender identities or to appropriate and write back (Chapter 6); and in more recent times, we see students navigating issues of language and race anew (Chapter 7).

And ultimately the third step towards criticality is feeding students' language narratives back into the course so that they become part of the collective pool of contextualized, local knowledge about linguistic diversity and language inequalities. The pedagogy aims to develop critical awareness through the analytical lenses (or metalanguage) provided by a critical orientation to sociolinguistics and for these to be used as tools for the students to action in their own lives as they navigate diverse and unequal language practices. This is reminiscent of the early work on critical language awareness (Fairclough 1992; Clark et al. 1990, 1991; Janks and Ivanič 1992) which sought to move beyond a benign pluralist approach to linguistic variety so as to place under scrutiny the relationship between language variation and inequality. In the section that follows we look at some of the key ways in which this pedagogy has been enacted over the years.

Enactment: Operationalizing the pedagogy

Writing about one's own pedagogy is strangely akin in level of exposure to one of those dreams where you are walking down the road naked and everyone around you is clothed. It is one thing to expound on carefully thought-out pedagogic principles, but the proof of the pedagogy is in the doing. In this section, we demonstrate ways in which we have enacted aspects of the pedagogy. In the first part, we demonstrate some of the interactions we seek to set up in the classroom/ lecture theatre space; and in the second section, we show some examples of the ways in which we work with texts.

Activities between self and other: Classroom as contact zone

Conceiving of the classroom as a contact zone means that interactions across difference are prioritized. In a context of high diversity like ours, these differences take multiple forms and operate intersectionally but it is through the prism of language that these differences are arranged. Thus in this section we present some of the activities/tasks that we have used over the years to surface and share students' diverse linguistic repertoires.

#1 MULTILINGUAL ICEBREAKERS have proven to be a quick and engaging way to start off the opening session, especially given that as a first-year course positioned at the start of the academic year, students are usually new to the institution and to one another. One form which this can take is by simply asking students to turn to a person near them and introduce themselves in the language in which they feel most comfortable, and then to explain why that is so.

Working with names in linguistically and culturally embedded ways (Orlek 1993) is an extremely productive way of extending on the usual round of introductions. In small groups, students tell one another about their names, addressing questions such as: How many names do you have? What information do my names carry about my family, my history and my future? How do I feel if someone uses my name wrongly? How much do I feel my name suits me or is part of my identity? Would I ever change my name or have I changed it?

Both of these kinds of activities are designed for maximum access – everyone has a language and a name and can thus participate. Not only do they begin to set up the inclusive language regime of the classroom but in groups such as ours, they begin to raise awareness of linguistic diversity and the relationship between language, culture and identity. Even when black students are numerically in the majority in our classrooms, the university itself is still experienced as a white space where white, western cultural norms are dominant. Common micro-aggressions in such a space would include mispronunciation of names in African languages. For students routinely marginalized in the English classroom, working with student names has the potential to function as a micro-affirmation (Rolón-Dow and Davison 2021; Rowe 2008).

#2 THE LANGUAGE DIARY ACTIVITY, also originally from Orlek (1993), has consistently stood the test of time because in a highly accessible way, it communicates how the individual language user adapts language use to places, circumstances and relationships. Students are presented with a visual-spatial mapping of Dimakatso, a young Tswana- and Sotho-speaking schoolgirl's daily language interactions (see APPENDIX 2), and asked to produce one of their own.

Figure 3.1 shows the language diary produced by Mpilo, an isiZulu-speaking student who has acquired English alongside his home language, isiZulu. While Figure 3.2 is the language diary of Julie, an English-speaking student who has

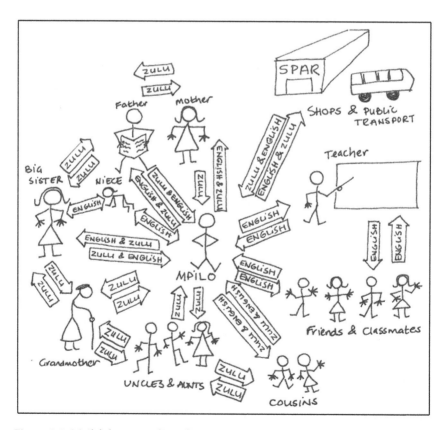

Figure 3.1 Mpilo's language diary diagram.

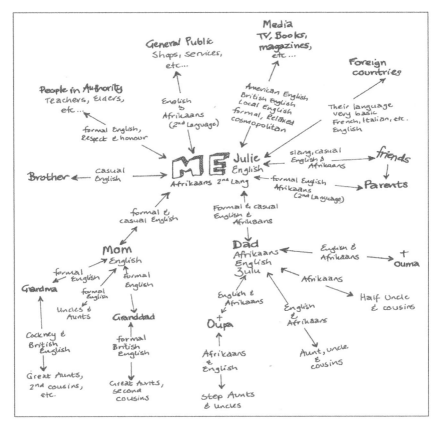

Figure 3.2 Julie's language diary diagram.

taken a heteroglossic orientation to language in order to identify different varieties of English related to formal and informal interactions, as well as to media and popular culture.

#3 PAIR INTERVIEWS ON LANGUAGE HISTORIES take place in the first week or two of the course and form the origins of the language narratives that students write. Students are encouraged to find a partner from a different language background and then interview each other using the questions provided to guide them. See Table 3.1 for the instructions. This plays an important step in beginning to expose students to experiences with language that are, in some cases, vastly different from their own, and in other cases, affirming of their usually marginalized language experiences.

#4 CREATING LANGUAGE METAPHORS has come to play an important role in preparing students to write their language narratives. Students are

Table 3.1 Activity on language history interviews

Part 1

Work with a partner, preferably someone from a different background to you. Introduce yourself to your partner and tell them something about yourself. Then interview your partner about their language history, using the following interview questions. Make notes of key points.

1. What language or languages were spoken around you when you were a baby?
2. In what language did you utter your first word?
3. Who influenced your language development?
4. In what language did you begin to read and write?
5. What other languages have you learnt? How and where did you learn these?

Positive and negative experiences of language (to answer these questions you may draw on a range of relevant contexts such as school, home and community)

6. What positive experiences of language(s) have you had? Describe these in detail and identify what made these experiences positive.
7. What negative experiences of language(s) have you had? Describe these in detail and identify what made these experiences negative.
8. What languages do you speak with your peers in everyday social interaction? How does this differ from the languages you use at home and for learning?
9. What languages do you use for learning purposes? How do you feel about learning in this language? Is there another language that you would prefer as a language of learning? Why or why not?
10. How many languages do you speak? If you are proficient in one language, how do you feel about this? How does this impact on your interactions with people who speak other languages?

(Adapted from Eltic, 1997)

Part 2

Report back to the class on what you learnt about your partner. What did you find most striking or most interesting about your partner's language history?

---

advised of how powerful a well-chosen metaphor can be when attempting to capture how they feel about their language(s) and how it could be effectively incorporated into their language narrative. Many of the narratives they engage with involve evocative use of metaphors and in preparation for writing their own metaphor, they are shown metaphors created by and used by previous students in their language narratives. Table 3.2 provides a selection of metaphors from over the years.

In the 2020 online iteration of the course, students posted their metaphors in the discussion forum and were required to read and respond to three to four metaphors posted by other students.

Table 3.2 Metaphors by students on their language(s)

My language, Zulu, is like travelling through bumps in the desert – hot, dry and challenging. Whereas English is like a cold lake in the desert – refreshing. It's free and allows you to be free and express your freedom yet it can be dangerous, cold and completely deadly.

*

To me, my languages are like chameleons. They change according to places. Like water they fit into a lot of shapes. After they have changed, like a key they fit into a specific lock at a specific time.

*

isiZulu: Like sounds and clicks rolling off my tongue. Making sense to me and others. Coming from my deepest most innermost being. Making others feel safe, feel comfortable, feel wanted and most of all feel loved. . . . It makes me feel like I belong to something more and bigger and better than even I am to myself.

*

SiSwati . . . it is deep, dark and juicy. No other language is as smooth and sexy as my one.

#5 LANGUAGE ROLE PLAYS have been used to show how language usage is intricately linked to context, purpose and power relations (Table 3.3). Students work in pairs on their dialogue and volunteers perform them for the class. Once the dialogues/commentaries became a major assignment, the role play activity began to function as scaffolding or rehearsal for the written assignment. The key issues emerging from each role play are framed using the relevant sociolinguistic discourses, thereby modelling the process of analysing dialogues in preparation for the assignment. Chapters 5 and 6 discuss these tasks and the dialogues students produced in detail.

Synthesis

Five sets of tasks have been presented. They range from icebreakers to interviews, role plays and individual writing. Activities such as icebreakers and the name game (#1), for example, may seem trivial but they in fact signal the inclusive and heteroglossic language regime of the course. In seeking to draw in students' full linguistic repertoires, students who are routinely placed in positions of deficit in the English classroom and do not see themselves as carriers of valued knowledge are being invited to contribute to the discussions around language and positioned as knowers.

Interactive teaching methodologies are harnessed so that students do not focus only on their personal explorations of language experience but are exposed to those of other students. In order to achieve this collective exposure to the

Table 3.3 Activity on language role plays

Part 1

In pairs select one of the following situations and work out a short dialogue (approximately six or seven lines) appropriate to the situation you have chosen. Feel free to use a range of languages where appropriate. Volunteers will read out their dialogues or role play them for the group.

1. Ask your neighbour's son, who is a gang member, to return your jacket which he took from your house.
2. Ask your lecturer why she has not returned your assignment (which you submitted six weeks ago).
3. Ask your boyfriend why he did not turn up for your twenty-first birthday party.
4. Ask your twelve-year-old sister, who is a very sweet and sensitive child, to go to the shop and buy some biscuits.
5. It is 3 a.m. and you have an exam tomorrow. Your neighbour is hosting a wild party. Ask your neighbour to turn the music down.
6. You are the manager of a large banking corporation. Ask a junior member of staff to photocopy a report for you, which you need urgently.
7. You have a part-time job as a waiter/waitress in a trendy restaurant. Your employer is very rude and aggressive. Ask him for an increase in wages.
8. Ask the warden of your residence for special permission to attend a concert during the week.
9. Ask a stranger in the street to direct you to any place of your choice.
10. Try to persuade your best friend to accompany you to a party instead of studying. Your parents have insisted that you do not go to the party alone.

Activity adapted from: TELIP (1998).

Part 2

What kinds of changes did you observe as contexts changed in:

- Language choice
- Accent
- Level of formality (colloquial/formal)
- Levels of politeness (modality, e.g. May I? Can I? Will you?)

Why? How would you explain these shifts? Consider the following:

- The power relations between the people in each context
- The nature of the relationships (e.g. family/friend/boss)
- The social status of the people in each instance
- What is at stake?

---

diversity of language experience, we needed to work against the usual flow of information – from teacher to students – to a more distributed, dialogic pattern of interaction. Students need to listen, share, respond and talk to one another in order to learn from one another. Activities #3 and #5 are designed to achieve this. After these break-away discussions, which can be quite brief, it is imperative to have students report back on what came up. First, this enables insights gained in discrete groups to be shared with the whole class. Second, it enables the lecturer to begin modelling the process of identifying and developing key ideas, and relating them to core sociolinguistic concepts. The vignette at the start of this chapter, taken from Ariela's language narrative, evocatively captures the way in which this student experienced the richness of this contact zone.

It can also be valuable to move beyond discussion, which not all students participate in, to the performative. In Activity #5 students perform role plays demonstrating the shifting use of language in different contexts, often using a mix of standard and non-standard varieties in a space that is usually the domain of standard English only. Volunteers present their role plays to the whole class with each role play often eliciting different responses and significant audience appreciation. If left unanalysed, they can simply reproduce dominance. However, the reflexive questions and the use of sociolinguistic concepts facilitate an unpacking of the meaning of the role play.

Whether we work face to face or online, we make every effort to create a suitable environment for this kind of student–student interaction and sharing. This includes creating space for the difficult and uncomfortable conversations which can arise. However, while we would like to create an inclusive space for discussion and to position every student as having something to contribute, we realize that the 'safe space' metaphor is problematic. Critique warns that students' experiences of safety differ according to their social locations (Adams et al. 2016); and, as Arao and Clemens (2013: 140) argue, 'the language of safety' can reinforce inequalities and entrench positions of privilege. We thus align ourselves instead with Boler and Zembylas's 'pedagogy of discomfort' (2003; Zembylas 2018), which resonates with our work in various ways. It invites students to examine and critique their deeply held assumptions; it attends not only to the intellectual but also to the affective domain; and 'it open[s] possibilities for challenging and extending the safety and security of our personal comfort zones' (p. 128). Thus while activities #1 to #5 present as unthreatening and inclusive, given the level of difference at play, the contact zone is not a comfort zone. The thought-provoking and controversial texts and activities discussed in the section that follows reinforce the learning potential of this productive discomfort.

Activities with texts

Selecting multiple and diverse texts and placing them alongside one another speaks directly to the heteroglossic aspect of our pedagogy. This is what

Busch and Schick (2007: 226) refer to as the 'multi-perspectivity' and 'multi-voicedness' of teaching materials that reflect heteroglossia. But we are acutely aware that texts don't have fixed teacherly or pedagogic meanings in and of themselves – it depends on how they are framed, sequenced, juxtaposed and so on, and what questions and activities are attached to them. For this reason it feels important to include a section in which we provide examples of *how* we use the texts we select. We touch on four different ways in which we work with texts, providing examples of the texts we use as well as the kinds of questions or activities attached to them. In each case we try to provide not only tried and tested texts but also more recent ones. Multimodal, multimedia texts such as short videos clips have become a useful way of bringing in additional ideas or new narratives, and are intended to provide multiple entry points for student engagement.

#1 RESPONDING

At the most basic level of pedagogy, all the texts used raise issues and perspectives about language and identity that we want students to consider and respond to. Some texts come to function as touchstones for students' emerging ideas, featuring frequently in students' narratives. A particularly popular text has been a local newspaper article by Fikile-Ntsikelele Moya (2006) titled 'Ekasi Is My Roots' where the writer defines himself as 'urban black'

Table 3.4 presents a reconstruction of a classroom discussion that took place in response to the Moya text. This is an example of the kind of robust class discussion that frequently takes place early in the course while students are still surfacing the resources and experiences that they bring. As lecturers, we play an important role in beginning the process of reframing in relation to new sociolinguistic lenses so that by the time they write their language narratives, they are able to interweave the personal with the key sociolinguistic concepts.

More recently we have included the video of a speech delivered at the 2019 Race Unity Speech Awards by Takunda Mazondiwe. She speaks about being an immigrant from Zimbabwe living in New Zealand, seamlessly blending spoken word poetry into the more conventional elements of public speaking. Takunda shares her experiences as an ethnic minority growing up in New Zealand, dealing with the power of language and the relationship between language, home and identity. As with the Moya text, students are asked to engage and respond in open-ended ways.

Table 3.4 A reconstructed classroom dialogue generated by the Moya Article

Belinda:	*So, I assume you've all read the Moya article and answered the questions. Now let's have some responses to the key question: How do we define our roots? Is it about the places that our families/ancestors originate from and their language heritage? Or is it about the community, culture and social group that one connects and identifies with?*
Student 1:	*I don't want to be defined by others, by history. I want to be myself.*
Student 2:	*I agree with the previous speaker. I will not let someone else call me a coconut because I speak English. I am black even if I speak English with a particular accent.*
Student 3:	*I'm a third-generation Sowetan. What is home for me? My ancestors come from KwaZulu Natal and that connects me to KZN, but it is not home. Home is Soweto.*
Student 4:	*I want to agree with [student 3]. Identities and languages are created by communities. It's about where you are at a particular point in time. Language and traditions change over time!*
Student 5:	*As a black person you should never forget your roots. You will become a lost sheep and a lost soul.*
Student 6:	*In African culture home is where your forefathers are buried. There's no getting away from that.*

Source: Constructed from overhead transparencies where students' responses were written (2008)

#2 JUXTAPOSING

It is the juxtapositioning of texts that foregrounds the co-existence of multiple voices and perspectives. Texts don't just tell stories, they provide ways of looking at the world. Placing different texts on similar issues side by side encourages metacognition. Students are able to see each text as one possible perspective among many and then consciously take up a perspective of their own, sometimes shifting as they hear other perspectives in discussion with peers.

In the early years we placed wa Thiong'o's (1986) autobiographical extract on being forced to learn English as a colonial language alongside Richard Rodriguez's (1982) autobiographical extract where, as a Mexican American immigrant, he welcomed the learning of English. We soon replaced the Rodriguez narrative with an extract from a local novel which portrayed similar conflicts between language and identity – Kopano Matlwa's *Coconut* (2007) – again providing a perspective that diverged from that of wa Thiong'o. Table 3.5 shows the comparative questions that accompanied these juxtapositionings.

Table 3.5 Juxtaposing narratives: Ngũgĩ wa Thiong'o and Kopano Matlwa

ACTIVITY: Questions contrasting Ngũgĩ and Matlwa's narratives

In this tutorial you will debate and compare the key issues that emerge from the extract taken from *Decolonising the Mind* (Ngũgĩ wa Thiong'o 1986) and *Coconut* (Kopano Matlwa 2007).

On the *Decolonising the Mind* extract:

1. Discuss the role that storytelling played in Ngũgĩ's childhood. What did he learn from these stories?

2. Ngũgĩ argues that there should be harmony between the home language and the language of learning and teaching, that is the medium of instruction. What does he mean by this? Do you agree with his argument? Give reasons for your position. You are encouraged to draw on your own experiences of learning in a home language or an additional language to answer this question.

3. Why did English become the language of learning and teaching at Ngũgĩ's school after 1952? How did this shift in the Kenyan language in education policy impact on the status of Ngũgĩ's home language and English?

4. Why do you think the school punished children for using their home language? What do you think are the effects on children of forbidding them to use their home languages at school?

5. How does Ngũgĩ illustrate the way English as medium of instruction affected the career opportunities of some learners? Discuss specifically Ngũgĩ's example of the boy in his class of 1954 who eventually became a turn boy in a bus company. What point is Ngũgĩ making by using this example?

6. Ngũgĩ begins this chapter by talking about storytelling in his home language and ends up by referring to the replacement of local Kenyan oral literature with English literature. What was his attitude towards this shift? Discuss his final comment (the last line) on the effect that the shift to English language and literature had on himself and other learners. What point is he making about the connection between language, learning and identity?

On the two extracts from *Coconut:*

1. In extract 1, Ofilwe writes 'I knew from a very young age that Sepedi would not take me far. Not a chance!' What reasons does Ofilwe give for her position? Do you agree with her argument?

2. As a student teacher, what is your response to the incident in extract 1 when Mrs Kumalo and the three men from the school governing board attempt to compile a list of learners' home languages? Comment on their assumptions about Ofilwe's home language.

3. In extract 2, Ofilwe sees herself through her brother Tshepo's eyes. What are Tshepo's criticisms of Ofilwe? Do you think that his argument that she is 'stuck between two worlds' and will never be accepted by either world is convincing? Give reasons for your responses.

Whose argument do you find most persuasive and why? Ngũgĩ's, Ofilwe's (in Matlwa's first extract) or Tshepo's (in Matlwa's second extract)?

Bear in mind that Ngũgĩ and Matlwa are referring to two different contexts. Ngũgĩ writes about his experience of British colonial rule in Kenya, while Matlwa writes about her experiences in post-apartheid South Africa in 2007.

Further ideas to consider:

- How do Ngũgĩ's and Matlwa's arguments relate to debates about language, learning and identity in a South African context?
- How are their experiences and ideas similar or different to your own language biographies?

Figure 3.3 A cartoon strip used to convey key sociolinguistic concepts.

#3 DEEPENING

Everyday texts are those texts that students would encounter out in the world, not associated with formal study or learning; for example, cartoons, billboards, street signs, newspapers, social media platform messages, clothing, website pages, television or radio shows and so on. For a language course that views language as embedded in real social practices, everyday texts that include language in written or spoken form are valuable sources of authentic language use. In this sense they offer a useful extension of the authenticity of autobiographical/ memoir writing of the language narratives.

Figure 3.3 shows a local, South African cartoon that has been on the first page of the course pack alongside the introductory blurb since the course began. This makes students' first encounter with the course a humorous one in which locally embedded racial and linguistic stereotypes are challenged through irony. It also perfectly reinforces a statement in the course blurb that tells students that they will be 'encouraged to challenge [their] taken for granted assumptions about language'.

In the same way, academic texts or language narratives can be paired with suitable everyday texts that can then function as additional entry points to complex sociolinguistic issues or to controversial language debates. One such pairing has been Gloria Naylor's language narrative, 'A Question of Language' (2000) and a comedy skit by the South African comedian Trevor Noah. Naylor's text first appeared as an article in the *New York Times* in 1986, and it is one of the handful of texts that we continue to use year in and year out. In it she paints the memory of an incident in the third grade when a classmate used the 'n--word' to insult her; and then she proceeds to undertake a nuanced analysis of the word and its shifting meanings according to context and insider/outsider speaker positions. It is a powerful example of the reappropriation of racist terms which also speaks to community, connection and reaffirmation of identity. Two broad questions originally accompanied Naylor's text. The first question asked students to extrapolate the rules for speaking implicit in Naylor's narrative; while the second one asked them to draw connections to their own context and experiences of pejorative labels, and to comment on their own position on the use of the term – making it clear that multiple positions on the issue were possible.

The other everyday text is similar yet different. Trevor Noah, who has been hosting the political satire television programme *The Daily Show* in the United States since 2015, is on stage doing stand-up comedy in front of a live audience (from *Son of Patricia*, 2018). Noah recounts an incident when a white motorist in Chicago called him the n-- word while Noah was jaywalking across the road and how he – drawing on a lesson learnt from his mother, Patricia – redirected this negative racist energy and greeted the surprised man with alacrity also using the n--word but in its appropriated, insider mode as if greeting a friend. He recognizes the oppressive history of the n-- word, arguing that in the South African context that he grew up in, it is not the loaded term that it is in the United States. He is transparent about his own positionality, admitting his own ease with using the n-- word, saying: 'It's a privilege I have in dealing with the n-word. In South Africa no one was called a n--. In Africa no one was oppressed by that word so that word has no power.' Both the Naylor and the Noah texts are risky and potentially triggering choices but they are authentic texts dealing with real issues of linguistic racism and thus have pedagogic value. In our 2020 iteration of the course, we placed a new text alongside Naylor and Noah – an article from the *New York Times* titled 'This Is the Casual Racism I Face at My Elite High School' written by Rainier Harris (September 2020). Rainer describes a number of racist incidents he experienced at school, and then writes about how the school addressed them through dialogue and restorative justice work.

When dealing with controversial issues it is important that it is clear to students that there are multiple possible arguments and positions. This does not mean all points are equally valid nor that positions cannot be challenged but it does alert them to the complexity of the issue and the need to develop reasoned arguments from informed positions. Indeed, when dealing with the issue of racial epithets, bringing in accessible texts with multiple voices and perspectives is particularly important for us as white middle-aged female lecturers of English in South Africa. Setting up the debate between/among texts and students removes the focus from the lecturer and does not allow her perspective of the issue to dominate discussions. However, we cannot pretend that we do not continue to occupy a position of power in the classroom/lecture theatre but the act of stepping back and focusing attention on other voices is one that we work on throughout the course.

On a more mundane level, key sociolinguistic concepts are being mediated through everyday texts, deepening the conversation and thereby the learning. The fact that these everyday texts occur in multiple modalities and genres – visual, colour, kinaesthetic, aural and so on – and not in dense academic writing facilitates student engagement, functioning as scaffolding to academic discourse and disciplinary knowledge. Their everydayness is ideal because it demonstrates how language is embedded in real life in real texts which have real purposes and position readers in ways which can have real effects on their lives. From a decolonial perspective we also recognize the disruptive potential contained in the mundane. Everyday multilingual texts contain other knowledges and experiences. Including them interrupts unmarked colonial knowledge and repositions these marked forms of knowledge as having more than limited local validity (Menezes de Souza 2021).

#4 CRACKING

Finally, there is a type of question to ask of texts that is radically open and operates by cracking texts wide open. These are questions that go beyond the texts at hand and throw open the universe. Two examples are as follows:

Example 1: One set of texts that we have used almost every year since it was published in 2005/6 was an insert from a weekly newspaper, *The Mail & Guardian*, titled Language and Culture. It consisted of four different articles, each with a different cultural focus – an urban black identity, minority ethnic communities and so on – and a different take on the relationship between language and culture. The articles were short and grounded in contemporary South African realities and collectively represented the following cultures: Xhosa, Zulu, Chinese, Jewish and 'Cape Malay'. After working through the issues they raised, we asked students to comment on what they could relate to but also asked the following question:

   Q1: If you don't identify with any of these articles, what article would you
       write/include to represent you? OR

   Q2: If you don't relate to/identify with any, what article would you write about
       the relationship between language, culture and identity? Are there other
       articles in the pack that represent you/that you can see yourself in? If not,
       what articles/texts would you want to add, or to write yourself?

Example 2: Another question that worked well once we had worked through the bulk of the language biographies was the following:

   Q: Of all the language biography writers/authors, who would you most like to
      meet for a chat (before writing your language narrative assignment)? Why?

How students took up this question gave some insight into what they were getting out of their reading, and again revealed multiple possibilities for engagement. A summary of the students' responses, reconstructed from lecturer's notes to feed back to the class is provided in Table 3.6.

Table 3.6 Conversations students wanted to have with authors

Most students wanted to chat with a particular writer because:
- They agreed with their ideas
- They related to their experiences
- They shared similar social/political contexts (e.g. Kenya and South Africa)
- They wanted to argue with them
- They could then see things through their eyes

Other examples:
- Students wanted to ask for advice from writers who had been in the same/similar positions to them and succeeded
- Because understanding a particular writer would help them as teachers (e.g. Anzaldúa and her teaching)
- Because they were impressed with and respected the way the writer had tackled issues around identity
- Ngũgĩ: 'because some students had never experienced that and so wanted to ask him more'
- Matlwa: 'because she gave some students an outsider's perspective of English'

This activity had no right or wrong answers – not even any predetermined answers. As teachers, we didn't have foreknowledge of the answers. Although some may have been predictable, there were always those that were surprising, often insightfully so, giving us new ways to think of how students were reading these biographies. What was also interesting was that students did not necessarily relate to a writer because of a shared language but rather because of a shared experience of language.

Conclusion

So we return to the question we posed earlier about what it could mean to bring this course into the decolonial era. While the origins of this course preceded the decolonial turn (Grosfoguel 2007), we are finding it generative to turn our relatively recently acquired decolonial lens onto the course. While there are aspects of the course that suggest that it remains trapped in a colonial logic, there are others that seem to align with a decolonial praxis. As theoretically informed practitioners, perhaps we can start from the ground up – moving from practice to theory – instead of trying to imbibe and digest the theory before making a move. Walsh (2020: 606) suggests as much when she writes of decolonial praxis that it requires 'ongoing processes of thought-analysis-reflection-action, processes that encourage *a theorising from practice* and a practicing of theory' [our italics]. In fact, as we begin to grasp the enormity of the work the needs to be done, the contradictions embodied in our own positionalities and the corresponding institutional constraints, it can be disheartening. For this reason, we have been inspired by Walsh's metaphor of the cracks – that when she shifts her gaze from the totality of the (system's) cement wall to the fissures in it, she is able to think of her work as 'not just within the cracks but part of the crack-making' (2020: 609). We can begin to think of some aspects of our pedagogy as working in the cracks. One such aspect could be the embodied ways of knowing that are centred in the pedagogy, enabling us to work beyond the theoretical in onto-epistemological ways. Another aspect could be our efforts to work in epistemically just ways, enabling marginalized voices to be heard and creating space for indigenous African languages where these exist in the students' multilingual repertoires. And a third aspect could be that alongside the embodied nature of the narratives, their locatedness enables us to work with the local in ways that are deep, critical and not parochial. The chapters that follow work directly with student narratives. These narratives emerge from the pedagogy and show how students have taken up the writing space and made their voices heard, sometimes with pride, sometimes painfully, sometimes in defiance, but they speak volumes about language as personal, as collective, as political, as always in flux and continually being shaped and reshaped.

Voices II

My father believed that if I could learn how to speak English very well then I would be educated or rather be considered an educated man. But does speaking good English mean that a person is educated? Is it right to say a person who speaks many languages is educated or a person who speaks English is educated? Is my language not sufficient for me to become educated, is English the only way to be educated? Is English the only way to study biology, the only way to study mathematics, science and all these other subjects?

Thabang, 2007

My proficiency in Tswana was quite impressive on paper, but orally I was a laughingstock. I remember black girls in my class giggling behind their hands when it was my turn to stand in front of the class and recite my Tswana monologues. I don't blame them. I would have simply lashed out at the girl who viciously murdered my mother's proverbs in front of an audience: spitting with every click and introducing an American twang into the greeting Dumelang.

Carmen, 2009

On my first day at a multiracial school my teacher asked me to stand up and read for the class and before I could even get up from my chair the whole class was in stitches as they were imagining my 'rural accent'. The disappointed look on their faces when I read so well that I even got a golden star was priceless. I walked back to my chair tall and proud.

Phaphama, 2018

I grew up with stares and whispers as society has not learnt to readily accept people with disabilities. People would stare if we were shopping or just having a Sunday lunch. I will never forget the day someone came up to us and placed a R200 note on the table. I was appalled! The fact that my parents are deaf does not mean that they aren't capable of earning. Personally, I find that there are some words that don't have an English equivalent, and I have yet to find an English word to describe them. Sign language is an energy that flows through me and processes my feelings and thoughts into something pliable.

Sabah, 2007

A six-hour drive later we arrive at my grandmother's birthplace and upon our arrival we are greeted by a full house of women clad in Zulu traditional casual wear and old men with large bellies, all bearing warm smiles and hugs. All was well when one of the men who are supposedly one of my uncles asked me how old I was in a fluent and deep Zulu accent: 'wePhumlani usuneminyaka emiy'ngakhi manje?' (Phumani, how old are you now?) Well, that part I understood, I was trying so hard to reply in fluent isiZulu myself but I could only count up to ten in isiZulu, so I replied: 'ngina18 malume'. (I'm 18 now, Uncle.) He replied with '18? Umsangano wani loyo? Awusazi na isiZulu sakini wena mfana?' (18? What madness is that? Don't you know isiZulu, your home language boy?), in a rather condescending manner which made me very uneasy, but I had to respect it since I was a boy and I would easily receive a violent punishment if I showed any sign of disrespect. I replied, 'Ngiyasazi malume' (I do Uncle). He got very irritated and dismissed the conversation with 'haaii kulungile mfana womlungu hamba uyodlala.' (It's okay white boy, go outside and play.)

Phumlani, 2017

My grandmother then said 'ungubani mtanami?' Puzzled, looking at her with a straight face, how could my grandmother not know who I was? It could not be her vision, she had glasses on. Maybe Alzheimer's is taking its toll already? I responded, 'NginguZonke, Gogo'. My aunt jumped up in hysteria saying this is exactly what she was talking about. She stated that if it wasn't me trying to be better than everyone else because of my English it was my crippled Zulu accent. My dad tried to save me from this saying that I've been schooling in Mpumalanga for two years already and this was bound to happen. 'Haaaaaaawu, wayibulala ingane, Mbuleleni!' screamed my aunt. No Zulu man will marry this child, her talk sounds too smart. Too white. Too English. She must start speaking like a Zulu girl again, or else this is trouble, said my aunt. As said by Moya that Africans with their rural roots still intact, good for them. For others it doesn't make them less African.

Zonke, 2018

When my grandmother eventually decided to take me to her employers, she gave me ground rules. 'Smile at everything they say, and agree with everything they say,' she said with a very serious face. I woke up early that morning. I wore my best dress and a pair of sneakers she got for me last Christmas. No one was in the kitchen when we got there. I waited patiently as my grandmother was starting with her everyday duties. I kept asking myself if they would look at me and think less of me because I couldn't speak their language, or would they understand that I am not one of them. The master came first and greeted me, 'good morning young lady.' Scared as I was, I greeted him back. I kept smiling and he looked at me as if there was something wrong with me. He asked my name and when I told him my name, he raised his eyebrows. For a minute I thought I had said something very wrong. I kept quiet for some time and awaited his reaction. He looked at me and asked me if I didn't have another name. For the first time I spoke to a white person, and it wasn't as nice as I thought it would be. I was very offended. My grandmother could see that I was very irritated or maybe she thought I didn't understand the question. She quickly answered him. 'Her other name is Priscilla, Master,' she said. 'That's much better,' he said. He didn't even attempt to call out my name. He just assumed it was difficult to say. Who said English names were better? Why do I even have a second name? My head started crowding itself with dozens of questions. Why didn't my grandmother say something in my defence? She just stood there and smiled.

Thando, 2015

(Re)Constructing Identities across Languages

English is like a tower shadowing over the houses of other languages, but it is the weeds among the grass and the rose among the thorns. To me it flows with my blood, but for others it twists their tongues.

Zinhle's language metaphor, 2015

SiSwati is that quick but gentle breeze that lightly touches your skin under the shade of a mango tree. The only thing that pierces my heart is that I feel more and more disconnected from it every day. Three years in KZN and now living in the City of Gold has made my tongue betray and dilute the sweet honey that is my language.

Nonhle's language metaphor, 2020

I never hold back when speaking IsiZulu. I feel like I am wearing shoes that fit when I speak my language.

Khwezi's language metaphor, 2017

From the first assignments in 2005 onwards we were struck by the richness of these diverse narratives and the window they offered into how students negotiated their linguistic identities in South Africa's second decade of democracy. Each year brought with it new insights and continues to do so, enriching students' and lecturers' evolving understandings of self and others' lived experiences of languages. The foregoing extracts from students' language metaphors give the reader a taste of how these narratives capture aspects of students' relationships to various languages in their repertoires: ambivalence towards English as hegemonic language and its impact on their other languages; shifts, losses and gains; the different selves constructed through specific languages and the conscious choices students make at the intersection of language and other significant social categories and experiences.

In this chapter we aim to illustrate how language works as a significant element of an intersectional identity, and how students' identities are (re)shaped by the confluence of multiple experiences. We offer a close reading of three narratives drawn from the first three years of the course (2005 to 2007) in order to explore students' identity shifts in relation to the dynamic positions of English, various African languages and Afrikaans in their linguistic repertoires.

After coding the full set of 140 narratives from 2005 to 2007 in relation to key sociolinguistic themes, we selected 20 for detailed analysis and for use as case studies. Although all were rich and fascinating, three narratives serve as exemplars for this chapter of what for us are the most striking themes.

The sections that follow begin with a brief overview of identity theory which is followed by three detailed case studies of student language narratives that highlight the following key themes:

- The impact of mobility on students' linguistic identities
- Conscious constructions of multilingual, hybrid identities
- Writing back to labels and assumptions

While the focus of each case study is on a different theme, they share many intersecting themes. For example, all three students are concerned with (re) positioning themselves, but this process unfolds in different ways in the individual case studies, shaped by the particular crisscrossing of key identity elements and experiences. We explore the specific microlinguistic choices students make about (re)positioning themselves in relation to macro aspects of their interactions, stories and journeys (Horner and Dailey-O'Cain 2019).

Shifting theorizations of identity

In this brief overview we draw on shifting identity theories from applied linguistics, second language acquisition (SLA) and sociolinguistics research. Norton's seminal work (Peirce 1995, 1997, 2000) changed the way identity is understood in the field of SLA and has had a significant impact on our thinking about linguistic identities. Norton challenged the static conceptualization of identity then dominant in SLA research, arguing instead that identity is multiple and fluid. She made connections between the language learner, the language learner context and the broader sociocultural context, with a specific focus on how the 'relations of power in the social world affect social interactions between second language learners and target speakers' (Peirce 1995: 9).

Her work was published at a time of growing interest in language and identity, a slowly shifting zeitgeist in SLA and educational research as evidenced by an increased number of journal articles, special editions and doctoral theses in the 1990s (Norton 2000). At the same time, Gloria Ladson-Billings (1995) published her seminal article on culturally responsive pedagogy, which made a compelling argument for reconfiguring curricula to meet the needs of black students in the United States. Alongside these increasing engagements with identity and power, some SLA researchers began to draw on critical pedagogy, raising questions about the relationship between the micro and the macro and debating what empowerment meant, for example whether teachers should provide students with access to dominant discourses or help students develop resistant voices (Canagarajah 2006).

Our initial conceptualization of linguistic identity was also shaped by Pavlenko and Blackledge's work on the role of agency and choice and the way in which 'many individuals find themselves in a perpetual tension between self-chosen identities and others' attempts to position them differently' (Pavlenko et al. 2004: 20).

Stroud's research on multilingualism (2015, 2018) has shifted the focus from linguistic identity to linguistic citizenship. Stroud explains that the notion of linguistic citizenship was 'born out of the felt need for a perspective that situated linguistic practices and representations of speakers firmly within their everyday socio-political strivings for agency and transformation' (2015: 22). He makes important connections between linguistic identity, agency and positioning and argues that linguistic citizenship is concerned with 'what people do with and around language (s) in order to position themselves agentively' (Stroud 2018: 7). Hence, linguistic citizenship foregrounds speakers' refusal to take on imposed linguistic identities and their crafting of identities outside ethnolinguistic stereotypes. This act of asserting linguistic agency enables a process of 'being through language' (Stroud 2015: 34) and becoming through language on one's own terms. Stroud's reconceptualization of multilingualism and his focus on agency and 'being-together-in difference' (2015: 54) resonates with the work we are doing and what we strive to achieve in the teaching of the sociolinguistics course.

Ndhlovu (2016) provides a valuable framework for a decolonial conceptualization of (diaspora) identity theories. While our focus is on our students' African locus of enunciation rather than on diaspora identities, we draw on some elements of his framework and put them to work in our context as the theme of mobility and migration is so powerful in our dataset. Ndhlovu

(2016) argues that traditional markers of identities (race, class, gender, etc.) frequently produce homogenous analysis and are increasingly problematic and contested because they fail to provide useful insights into how people construct their identities in the real world. Bucholtz and Hall (2005) and Soudien (2021) also argue that traditional identity categories have limitations and that we need to rehumanize identity discourses. These arguments have implications for the way we position ourselves as researchers and the way we engage with students' narratives: while not abandoning these categories, we try to use a more open, nuanced approach.

Ndhlovu argues for alternative categories of thought about identities that take into account the range of resources and experiences people bring to their 'multi-formed, multidimensional and convoluted migration histories, journeys and itineraries' (2016: 33). In his view a decolonial theoretical framework could be used productively to capture 'the multiplicity of histories and experiences' (2016:37) in open-minded and sensitive ways. Central to his thinking is the notion of 'the coloniality of being' which 'seeks to provide counter-narratives in identities and identity formation processes' (2016: 37), disrupting the binaries of them/us, developed/developing. He draws on decolonial epistemologies to argue for 'recognition of alternative knowledges and alternative ways of conceptualising cultural identities in order to both counter and complement dominant Euro-American epistemologies' (2016: 37).

We agree with Ndhlovu that there is no one theory that can do all the work needed for understanding identities as every theory can tell only a partial story. He has opened a conversation that we would like to join as it resonates with our flexible, intersectional approach to the analysis of students' identities in this chapter, and elsewhere. We regard the students as constructers of knowledge from their particular African locus of enunciation, (re) telling stories about their linguistic identities. We do not approach the reading of these narratives with preconceived ideas or with a specific argument in mind. Rather we read and learn from each narrative and our analysis is guided by 'the multiplicity of histories and experiences' (2016: 37) that students bring to their narratives in the act of knowing/being/becoming, within the limits of our positioning and loci of enunciation.

Finally, we use the sociocultural linguistic analytic tools of Bucholtz and Hall (2005) for the micro analysis of identity as produced in linguistic interactions. They argue that language plays a significant role in identity construction. They provide tools for analysis of 'social positioning within discursive contexts' (Horner and Dailey-O' Cain 2019: 7) enabling researchers to make connections between the micro and the macro of social interactions. We find the following tools helpful for analysing students' narratives, particularly their descriptions of critical incidents and social interactions:

Relationality: People construct identities by comparing themselves to others – making distinctions between self and other using concepts such as 'similarity/ difference, genuineness/artifice and authority/delegitimacy' (Bucholtz and Hall 2005: 598). Language can play a significant role in providing access or barriers to group membership.

Authenticity: The process of authentication entails members of a social group determining 'what sorts of language and language users count as "genuine" for a given purpose' (Bucholtz and Hall 2005, 2010: 24). However, individuals can disrupt and denaturalize the assumptions underlying authentication, and this process is strongly evident in the student language narratives that follow. This process of discursively verifying identities often causes linguistic prejudice and persecution within a given community. Anzaldúa (2000b) refers to this as in-group linguistic persecution.

Micro and macro: Identity is a strange combination of conscious and less than fully conscious choices and is simultaneously shaped by local interactions, other people's perceptions and broader structures of power and ideology.

Analysis of students' language narratives

In the sub-sections that follow, we discuss and analyse three students' language narratives. For each sub-section a broad discussion of the relevant theme is followed by the related case study.

The impact of mobility on students' linguistic identities

In analysing students' narratives, we have been struck by the extent of the mobility that many have experienced. Mobility refers to the flow of people across borders and 'the relationship between newcomers, their places of origin and their current places of living, as well as the more ethereal social spaces within these places that they create' (Horner and Dailey-O' Cain 2019: 3). It also includes smaller movements within a single country, across regions and even neighbourhoods or buildings. We use mobility to refer to these smaller movements across regions, neighbourhoods and schools. While geographically these are smaller moves, linguistically, emotionally and socioculturally such moves frequently require students to rapidly acquire new languages or varieties and to make substantial identity shifts in formal classroom settings as well as in informal social domains

What follows is an illustration of identity shifts, related to mobility, that are evident in the multiple journeys of Mashudu.

Mashudu's language narrative: I am proud of my shifting identity (2005)

Mashudu is a Tshivenda-speaking, black male student. In his narrative, he reflects on the impact of attending an English-medium boarding school, identity shifts and the positive and negative implications of these shifts. The full narrative is included, followed by discussion and analysis.

> *I was born on the third of January 1986 in a diverse background consisting of a white droplet along the family tree, which resulted in my brother adopting the genes of our great, great grandmother. My home language was Tshivenda during the period of 1986 to 1993, until I was sent to a boarding house in Johannesburg. The boarding house consisted of sixty to ninety boarders from diverse backgrounds, cultures and religious beliefs which contributed to the difficulties that I faced in terms of communication and understanding. I had to learn English in order to communicate with the other boarders. It was more difficult in my dormitory because a lot of the people were foreigners, but it didn't take long for us to learn English as we attended Extra English lessons after school.*
>
> *I passed Grade 1 but was told to repeat Grade 2 because I was too young to go to Grade 3. This sounded true at the time but now I look back and question why I was sent back to repeat Grade 2. It was because I was illiterate and not yet competent to the standards that were required. By that time, I could only speak English by code switching sometimes to my home language. By the time I completed Grade 2 I was declared literate and carried on with my studies.*
>
> *I was a termly boarder and I only went home every six months for the June and December holidays. My identity was shifting slowly but before I went to boarding school it was static as I used to follow cultural practices and traditions. My cultural beliefs, traditions and practices fell away as my identity became a more flexible one. It was difficult to rebel against the boarding house system as every Thursday and Sunday night we had to attend chapel services which was part of a long tradition. Even though the majority of the boarders were white, I adapted to the society around me because people respected the fact that some of the people were learning English and there wasn't any segregation or discrimination as we treated each other like brothers.*

Although the boarding house facilitated for everyone, I think the key factor that contributed to unity was the learning of a language that we could communicate in and relate to each other. My literacy development was important so I could understand and communicate.

My parents sent me to the boarding institution because they thought that I would have a good education. I completed primary school and refused to go home because I was enjoying it. I rejected the opportunity because every time I went home, I had a problem communicating with my siblings and neighbours. I was given labels such as 'coconut' as I had adopted the white man's accent. 'Coconut' means black on the outside and white on the inside. This label was discriminatory towards me. There were other labels I was given because of the way I spoke including my illiterate skills of other languages. 'Oreo' was another negative label that made me angry. Basically, the way I spoke English resulted in 'linguistic terrorism' (Anzaldúa 2000:316) as people made judgements about how I spoke, my accent and my change of identity. I couldn't handle being discriminated against whenever I went somewhere with my brother and his friends, so I preferred to stay away from home. I enjoyed the boarding institution – I felt more at peace and ease with people who didn't judge me or had anything against me.

Boarding school gave me the opportunity to communicate in the same language with people from diverse cultures, beliefs, and religions. I can reflect back and be proud of my shifting identity because at the beginning I had no choice but then I chose the choice not to leave as I had adapted to the changes. Some people will see it as a disadvantage, but my switch of identity has brought a lot of joy to me and has become a positive element as I speak and understand English well. I have been offered opportunities to study, work and teach other children to communicate in English, as I am a Housemaster in a boarding institution.

We found this to be a particularly interesting narrative in its articulation of the tensions and disjunctures frequently experienced by students when they are required to shift from an African language to English as the medium of instruction and as a medium of communication outside the classroom. In the case of Mashudu, this tension is articulated particularly strongly because he was a boarder at a historically white, English-medium public school from an early age and was thus immersed in this sociocultural environment at a formative stage in his life. The usual pressures of Anglonormative educational environments (McKinney 2017) on English additional language learners were intensified and he needed to master English rapidly for social and educational survival.

Mashudu begins his narrative by describing his limited proficiency in English as an obstacle to group membership and academic success at his new school. His home language, Tshivenda, is sidelined from the narrative after line two, when the watershed event of attending boarding school begins. It is also striking that he provides no information about his home linguistic, social and cultural practices prior to attending boarding school, other than that his home language is Tshivenda. His own writing mirrors the ways in which his linguistic and cultural resources were rendered invisible in the assimilationist school environment.

Mashudu's journey entailed multiple moves, from a township school in Tembisa[1] to an English-medium, historically white public boarding school located in a previously white suburb. Geographically, the distance between the two schools was not significant – both being located in the eastern part of Johannesburg. However, culturally, linguistically, socially and emotionally the move was substantial. His journey illustrates the point that 'language in motion (physically or virtually) can potentially gain or lose value along the journey with its speaker/s' (Horner and Dailey-O'Cain 2019: 3) After repeating grade 2 he began to acquire fluency in English, and he assimilated into the culture of whiteness that predominated.

Mashudu locates his narrative within the framework of identity issues although he seems to be working with contradictory notions of identity as simultaneously shifting and fixed, ultimately arguing that he has made an 'identity switch' that leaves no space for the synthesis of the traditional, cultural identity (as a Venda) with his 'white', western English-speaking identity. He works productively with new ideas and concepts, such as 'linguistic terrorism' (Anzaldúa 2000b) to explain a painful aspect of his experience, in particular the way he was judged by family and neighbours for taking on a new linguistic identity that conflicted with his home linguistic identity. This is an example of in-group linguistic persecution (Anzaldúa 2000b). He harnesses sociolinguistic discourse in ways that enable him to reinterpret this difficult memory within a broader, analytic framework.

The only time Mashudu references Venda cultural practices and traditions is in the third paragraph and it is significant that these are mentioned in the past tense, as something that 'fell away'– which seems to suggest an inevitable and natural process of replacing one set of linguistic and cultural practices with another 'more flexible one' in the context of the boarding school. He narrates his story from the perspective of his current self, detaching himself emotionally from his life before attending boarding school. Mashudu emphasizes the importance of English as a language that facilitates communication and unifies the boarders. However, while he gained access to group membership at school, he begins to feel alienated whenever he returns home.

An important aspect of Mashudu's narrative is the recurring theme of the significant role of language in creating access or barriers to group membership (Bucholtz and Hall 2005). At boarding school mastery of English provided Mashudu with access to group membership, while on his return home his 'white' accent and limited proficiency in African languages resulted in social exclusion and negative judgements. He is judged by his siblings and neighbours to be lacking 'authenticity' (Bucholtz and Hall 2005), a concept that refers to a social process of verification 'played out in discourse' (Bucholtz and Hall 2005: 601). In Mashudu's case, he is found to be not black enough and not Venda enough, a judgement that applies to both contemporary Venda linguistic–cultural practices and 'a claimed historical tie to a venerated past' (Bucholtz and Hall 2005: 602). On his home visits, he finds himself 'in a perpetual tension' between his self-chosen identity and others' attempts to position him differently (Pavlenko and Blackledge 2004: 20). His parents had sent him to boarding school 'because they thought he would get a good education'. However, his parents and extended family were unprepared for the 'unexpected sociolinguistic effects' (Blommaert 2010: 4–5) of educational mobility: that learning is deeply tied up with identity, especially when it involves linguistic shifts.

Despite the manner in which Mashudu's identity is contested by his family and community, he rejects this social pressure and becomes more determined to position himself differently. Mashudu's investment in English (Darvin and Norton 2017) is partially driven by his perception of the economic benefits of English as the language of 'global access' and social mobility. For example, being a housemaster at a boarding school

One of the striking features of this narrative is Mashudu's insistence that he has made a conscious choice that is beneficial and positive, illustrating Darvin and Norton's (2017: 7) argument that 'learners exercise agency by choosing what they perceive as beneficial to their existing or imagined identities'. He is emphatic about having made this choice with agency: 'at the beginning I had no choice but then I chose the choice not to leave as I had adapted to the change.' This powerful play with language points to elements of a counter-narrative in his refusal to tell his story as a story of loss and victimhood but rather a story in which he ultimately navigated difficult schooling and family dynamics on his own terms. But it is important to acknowledge that Mashudu's agency is embedded in a web of power relations with family and institutions, highlighting how students navigate and (re)construct their identities in relation to powerful and marginalized languages. He had to make difficult choices that English first language speakers never have to contemplate: their narratives provide accounts of seamless matches between home and school.

Mashudu concludes his narrative by reiterating his positioning as a westernized, English-speaking black male who is comfortable in diverse social contexts. In a moment in time, he constructs a textual identity that speaks back to an imagined audience who are critical of his choices. In contrast with Mashudu's, the narrative written by Mandla serves as an exemplar of students who embrace their urban multifaceted linguistic identities. While Mandla and Mashudu are both from Johannesburg and both moved from township schools to historically white public schools, their narrative journeys entail significantly different identity shifts.

Conscious constructions of multilingual, hybrid identities

At the outset of the course, when we invite students to share their language metaphors, there are always some who foreground their multilingual repertoires, embracing linguistic and cultural hybridity. They often use food metaphors such as that expressed by Londiwe, the multilingual chef who 'can proudly dish up five different meals for five different cultures.'

In reviewing educational research in South Africa post-1994, Ferreira (2016) concludes that 'these studies draw attention to the fact that social change is experienced and taken up differently by young people whose identity locations are racialized, classed and gendered in different ways' (2016: 1249). Together these studies present a portrait of youth taking up fluid identities and frequently 'straddling different worlds' resulting in tensions and alienation (Stevens and Lockhat 1997: 258). Other studies foreground students' agency as they reconstruct their identities in new contexts (Salo 2003; McKinney 2010).

As stated in Chapter 1, the labelling of the 'post-apartheid' youth generation as 'the rainbow nation' and the 'born frees' has been critiqued. Chikane (2018) problematizes the 'rainbow nation' trope, arguing that it elides difference and structural inequalities. Nwadeyi (2021) argues that neither of these labels is complex enough to capture the nuances of South African youth identities. He concludes that youth need to name themselves and tell their own stories on their own terms. Mandla's narrative is an example of such a telling and illustrates the intersection of language, race, class and disability in the construction of his identity.

Mandla's language narrative: Camouflage (2007)

Mandla was born in Katlehong, a township in the eastern part of Johannesburg. From the outset of his narrative, he foregrounds the creative aspect of identity (re) construction and the use of his multilingual repertoire as tools for deployment in different domains. His narrative powerfully illustrates Botsis's (2017: 91) argument that 'students use language flexibly to negotiate their identities and social positions'. His intriguing title 'Camouflage' contributes to the impression of multiplicity and strategic adaptability that is threaded through the narrative, illustrating Darvin and Norton's argument that 'the feel for the game' (2017: 7) is an important aspect of learner investment in a language. We turn to Mandla's narrative.

Being born in Katlehong, a township in the East Rand, identity could be something that one has to create or should I say develop for oneself. This is due to the diversity in culture, traditions, customs, and different ethnic groups that you would find yourself being brought up in. I for one was a victim of such nourishment. Well, what I am actually saying is that I was fortunate to be raised in a community that is so rich in culture because all the ethnic groups were united. So, I was spoilt for choice.

I grew up in Katlehong for the first seven to eight years of my life. Now one could ask what possibly a kid/toddler would learn about language. I, as a matter of fact, speak from plentiful experience. With Zulu and Sotho being the first two languages that I was introduced to I could interact with various groups of people. I was given the platform to showcase my ability of being bilingual in the streets because most children had their fun and games there and I could interact with a variety of languages when participating. I soon learned Tsotsitaal[2] which was a medium that enabled the people that lived in the township to communicate with one another. This was mostly amongst the youth whilst the elders spoke dialects of Zulu or Sotho.

The downside to all of this would be that I would never master any of the languages and this has been a factor that has played on my conscience from time to time. I am a person who loves accommodating others. When going to the rural areas when there would be an elderly person who has visited our family from the rural area, I found it uncomfortable to speak to them. I would feel ashamed at times. The other elderly people within the community would be the ones to make remarks on how the youth's usage of language was so awful. But the irony in all of this would be that they are the ones who should be taking the initiative of teaching their young ones their home languages. So, I would often ask myself the question: who is really at fault?

Nonetheless, I persisted in making use of the tools I had. I attended school at an early age in Katlehong. Fortunately, or unfortunately, I failed to cope due to my disability; I am visually impaired. I then attended school in Pretoria, which was a totally different environment to Johannesburg. The school was both an Afrikaans and English medium school. The significance of all of this was that English was no longer a language that I heard only on the television, but I had the opportunity to speak the language with people who understood it and who would not find it problematic when I spoke the language. Whereas back at the township it would be said that I was better than the rest when I spoke English. My family also had decided to move to Jameson Park, a semi suburban area next to Nigel still in the East Rand.

At first, I was reluctant in learning Afrikaans. I did not see the necessity to know the language. I had no choice though. Learning Afrikaans was compulsory. There were times when I felt as if I could not express myself when speaking to teachers or fellow learners. It was so frustrating, but it encouraged me to learn the language to such an extent that I even spoke the language with the so-called appropriate accent. At the time when I started the school other learners were rather discriminatory towards me or any other black learners. This would occur when I mispronounced a word. Like for instance: When I was asked a question by the teacher when answering I would start off by saying 'teacher it is', which I would say as 'teasha it is'. I guess the feeling would be similar to what Anzaldúa felt when she was told by her teacher to go back to Mexico as she could not speak with an American accent. (Anzaldúa 2000: 312)

As time went by and I adapted to my new surroundings, I felt the need to create an image. An identity of some sort, something that people would be able to relate to me. I also had realised that identity need not necessarily be the way one walks or talks, but also how one conducts one's conversations socially. This had been a dilemma for me. I was confused. I did not know whether I should be your typical traditional Zulu boy who spoke rural Zulu or your typical urban Zulu boy who spoke urban Zulu. Or perhaps should I speak English since it had been a language that dominated my life in all aspects. At school I was taught in English! Books at the library were written in English! And of course, then, the most influential monster, the media, where information was predominantly available in English. It was a continuous phase of colonization I had thought to myself (wa Thiong'o 1986: 11). I came to the conclusion that rather having the privilege of being able to speak four languages I should use it to my full advantage.

Through all of these different experiences and a little innovation, I managed to come up with a system that works in such a manner that I could interact with all types of individuals as diverse as they might be. Something that has always been a part of me is that when talking to my grandfolks I would try my best to use the ideal register which would be speaking formal Zulu. But it is not only about the register, but I have got to be gentle and very descriptive especially during serious discussions. A casual chat with my mother would be a mixture of English and Zulu. This often occurs when discussing general issues that we would hear on the news. My cousin whom I spend most of my time with when I am home speaks to me in English and we will switch to Zulu occasionally. In the groups that I used to hang around with during my school career, a mixture of all these four languages that I am acquainted with would be spoken. But then we used to use English in our deep discussions. It seemed to be the language that all the members could express themselves freely in.

Ultimately, I believe that your identity is partially how you portray yourself and the other portion how people perceive yourself. That is why I incorporated all my languages. I view this as a form of liberation. I am enabled to communicate with people in a medium in which they are feeling comfortable. This in turn puts me at ease when they are feeling free having a conversation with me.

Mandla embraced the cultural and linguistic diversity of his formative years. His fluency in isiZulu and Sesotho created opportunities for interactions with various groups of people. He shows an awareness of the performative aspect of language, showcasing his multilingual repertoire on the streets. Despite his predominantly positive experience of multilingualism, he experienced discomfort and shame when he visited family in rural areas because of his urban varieties of isiZulu and Sesotho.

Mandla's narrative takes another turn as he describes the move to a school for the visually impaired in Pretoria (a historically Afrikaans city, forty minutes away from Johannesburg) because he was not coping with mainstream schooling. His visual impairment is mentioned in passing – he seems to make a conscious choice not to foreground it. The new school environment and Pretoria itself was 'a totally different environment to Johannesburg', having been the seat of the apartheid government until 1994. In a dual-medium English/Afrikaans school, where the majority of students were white, Mandla took the opportunity to further develop his English proficiency.

Mandla is subjected to linguistic prejudice both at home in Katlehong and at school in Pretoria for very different reasons. He explains that his English improved both because of immersion in an English-speaking environment and because he could use English without being judged as being 'better than the rest' as had been the case in Katlehong where he encountered in-group linguistic prejudice. He is also subjected to linguistic prejudice from white learners at the new school because of his pronunciation of English words, a form of racial discrimination.

The link that Mandla makes to Anzaldúa's narrative (2000b) strengthens his point about feeling othered in this new context by white learners ostensibly because of his black South African English accent. Although it is not clear what roles the teachers play in this othering, given what we know from research about newly desegregated schools at that time, we can assume that an assimilationist discourse was dominant (Soudien 2004). Hence, even if teachers didn't specifically criticize his accent, the idea of accents as markers of a range of identities, would not have been foregrounded. Mandla chooses to background his experience of racial discrimination at his new school, refusing to take up a victim position. Instead, he positions himself as agentively crafting a new image and identity in the context of various struggles and oppressive experiences in institutional, family and social spaces.

He elaborates on his identity dilemmas and confusion, illustrating the psychological tensions resulting from 'straddling different worlds' (Stevens and Lockhat 1997: 258), spinning between traditional and urbanized identity options. In all these deliberations, language plays a key role as a tool to index his identity and group membership options as reflected in his comment:

> *I did not know whether I should be your typical traditional Zulu boy who spoke rural Zulu or your typical urban Zulu boy who spoke urban Zulu. Or perhaps should I speak English since it had been a language that dominated my life in all aspects.*

Unlike Mashudu who chose an English western identity, Mandla ultimately embraces a hybrid, multilingual identity that draws on all four languages (English, Afrikaans, isiZulu, Sesotho), which he deploys in different contexts and with different participants. His linguistic repertoire includes shifting registers and varieties with family, especially parents and grandparents.

The conclusion to Mandla's narrative is powerful, showing a shift from seeing English as a form of colonization towards seeing his multilingual repertoire 'as a form of liberation', illustrating Ferreira's argument (2016) that social change has the potential to destabilize previous identity locations and to offer new identity positions.

Writing back to labels and assumptions

While Mashudu and, to a lesser extent, Mandla both encountered some linguistic prejudice, neither of their narratives foregrounded this issue. In the narrative that follows, Gillian foregrounds linguistic labelling and writes back to discursive assumptions imposed on her. There is a powerfully recurring theme about resisting linguistic and racial assumptions, labels and stereotypes through adopting a strong voice and telling a counter-story (Morrel 2008), a story that resists dominant narratives. As discussed in Chapter 2, voice is a significant aspect of the narrative writing process. Gillian's narrative powerfully illustrates Chadwick's (2017: 12) argument that 'Stories are constructed in the cracks between multiple and at times contradictory collective voices, and identity/narrative is thus radically dialogical'. When we refer to voice, we have two dimensions in mind: the first is from a literary perspective – the writer's presence in the text as distinct and resonant in ways that engage the reader's imagination. The second, and the more significant for narrative analysis, is the understanding of voice in a Bakhtinian sense as dialogic and multiple. Each individual voice draws on other voices from the past, present or imagined future. This notion of voice emerges from Bakhtin's (1981) conceptualization of language as heteroglossic, always a site of struggle that traverses the individual and the social.

The presentation of Gillian's narrative is followed by analysis and discussion which draws on the theoretical framework for understanding the role of voice in narratives included in Chapter 2.

Gillian's language narrative: *Freedom to speak – A matter of choice* (2005)

The assumption goes as follows: All coloured persons are bilingual in English and Afrikaans.

Well, I am about to rectify a common misconception. My name is Gillian Linda Charmaine Peterson. It is quite evident that this is an English name and not the latter. My surname travelled all the way from Ireland, many thanks to my great-great grandfather in the late 1800s. An Englishman who found love in the arms of a Swazi chief's daughter. Sounds terrific, doesn't it? Thus, mixing of cultures, the possibility of a multi-linguist. Unfortunately, it all ended there for both my parents are Afrikaans speaking coloureds.

History dictates that 'the so-called coloured persons' were slightly more favoured by the apartheid regime than others. For this reason, many had to use Afrikaans as a medium at school. This became a tool especially used for employment purposes. Over 30 years ago, banks in South Africa required bilingual staff who could cater for their clients who largely only spoke Afrikaans and English. Sadly, this has only recently come to pass with black people being employed to accommodate for the rise in the bank's non-English and (non) Afrikaans speaking clientele.

My mother became one of the chosen few, guaranteed employment in the bank, based on her efficiency in both languages. Soon she discovered that English would become the most dominant of the two. This is why it was decided long before our birth, that my brother and me would be called by the English names 'Larry' and 'Gillian'. However, the onset of motherhood let sound reasoning evade her mind, allowing Afrikaans to dominate the first three years of my existence. Then snap! Prior to attending nursery school, I had to adopt the English language. My mom's predictions were true. English has seized our schools, streets, homes, and businesses.

The majority of coloured parents scrambled to get their kids to speak the language. So easily they gave up their language, their identity. But was it truly ours? Or was it borrowed from our oppressor to make us feel whole?

Nonetheless, I was a bright one, that I was. Ever so proud (at the age of three) of my broken English. One of my infamous first words uttered being, 'I did wash my tandes (teeth).' Yet, I persevered and loved this new language. I loved it so much that I completely stopped speaking my home language. My circle of friends spoke my new language and my parents only spoke English to us. People had to adapt to my new language, the old one becoming a thing of the past.

At school, Afrikaans speaking children were seen as stupid, poor and coming out of our roughest neighbourhoods. I stayed clear from these images. But I could never completely eradicate Afrikaans from my life. I still possess the dialect of English restricted to coloured people. I have the accent to prove it. If you were to phone me and guess my race, immediately you would identify the Afrikaans undertones. Especially the pronunciation of the letter 'r'. Harsh and quite notorious in our culture.

Still, I have restricted myself to monolinguistic people irrespective of creed, sticking close to coloured English speakers. Like them, I fully understood my mother tongue, but could not speak it.

After I completed school, I chose to work, what better place than the good old bank with that famous assumption that because I am coloured therefore, I can speak the two dominant South African languages. Amongst my peers, I found that they addressed me in Afrikaans whereas I would reply in English. As you would already know, for this reason they remained just acquaintances. The church I attend is also predominantly Afrikaans, with only myself and two English speaking people attending.

Yes, I do blame myself for my lack of interest in speaking my home language. Yet I think it's safe to say that I am English and have been since a young age. So do not judge me by the colour of my skin, rather by my tongue. For the tongue is a powerful tool. In it lies the secret of who I truly am. It encompasses my coloured identity and makes a completely special individual of me.

The title of Gillian's narrative – 'Freedom to Speak: A Matter of Choice' – is powerfully consolidated in the final paragraph where she concludes with an instruction to the reader: 'do not judge me by the colour of my skin, rather my tongue.' Both her title and her concluding instruction to readers signal that this is a highly agentive narrative in which she asserts her voice and (re)positions herself. Her title and her focus on individual and intergenerational choices throughout the narrative illustrate Bucholtz and Hall's (2005) point that people can make conscious and active choice to use language to index their identities. In

Gillian's case, her choices entail both embracing an English-speaking coloured identity and an explicit refusal to take up imposed identities (i.e. Afrikaans-speaking coloured identity).

The narrative captures a process of becoming, a moment in time where various elements of her identity come together in a particular way, a coalescence of multiple selves and voices. Gillian regards her tongue as a powerful tool for asserting her voice and writing back to stereotypic assumptions and labels.

As she puts pen to paper, Gillian makes a number of conscious choices about how to position herself and her audience. Writing a narrative always entails making choices about what version of a story to tell and how to represent the self. From the outset, Gillian consciously repositions herself as an English-speaking coloured South African by challenging the assumptions that her imagined reader has of her as a bilingual coloured South African. Like Mashudu and Mandla, Gillian's struggles are shaped by a multitude of experiences, histories, social relations, race, ethnicity, places, communities and family. Her specific identity is deeply connected to the historical marginalization of coloured South Africans and her need to 'revoice' (Stroud 2015) or retell her story on her own terms.

Audience is always implied in any narrative, but Gillian foregrounds her relationship with her audience in explicit ways from her first line: 'The assumption goes as follows: All coloured persons are bilingual in English and Afrikaans. Well, I am about to rectify a common misconception.'

Her use of direct address to her audience is an interesting device – setting her reader up for a particular response and then indicating that the assumption is incorrect. For example, in the first paragraph she poses a rhetorical question to the reader in a colloquial style: 'Sounds terrific, doesn't it?' and then proceeds to tell a counter-story that undercuts celebratory notions of diversity. It makes for engaging and challenging reading, pushing the reader to reconsider their assumptions. There are interesting dynamics at play with voice and audience. First, Gillian is making assumptions about her imagined reader and positioning them as embracing stereotypes about coloured linguistic identity. Secondly, Gillian repositions herself by challenging the multiple voices in her world – some of which she may have encountered directly in educational, family and social spaces while others may have been encountered in the media.

Gillian's conscious play with audience is also a strong illustration of Thesen's (2014) argument that voice is not only located in the text but also at the point of reception, for the reader. We write to make a point, to be heard. We want our voices to carry ideas across spaces and to reach receptive readers with whom we establish a relationship. From this perspective voice has a journey, from the point of construction on the written page to the point of reception. A fundamental aspect of this journey is voice as 'writer agency across space' (2014: 3). Re-reading Gillian's narrative sixteen years after it was originally written, we find it a powerful narrative, one that has carried successfully across space and time and still has resonance.

One of the multiple voices in the narrative is that of her parents (especially her mother) and the choices they made at an early stage about the role that English would play in Gillian's life. Her mother predicted that English would become the more dominant of the two languages and her parents made a conscious decision to give their children English names and to raise them as English speakers. So, while Afrikaans dominated Gillian's first three years of life, thereafter English was prioritized in her family. This process highlights how language permeates multiple aspects of students' lives in intergenerational ways.

Gillian captures the hegemony of English and its reach in her description of its seizure of schools, the economy and even naming practices. Her point about how 'coloured parents scrambled to get their kids to speak English' is elaborated in Adikhari's (2006) research about the negative attitude of middle-class coloured parents towards Afrikaans and the preference for English. This moment in the narrative surfaces a more critical voice when she writes: 'So easily they gave up their language, their identity. But was it truly ours? Or was it borrowed from our oppressor to make us feel whole?' Gillian reinforces this point in a school context, pointing out the judgements made of Afrikaans-speaking children at school and her conscious decision to escape these judgements by taking up an English identity. In the rest of the narrative, Gillian embraces English as her language and her most 'powerful tool'. As it did for Mashudu, English ultimately replaced her home language which 'became a thing of the past'.

Despite her rejection of Afrikaans, it is still important to her to identify herself as a coloured South African through her specific accent which carries traces of Afrikaans. She unpacks her ownership of English as part of her coloured identity in the conclusion where she asserts that 'the tongue is a powerful tool' and the key to the secret of who she really is.

We find it interesting that although assumptions and labels pervade the narrative, Gillian does not provide a specific detailed example of an incident in which she needed to engage these assumptions. Instead, she bypasses the specifics of incident description and proceeds directly into the interrogation of discursive spaces. Her narrative illustrates that the course and narrative assignment facilitate multiple entry points, multiple ways of knowing and telling stories.

Conclusion: Agency and conscious choices across the three narratives

Many pieces of ourselves are lost and scattered in history – as young South Africans, we do not fully know who we are. We deserve the right to put our stories back together as a way of putting ourselves back together. (Nwadeyi 2021: 23)

The three narratives all raise complex themes and illustrate the interweaving of multiple threads that constitute the students' linguistic identities, written from their loci of enunciation. Our discussion of each narrative has aimed to capture the 'multiplicity of histories and experiences' (Ndhlovu 2016: 37) that Ndhlovu argues for in his conceptualization of a decolonial identities framework. In this final section we bring these interwoven themes together. All three students exhibit high levels of agency. However, their agency is 'contingent on the conditions of possibility of the particular moment' (Ferreira 2016: 1250) and is influenced by their social locations. The students juxtapose past and present selves as they put their stories and themselves 'back together' (Nwadeyi 2021: 23), foregrounding their languages and tongues as powerful tools for telling and retelling their stories.

It is not surprising that the titles of two of their narratives foreground conscious choices about crafting their linguistic identities: 'I Am Proud of My Shifting Identity' (Mashudu) and 'Freedom to Speak: A Matter of Choice' (Gillian). Mandla's title 'Camouflage' alludes to disguise and strategic adaptability. The students' strategic choices illustrate Stroud's (2015) argument that people position themselves agentively and consciously craft identities on their own terms, and that one cannot make assumptions about the linguistic identities students take up in terms of rigid categories.

English is viewed positively by all three students. They take ownership of English, especially Mashudu and Gillian. While Mashudu's and Gillian's home languages become marginalized and replaced with English, Mandla foregrounds his multilingual repertoire, viewing English as just one of the languages that shapes his hybrid identity across different contexts and relationships. One of the findings of our analysis of the three narratives supports Botsis's argument that the value of English among South African youth is 'variable across different social spaces' (2017: 102) and might be perceived as an asset in some contexts and as a liability in others. English plays a significant role in providing access to knowledge in school spaces and also in facilitating economic opportunities and communication in some informal social spaces. However, in certain contexts students' take-up of English makes them vulnerable to linguistic judgements and in-group linguistic persecution as is evident in the way Mashudu is labelled negatively by family and community. Mandla is also subjected to in-group linguistic persecution as well as linguistic prejudice and racism at the Pretoria school. Their descriptions of these experiences illustrate how relationality and authentication play themselves out at both micro and macro levels (Bucholtz and Hall 2005), but the three students subvert these assumptions and ultimately (re)construct their identities on their own terms, refusing to take on imposed linguistic identities (Stroud 2015).

In all of the students' journeys, race, ethnicity and language interact in significant ways with other overlapping categories of identity. Gillian foregrounds race from the outset and highlights how her identity is deeply connected to the historical marginalization of coloured South Africans. While not foregrounding race as explicitly as Gillian, it clearly plays a significant role in Mashudu's and Mandla's narratives as their take-up of English changes their views of themselves and is associated with whiteness and western culture by some members of their communities. They experience both losses and gains simultaneously.

This chapter has shown that reflective language narratives are a powerful tool for providing a window into students' lived experience of language and a conscientizing tool that enables students to explore the role of language and power in their own lives and the lives of others. In particular, the chapter has shown how students have made conscious choices about (re)positioning themselves and their linguistic identities in relation to both English as hegemonic language of power and their home languages.

5

Juxtaposing Creative and Critical Genres in a Heteroglossic Pedagogy

When writing this dialogue, I had hoped to entice the attention of young women who are viewed as 'loose' by young men, treated terribly for who they date and just how simple it is for men, especially those who are friends, to describe a woman as a sexual object of amusement and fun. The term [village bicycle] is used as an insult by men to hurt and inspire[s] anger. However, as a woman you may accept the term as one of intense jealousy from a man who cannot be with you or one of anger from a family member in reference to how many male friends you have.

Extract from Olivia's critical commentary on her dialogue, 2010

Over the years that we have taught the sociolinguistics course we have always been interested in not just the power of narratives that are read and told in our classes, but the work that narratives do for students as writers. In 2010 we introduced an alternative assignment to the language narratives. We asked students for two pieces of writing: creative writing in the form of a dialogue that drew on an incident from their everyday lives in a language variety or varieties that they knew and a critical commentary to accompany it. Olivia's dialogue focused on two young men talking to each other in a kitchen about a young woman one of them had met. He was interested in her and was excited that she had given him her phone number. The dialogue is full of masculine posturing and sexist terms objectifying the woman. When the young man reveals Sumaiya is the name of the woman he is interested in, his jealous friend informs him that she is known as the highly promiscuous 'village bicycle'. Male solidarity and the 'bro code' that polices gender win out. This isn't just a dialogue about a conversation between two friends speaking in sexist discourses. Nor is it just a dialogue that captures linguistic diversity in its multilingual slang and seamless shifts between English and Afrikaans characterized by this coloured community, although it does. Olivia's dialogue and critical commentary were a way of writing back. She had been present when this event occurred but had not felt empowered enough to challenge these young men. This assignment, she told us, was a way of reclaiming her voice.

As outlined in Chapter 2, one of the goals of the course is for students to develop a critical narrative gaze, where they can make the familiar strange, deconstruct and reconstruct meanings, (re)interpret events and have opportunities to challenge identity positionings and imposed discourses. We think it is important that this course provided a space for Olivia, the silenced young woman in the kitchen, to write a counter-story. We also believe that it is as important that Olivia, the student, has the tools to apply a critical gaze, and that Olivia, the future teacher, is aware of the politics of language to both navigate the language classroom and teach language in culturally responsive ways.

This chapter focusses on the dialogue and critical commentary assignment as an example of the ways in which our heteroglossic pedagogy operates. To do so it begins by extending the definition of heteroglossia set out in previous chapters and outlines some key characteristics of a heteroglossic pedagogy. It briefly describes the assignment and draws attention to show how its construction is a heteroglossic move. A similar case can be made for the language narratives, but this is addressed elsewhere in the book. Here we concentrate on the ways in which this assignment forms part of a heteroglossic pedagogy that enables an entry point into academic discourse as students explore the relationships between self and others in critical and socially contextualized ways. However, our work is also affected by context and it is important to acknowledge the tensions between institutional conceptions of academic writing and discourse and creative work for first-year students. We present three examples of how our pedagogy is realized through classroom practice and student writing.

A heteroglossic pedagogy

Bakhtin's (1981) work has been useful in conceptualizing our understanding of language and language teaching. It bears repeating that he resists a monoglossic orientation to multilingualism as stable and distinct languages, favouring heteroglossia that includes other linguistic phenomena like registers, dialects, voices and varieties in addition to named languages (Bailey 2012: 499). Bakhtin's explanation of the two ideological forces in society that manifest in discourse enables us to acknowledge students' linguistic repertoires, the politics of language teaching in South Africa and our aim of fostering a critical awareness of language practices in students. On the one hand, centripetal discourses are monoglossic, aiming to fix meaning; on the other hand, centrifugal discourses resist this fixing by diversifying language and articulating alternative and often marginal worldviews. The coming together of these forces in conflict is the operation of heteroglossia.

We draw on Busch (2014), who identifies three elements that need to be distinguished when working with heteroglossia: multi-discursivity, multi-voicedness and linguistic diversity. Multi-discursivity frames discourse as socio-ideological where discourses are shaped by time periods, social worlds or spaces and belief systems. Relatively stable genres develop within these discourses. Multi-voicedness refers to the diversity of individual voices that speak in multi-discursive interactions. The word, according to Bakhtin (1981), belongs to the individual and the other. The speaker/writer has to appropriate the discourse adapting it to their semantic intentions, shaping it in their accents before it becomes their 'own'. Linguistic diversity is used in a particular way that complements the way we talk about diversity in terms of pedagogy. For Bakhtin, it does not refer to different languages; rather it refers to the traces left behind as a result of social differentiation (Busch 2014). Thus, the intentional use of language by speakers results in a dialogue of languages that disrupts monoglossic boundaries between languages and varieties.

These concepts can be operationalized to constitute a heteroglossic pedagogy (Busch 2014). Acknowledging multi-discursivity in the classroom means making space for students' own experiences, concerns, histories and ways of knowing to enter the classroom. Placing narrative genres at the heart of the course foregrounds 'voices which index students' localities, social histories, circumstances and identities' (Blackledge and Creese 2014: 18). A pedagogy that values multiple voices is underpinned by an understanding of the dialogic nature of teaching and learning. This shifts traditional power relationships because learning is multi-directional. We learn as much from our students as they do from us, from other students and the voices in published texts. This multi-voicedness enabled the existence of the dialogue assignment. It acknowledges the diversity of ways in which meanings are made without placing them in deficit. A heteroglossic pedagogy has an openness 'where the polyphony of voices, discourses and ways of speaking . . . is not kept out or segregated, but taken as a constitutive feature' (Busch 2014: 14).

Juxtaposing genres: The dialogue and critical commentary assignment

As is inevitable in a course spanning nearly two decades, not everything we have done has been successful nor does it meet the needs of all students. The value of teaching collaboratively is that conversations and concerns enable experimentation. One of these instances was the dialogue and critical commentary assignment. An issue that concerned us was the ways in which problematic discourses and stereotypes around race and gender were often unconsciously reproduced in writing. We knew that students did not always necessarily hold these positions based on the rest of their narratives. We also noticed that some students were overwhelmed by their experiences and memories or got trapped in a discourse of victimhood, rather than being able to make the reflexive move and relook at their history with some critical distance (Dixon and Mendelowitz 2016).

So, we wondered what would happen if we shifted the focus. We thought about how the stories students told in class gave the course a vitality and energy and how this might translate into a different form of narrative writing that enabled students to work creatively, critically and reflectively. We juxtaposed a creative text in the form of a dialogue with an academic text in the form of a critical commentary, thus creating a heteroglossic text that works across genres. In this assignment we asked students to write a dialogue between two or more participants. We wanted them to use their own experiences as a creative impetus. They could write about a real event they had participated in or observed, a fictional event based on a life experience or a fictionalized retelling of an event they were a part of. In terms of thinking about epistemological access, writing about an everyday experience presented a level playing field for students. Second, students were asked to write the dialogue in a youth or other language variety/ies they were familiar with. This built on the linguistic strengths of all students. Students could draw on languages, varieties and registers of their choice, making this text heteroglossic. There was no expectation that the dialogues be in English. We did ask that glossaries or full translations be provided to make up for our linguistic deficits. It also shifts the power relationship where students are placed in a position of knowers, whose linguistic expertise is valued and trusted. The second part of the assignment asked students to cover the following in their critical commentary:

- The intended audience
- Context and purpose

- Group membership and/or the expression of specific identities in the critical commentary

Slonimsky and Shalem's (2006) work on academic writing and epistemological access remains useful to us. Their use of the principles of appropriation and distantiation enabled us to justify our thinking for juxtaposing genres. Drawing on life experiences to write the dialogue is an act of appropriation and holds the comfort of the known. The successful creative construction of the dialogue requires a meta-awareness of how language functions in order to deliberately craft it and place it in the mouths of characters. This is critical-creative work. However, first-year student dialogues on their own do not necessarily show this critical orientation – and thus reproduce a constraint of the language narratives in a different genre. The critical commentary, however, requires an act of distantiation, where the familiar is rendered strange and becomes an object of critical enquiry. Separating the dialogue from the critical commentary has the advantage of explicitly foregrounding critical thinking in contrast to the critical reflexive stance implicit in the language narratives.

The inclusion of the critical commentary is an initiation into an academic way of evaluating the world, where concepts from sociolinguistics are mobilized by students. For students whose school experiences did not include critical analysis and for whom academic language is foreign, this assignment limits the high-risk nature of the academic essay and opens up a broader range of possibilities. Placing critical and creative genres together for this assignment meant that we needed to return to thinking about what constitutes knowledge in sociolinguistics and what was useful for first-year education students. We needed to be clear about which concepts were important for education students and that they could use as tools. But we were also mindful that 'a discipline is not the sum of all that can be truthfully said about something' (Foucault 1981: 59) and that disciplinary knowledge is not stable. This is particularly the case in the last five years where the decolonial turn has required a more intense interrogation of where knowledge has originated from and the ways in which it is colonially situated. Ideally, we want students to see sociolinguistics as one way of knowing. We want them to be able to use its discursive tools in ways that do not undermine the knowledges that they have which are embodied and connected to communities and place and (re)shaped by histories of mobility (Heugh et al. 2022), and but as part of a dialogic engagement in sense making. The conceptual tools sociolinguistics provides are not meant to be reified. Rather as language educators our responsibility is to be thinking about how forms of knowledge and the languages that express them can be harnessed for 'liberatory and empowering purposes' as a way of 'widening participation' by working critically with pedagogy and curricula (McKinney 2018: 174). As markers of assignments, we work at the intersection of centripetal and centrifugal forces that circulate within language education at universities. We can value the ways of knowing that reside in the dialogues, the ways of knowing that reside in the commentaries *and* the ways of knowing that emerge from the juxtaposition of texts that would not have existed if multiple voices were not at play.

A description of the datasets

Student dialogues have covered a range of topics over the years. The data sets we draw on for this book are from the 2010 and 2015 cohorts where we have analysed 30 per cent of the assignments from each cohort. Unsurprisingly there are many recurring themes: experiences of learning at school and university; navigating friendships; friends gossiping; and accounts of young people's social lives that include going to parties, meeting new people, dating or attempting to date. The dialogues are set across the country in rural and urban areas and located in communities the students are from or know very well. The settings for the majority of dialogues are ordinary: many are set in homes and, similar to Olivia's dialogue, often take place in the kitchen. There are walks home from school, altercations in the street and conversations between classes at school or university. Despite the fact that many dialogues are set in ordinary places, what is striking are the serious social issues they cover. Dialogues have been written about teenage pregnancy, drugs, gangsterism, homophobia, patriarchal double standards on sex, gender-based violence, sexual and gender identities, sexism, racism, violent bullying and the decision to attend initiation schools where young men are circumcised. It is in the minor politics of everyday life, for example of two women drinking tea one afternoon and complaining about their mothers-in-law, that students reflect macro issues, like the broader position of women in society. It has been fascinating to see how these dialogues present snapshots of students working through issues and problematizing them. One memorable dialogue is of a group of girls talking about a newspaper article that reported on an alleged affair between one of former president Zuma's wives and her bodyguard. They unpacked the double standard of President Zuma, whose sexual escapades, multiple wives and a rape case made headline news regularly, against traditional expectations for Zulu women in a patriarchal culture. The choice of female students to write in masculine voices, like Olivia to problematize gender, was also a trend. Overall, the dialogues have been funny; they have been disturbing; they have been pleasurable reads for markers who have also been strangled by the academic essay; and they have provided remarkable insights into students' lives, the communities in which they live and the issues they have to navigate. There is a startling honesty in these accounts. Above all, this assignment has an energizing freshness and vitality that most academic writing lacks. We would argue that it is because students can tap into a repertoire of voices they know and voices they use, which is fundamental to a heteroglossic pedagogy.

We now turn to a discussion of the ways in which narrative and heteroglossia work through classroom pedagogy and in two examples of student assignments.

A heteroglossic pedagogy in action: The Zulu boyfriend

It was important for us that in preparing students for an assignment requiring dialogue that we took a performative approach. We wanted students to create authentic, 'slice of life' dialogues that played with language varieties in interesting ways and to literally use their voices, first in small groups and then to the whole class. Bauman (2004: 9) sees performance as an 'act of expression . . . framed as display: objectified, lifted out to a degree from its contextual surroundings, and opened up to interpretive and evaluative scrutiny by an audience both in terms of its intrinsic qualities and its associational resonances'. A performance's affective relationship to the audience creates a collaborative and productive space to interpret and analyse what we watched, bringing voices together.

Students were asked to create short dialogues as an in-class task. Volunteers role played them to the whole class. They covered a range of interactions (e.g. an errant boyfriend and irate girlfriend, hostile neighbours, lecturer and student, employer and employee). Each role play elicited a different response, but there was a high level of audience appreciation (Bauman 2004) at seeing classmates take on roles, negotiate conflict situations with verbal dexterity and use of a mix of registers, varieties and languages in a space that is usually only the domain of (white) standard South African English. Laughing together as a class cannot be underestimated as a way of opening up space and removing some of the formalities of the lecture as a mode of interaction.

However, besides being engaging and entertaining, the role plays served a number of important functions in scaffolding and facilitating the assignment.

It provided students with opportunities to 'inhabit creative contexts' (Grainger, Goouch and Lambirth 2005: 24) using oral and kinaesthetic modalities and to rehearse ideas for the assignment in a relatively unthreatening, low-stakes context. The task encompassed the elements of a critical narrative gaze we wanted to foster: creative narration, critical reflection which was collaborative, and argumentation through analysis by the performers (experts in understanding their own characters and contexts) and the class (interpreters of the performance). It is important to state that this analysis of the role plays was never about critique or evaluation; it was about valuing and working with what was present in what were mostly impromptu performances to support students when they wrote their critical commentaries. In these class discussions we focused on linguistic choices, language varieties and register shifts in different contexts and explanations for these shifts. Drawing on key issues that emerged from each role play, identified by students or ourselves, we then connected them to the relevant sociolinguistic concepts and modelled how to use the concepts as an analytical tool. Both the performative and reflexive components of the lecture served as important support for the writing genres required by the assignment. From this perspective the lecture as a whole is an enactment of multi-discursivity where academic and creative genres and discourses are interrelated. This is an account and analysis of one of the role plays that took place during one lecture:

'Where were you?' Evasive boyfriend and angry girlfriend role play

Two female students volunteer to present their role-play to the class, taking on the role of a Zulu male and his Zulu girlfriend. The girlfriend is angry and hurt that her boyfriend didn't attend her twenty-first birthday party. She confronts him but he does not provide the response that she really needs: an explanation, an apology and confirmation that she is the 'main chick' (chick is slang for woman, but when combined with main, the term implies that men have multiple girlfriends, with one having more status than the others). The boyfriend replies that he was busy and has a lot going on. The girlfriend becomes quite shrill and continues to probe, to try and get the response she needs. The boyfriend paces up and down the room, mumbling to himself in Tsotsitaal [see body text for explanation], and occasionally spouting terms of endearment in standard isiZulu (e.g. '*isitandwe*') then reverting to Tsotsitaal. The role-play ends with the girlfriend's devastating realisation that she is not 'the main chick'. The dialogue alternates between standard English, standard isiZulu (used by the girlfriend) and Tsotsitaal (used by the boyfriend).

This was a fascinating, if disturbing, role play to interpret and analyse with our student audience. The performers and the class were clear that even though the 'boyfriend' was in the wrong and the 'girlfriend' had the moral high ground, the 'boyfriend' held the power in the interaction because of Zulu cultural practices around gender and, we would add, his use of Tsotsitaal. Tsotsitaal is made up of two words, 'tsotsi' meaning criminal and 'taal' from Afrikaans meaning language. The word 'tsotsi' was first used to describe young, male urban criminals living in mixed-race townships like Sophiatown of the 1930s and 1940s before apartheid's forced removals in 1955 (Brooks 2020). They spoke a secret criminal language that had a strong Afrikaans base. Over the years Tsotsitaal has evolved into varieties of street speech across the country that draw less on Afrikaans and more on urban vernaculars from African languages. Mesthrie (2008) refers to these as tsostitaals. For the most part, Tsotsitaal is still predominantly spoken by men and can carry with it displays of forceful masculinity and criminal connotations, although it needs to be emphasized that it is increasingly used as a creative act and an expression of youth identity (Bembe and Beukes 2007; Hurst 2009; Deumert 2018). The choice of isiZulu and Tsotsitaal in this role play introduces a gendered-power dynamic that makes it justifiable (if not entirely acceptable) for the boyfriend to withhold his explanation. The reaction to the role play was mixed. There were vocal protestations (mostly from female students) about the gendered-power imbalance alongside the acknowledgement of a particular social practice entrenched in certain communities.

The role plays (and our analysis that follows) illustrate Bauman's (1977) framework of performance in action. First, there was a powerful sense of 'audience appreciation' evident in laughter and gasping while watching the performance and clapping, commenting and engagement with the issues afterwards. The two female students displayed their verbal dexterity by using multiple voices, gender crossing and switching between English, isiZulu and Tsotsitaal. An understanding of the use of language was evident in their selection of language varieties to convey specific messages about language, gender and power. The students talked about the boyfriend's deliberate switch to Tsotsitaal as a way of escaping and avoiding having to communicate and account for his actions.

The students demonstrate multi-vocality not only by taking on the role of the male 'boyfriend' and speaking the relevant language variety but also by emulating the masculine body language and style. Particular body language, dress and style along with linguistic performance constitute the embodied communicative practice necessary to be a tsotsi (Deumert 2018). The 'girlfriend' speaks mostly standard English and standard isiZulu, which are high-status and dominant varieties in certain contexts. However, in this context this standard form is silenced. Although the girlfriend is articulate and assertive, she is ultimately silenced, and her voice is rendered less powerful because of the discursive practices.

Reflexivity, Bauman's (1977) final element of performance and an important part of our critical narrative pedagogy, was evident in the discussions that followed the role plays. Students drew on their everyday experience. However, the reflexive questions and the use of sociolinguistic concepts facilitated an unpacking of the meanings embedded in the role play. The role play task illustrates the fluid movements between appropriation of the students' everyday experiences and distantiation by making the role plays the objects of analysis, using sociolinguistic categories. The students are thus challenged to interrogate and critically analyse the role plays with disciplinary tools.

In this heteroglossic space the role plays generated a rich array of voices and social issues that we jointly problematized and analysed. The presentation and exploration of contentious issues through roles created important 'safety valves', enabling students to distantiate by exploring the issues with an outsider perspective. The students were required to take on two different roles: the role of creative dramatist and the role of emerging academic writer. When these two processes were in dialogue with each other, they generated depth and critical engagement with sociolinguistic issues.

We now explore the ways in which a heteroglossic pedagogy was realized in two student assignments.

A play of voices: You should have a sugar daddy

This assignment was written by Thandiwe. Her dialogue is set in Nongoma, KwaZulu Natal. Nongoma is a small town, about 300 kilometres from Durban. The area is predominantly rural, where levels of education are low as is access to basic resources like electricity and running water. The dialogue takes place in a yard where three high-school girls are talking. Two of the characters, Happy and Samke, are from Nongoma and Philile grew up in Durban but has moved to Nongoma. Thandiwe prefaces her dialogue by writing:

> Their conversation is about getting boyfriends which is not something girls at rural areas are paying attention into it, so Philile has been in relationships, then she wants to influence others.

This is more than just a conversation about boyfriends. Philile tries to convince Happy and Samke that they need to 'procure' a sugar daddy. This is an extract from Thandiwe's dialogue with her accompanying translations:

> Philile: *Ok, dizzy moon kumele nithole amadoda enu kodwa a-g8* [great]. (Ok, loose girls, you must find your own boyfriends, but they must be great i.e. rich.)
>
> Samke: *Ngicela ungaqalike nalesi silingu sakho.* (Please don't start with that English of yours.)
>
> Philile: *Duh, kumele niwathole nike nithole isincandu nani nje kancane.* (Obvious, you must find them and be kissed once in your lifetime.)
>
> Happy: *Hhayi mina anifuni lokhu ngicabuzana nomuntu ofeyiva iKaizer Chiefs.* (No, I don't want to kiss a person with yellow teeth that is like the colour of Kaizer Chiefs [a South African football team whose branding is bright yellow].)
>
> Philile: *Happy musa juba inyoni, bazokuthengela intseletsele awusiso phela isikhunba bonke abafana bayakythanda.* (Happy, don't be a fool, they will buy you cell phones, you're not an ugly girl, all guys love you.)
>
> . . .
>
> Philile: *Singabona ngesbati, thola umaqhoboza wangempela ongeke ase athimule.* (We don't want to see you with pregnancy, find someone who is rich and popular who will not let you down.)
>
> Happy: *iZ3 izohlale ikhona ifuna nina.* (HIV will always be there for you).

The multi-discursivity in this dialogue is clear as discourses of tradition and capitalism in the form of material consumption compete, setting rural and urban cultures against each other, and highlight the positioning of girls in relation to sexual behaviour and gender norms in this community. These discourses mix together; and when the dialogue and the critical commentary are read together what emerges is Thandiwe's nuanced, ambivalent, authorial voice.

One layer of complexity addresses young women's sexual identities. Later in the dialogue Samke expresses an innocent desire to have someone kiss her ('nifise sengathi nami bengangiqabula'), which reflects the emergence of sexual identity and curiosity about sex. This is set against Philile's rather mercenary exhortation to find a rich, popular boyfriend with the means to support them. Sexual identity in this narrative is discursively shaped by rural and urban belief systems. Despite their rural upbringing and acknowledging in the dialogue that they lack an urban sophistication, Happy and Samke are not naïve. They know that that these are older men, often referred to as sugar daddies or blessers, who provide young women with money or material goods for sex. Happy's horror at selling favours to unattractive old men is captured in her humorous description of the men's teeth being the same colour as Kaizer Chiefs Football Club. What is also interesting is that the peer pressure from Philile is not uncommon as girls often pressure, victimize or bully other girls into these relationships (Hoss and Blokland 2018).

We would argue that this dialogue is an example of multi-voicedness where the course creates a space for this social issue to be brought to the fore and explored in creative narrative form. This example of peer pressure also needs to be read within a complex set of socioeconomic relations that normalize transactional sex (Ranganathan et al. 2018). Thandiwe opens a space that enables centrifugal discourses emanating from a yard in Nongoma to be validated and analysed. During the period of writing in 2010, the subject of university students engaging in transactional sex had made the mainstream media in quite sensationalist ways. We knew from conversations with students that this was an issue that they confronted when living with other students in residences, or choices they were faced with themselves. We contend that Thandiwe uses the dialogue to work though the issue of transactional sex as being a survival strategy for women where intergenerational poverty is the norm, whose finances and living conditions are precarious, as well as a means to procure material items of status. In this dialogue, the character of Philile refigures young women's agency in exploiting sexual relations for increased status and the 'commodities of modernity' (Leclerc-Madlala 2003). However, Samke and Happy rebuff her at the dialogue's end. Happy explicitly notes the dangers of this risky sexual behaviour by referring to the BMW Z3, a township term that likens the spread of HIV to the speed of a BMW Z3.

The tensions between rural values and urban behaviour are evident in Thandiwe's intentional use of language varieties. The linguistic diversity spans languages, registers and modes and works in interesting ways. Philile, the urban sophisticate character's language draws on slang in both English (unmarked) and isiZulu (underlined):

Ok, dizzy moon <u>kumele nithole amadoda enu kodwa a-g8</u>.

Philile moves between isiZulu and English. Her use of slang and the inclusion of text-speak ('a-g8') reinforces her urbaneness and the playfulness of township varieties – in one turn she refers to herself as an MP3 to reference her talkativeness. This is in contrast to the formal isiZulu that the other girls speak ('*Ngicela ungaqalike nalesi silingu sakho*' is phrased using the polite form). The two characters from Nongoma say that they do not understand the language the urban sophisticate is using. Thandiwe recognizes the working of power through language: Philile's character is written as showing off and positioning herself as superior to the other girls. Thandiwe writes in her critical commentary,

> This is how youth now use the social functions of codeswitching as I have shown in the above example to accommodate each other and sometimes to exclude other participants who have never been in other places from home . . . that increases the social distance between them.

Thandiwe successfully 'speaks' in these conflicting voices and creates a space for her dexterity to be validated. Her own voice in the critical commentary adds to the multi-vocality of the text.

There is an ambivalence here. While Thandiwe seems to prefer more conservative rural values around sexual behaviour, referencing the importance of 'respect' in her critical commentary, she is also aware of the ways in which the monolingual orientation of the rural areas is a disadvantage for young people who aspire to be mobile. She writes:

> What I really noticed . . . to this generation is that we gained a lot from going to different places . . . rather than listening to our parents talking their deeply standard language that holds us back when we go to a place like Joburg.

This play of conflicting voices is also evident in how Thandiwe writes about gender norms in the critical commentary. She explains how

> Our cultures don't allow us to go about and play with our peers, girls have to do home chores . . . sometimes their parents do not want girls to be seen to gather together without an elder between them.

There is an unresolved tension in this assignment. The taboo nature of the girls' conversation is highlighted when Samke warns the others to keep quiet at the end of the dialogue. Thandiwe notes in her analysis, 'She [Samke] knows what they are talking about is wrong . . . and they do not want their parents to hear.' But at the same time, it is Samke and Happy who seek Philile out for the latest gossip.

There is also evidence of Thandiwe taking on the discourse of sociolinguistics and academic writing. This is evident in the first extract we have quoted from the critical commentary in her use of terms like 'social functions', 'code switching', 'accommodate', 'exclude' and 'social distance'. Her use of the phrase 'as I have shown in the above example' indicates an awareness of the formality and signposting prevalent in academic writing. The entire sentence demonstrates that she is able to use academic language as a tool to critically interrogate social practices. The construction of this sentence contains traces of other discourses.

The phrasing of 'never been in other places from home' has an informality that someone with full mastery of academic writing is unlikely to use. But there is a richness in the multi-vocality of this phrase that comes from the ways in which isiZulu has shaped English. Thandiwe's writerly voice begins to take on the authoritative tone from academic discourse, but her linguistic repertoire and the identity politics she is navigating have not been subsumed.

Tsotsitaal: The language of generations

The second dialogue returns to the topic of tsotsis and the critical commentary presents a powerful example of an 'African locus of enunciation' (Ndlovu-Gatsheni 2013) where embodied ways of knowing are spatially and temporally located in places that teach bodies how to be in the world.

This is an extract from Pete's dialogue with his accompanying translations:

> The dialogue occurs between me (Pete) and two friends, Thabo and Steven who are from the same neighbourhood as me, White City Jabavu in Soweto [a large township outside Johannesburg]. I am detained in a police cell for commuting in a train without a valid train ticket.

> Thabo: *Shesa lapho kaw!* (Greetings my friend)

> Pete: *Sho mfethu* (Greetings my brother)

> Steven: *Entlek nou wat soek hierso Pete my bra, e police station?* (And Pete my brother, what are you doing here in police cell?)

> Pete: *Kushubile* (It's bad) I was caught in New Canada station for not having a valid train ticket Stivovo and you, *wat soek?* (what happened?)

> Thabo: *Eish ntwana mina banithathe eMzimhlope, bengeza ispharaza mfana!, kanti bang'bongile* (Young man! The security caught me in Mzimhlophe for doing staff riding [train surfing], they caught me red-handed.)

> Steven: *Tjo deur manje la bantu abasibhekeki nogoba mina bangithathe eDube for ukubhayisa egadweni* (Wow! The security officers caught me in Dube station while selling some snacks inside the Metrorail train.)

> Pete: *Majimbosi okwenzekile kwenzekile, fede* (My brother what has happened was meant to happen, we have to accept it.)

The dialogue ends with Pete and Thabo asking if they could get Steven's older brother to bail them out, only to discover he has been incarcerated for armed robbery.

In Pete's dialogue there is a multi-discursivity that captures the 'language of generations' (Bakhtin 1981: 271) of tsotsis and it is full of 'associative resonances' (Bauman 2004). Pete's characters display a multi-voicedness as they move between an older version of Tsotsitaal and a more contemporary variety. Compare Steven's opening line where the base of his Tsotsitaal is Afrikaans (Afrikaans is italicised, isiZulu is underlined and English is unmarked),

Entlek nou wat soek hierso Pete *my bra,* <u>e</u> police station,

with a later turn explaining why he was caught, which has a predominantly isiZulu base:

<u>Tjo</u> *deur* <u>manje la bantu abasibhekeki nogoba mina bangithathe eDube</u> for <u>ukubhayisa egadweni</u>

In the first sentence apart from the locative form in isiZulu (e-) and the English 'police station' the rest is in Afrikaans. In the second sentence, there is only one Afrikaans word ('deur') and one English word ('for'), the rest is in isiZulu. Starting the dialogue with the older variety is not accidental. Pete explicitly states in his commentary that his intended audience for the dialogue are young men and 'those men who have lived in Soweto for a lengthy period and subscribe to this way of life'. They 'have backgrounds of prison life and are referred to as a menace to society'. While criminality is certainly an aspect of a tsotsi lifestyle, there is more to 'this way of life'. In apartheid South Africa an anti-establishment stance was a fundamental part of the tsotsi identity. Deumert (2018: 4) lyrically describes the tsotsi as also being 'about music and movement, with a walk as free and distinct as the language that accompanied it. It was an identity which was artful and powerful at the same time, expressing resistance to all forms of oppression.' These men were street smart, clever, quick-witted and had a sense of style and fashion. In some ways this piece is a homage to old-school tsotsis, who would appreciate how this way of being has manifested in these young men. The traces of quick-wittedness emerge in Pete's playful renaming of Steven as Stivovo in the dialogue. The street smarts are highlighted when Pete references Dell Hymes in the critical commentary to make a case for the importance of understanding context and register when one finds oneself incarcerated and needs to prove a 'level of township slang so that he may not fall victim to unscrupulous men'.

Narrative ways of knowing and being come from being deeply located in time and place. The multi-discursivity of layered time periods and social worlds has a particular vividness. This dialogue has deep historical roots. Jabavu is one of the oldest suburbs in Soweto. It is located next to Meadowlands, where people were located after the forced removal from Sophiatown in the 1950s. In the 1960s and 1970s Jabavu was known as the 'Wild West' for its violence, gangs and criminality (Glaser 2000). There is also an interesting movement in the dialogue as Pete brings the reader into the heart of these old Soweto suburbs at the mention of each train station. Pete is stopped by police at New Canada station which lies on the outskirts of Soweto. He likely came from the university, in the centre of town in Johannesburg, and caught the train south to Soweto. This journey back home is also redolent with the symbolism of trains as part of the apartheid machinery that moved people into and out of segregated spaces (Moroke 2015). The next stop is Mzimhlophe where the trainline bisects Meadowlands and Orlando, where Thabo was caught staff riding, and then to Dube, where Steve was caught selling snacks, which is near to Jabavu.

And, while place shapes who these young men are, their embodied ways of being have taken on a contemporary flair and style that still retain the element of risky lifestyle choices. This is evident in Thabo's participation in the dangerous pastime of staff riding, the slang term for train surfing (see Casino's (2014) short documentary https://vimeo.com/83486021). Moroke (2015) sees staff riding as a performance of an urban black masculinity in contexts of poverty, where there are few options for young men. The other side of risky lifestyle choices are those that are strategies of survival. This is evident in Steve's story of hustling to make money by becoming an illegal vendor selling snacks to commuters. It is evident in the decisions Pete has to make when the additional and often hidden costs associated with studying for a degree are not covered. Their masculine performances are carried through from the lively dialogue to the critical commentary where Pete paints an evocative visual image of the dress of these three petty 'criminals' that binds them together:

> All Star wearing men, Dickies jeans hanging beneath their butts without having been fastened with a belt and hats being put halfway down the face to camouflage identity. . . . The type of dressing is very important as the language variety does not exist independently from the person's behaviour at most times, the manner of dressing and greeting is meant to curb any possibility of having people who do not belong in the group saying and doing what they do not understand.

We believe Pete has taken on a critical narrative gaze. He has moved beyond telling a story of three young men in police detention cells to reflect on it analytically. He explicitly identifies how 'language varieties do not exist independently from behaviour and dress'. He demonstrates it is not enough to be able to speak

Tsotsitaal; rather 'what sociolinguists refer to as the speech community' requires knowing the 'norms and values' that constitute it. In this case, writing in an academic voice he backs up his claim with an example of embodied practice captured in an evocative image of a gesture and movement that show connected ways of being:

> For example, when we greet each other one has to open his palm and then click his finger with that of the other person being greeted.

Pete has made connections to the discussions and readings in the course where we covered language and identity, the role that language plays in group membership. He makes a case for how these concepts work in academic writing. But most importantly for us, his voice is made stronger by the echoes of the men in White City Jabavu, as he creates a contemporary account of rebellious young men.

Conclusion

In this chapter we have focused on Bakhtin's notion of heteroglossia and developed it to illustrate how our pedagogy in this course is heteroglossic. We present a particular narrative assignment, the dialogue and the critical commentary and advocate for the value of working with creative and critical genres. We also acknowledge that our work is located within the context of neoliberal regimes of accountability that can be in tension with providing epistemological access and appropriate enculturation into academic writing for first-year students. Examples of pedagogical practice and student writing illustrate the ways in which forms of embodied knowing enrich the classroom experience, how linguistic repertoires that arise from lived experiences provide a platform for critical analysis and how students' writing that on the surface appears to deal with mundane and everyday issues, in fact, reveals the workings of power relations that circulate in social spaces and the development of a critical narrative gaze for students.

Voices III

I am growing up in a country described as a rainbow nation due to its 'linguistic variety' and its assortment and mixture of cultures as a result of the individual's language backgrounds (Kaschula and Anthonissen 1995). I have been at war with myself as I have been taught that my language is not important therefore I am not important. I am obsessed with the perfection of my accent when looking at the standard English so as to avoid 'negative attitudes' and 'people's judgement' and because I am not seen as well spoken (Kaschula and Anthonissen 1995). Deep beneath the depths of my identity I feel as though my life has been a lie. I have worked so hard to become 'competent in the standard form of the (English) language' as to 'feel more at home in the school environment' where no one else actually cared about my culture and would act as though they cared about my culture once a year during Heritage day with the rest of the country. I was not at home; I will never be at home with a person that 'has a low estimation of my native tongue' as 'she also has a low estimation of me' (Anzaldùa 2000: 14).

Nobantu, 2017

I became better at this Standard English concept. I started enjoying learning more about this dialect. Its literature and poems captivated me. I was unconscious that I was also losing my mother tongue, Sesotho. I spoke less and less of it and the sad thing is that my mother said nothing. She just kept on praising how beautiful my English sounded. There was no one to mother my mother tongue. It was abandoned and left on Standard English's doorstep.

Dikgang, 2018

Languages are violent and once you stick to one language you learn to hate. You are left to think that your language is superior to others. You ignore the opportunity to grow and have beliefs about other languages that cause you to dislike them. The truth about language is that it's beautiful once you know the real purpose of it and that is to communicate with others. You don't really have to be in denial just because you don't follow the language's customs and traditions. Once all of us truly will ourselves to learn about other people's language, we can reach a new point in time as human beings. We can learn the beliefs of others, their customs, and their traditions. We can discover why they do what they do and think the way they think. We can finally bring truth to the whole point of language: understanding each other. I have no roots, I am no new breed and certainly do not belong to any culture. I am just Velaphi, the son of the new Africa, willing to learn about the world's languages so that I can understand others.

Velaphi, 2018

The A on my matric certificate is now a powerful thing for me, I feel one up on the oppressors who forced their language on me and deprived themselves of an opportunity to learn mine. I can stick a tongue out at them and say: 'who speaks more languages now?' . . . I am proud to have Afrikaans in my language repertoire.

Dikaledi, 2015

I am a child born in the Digital Age, part of the generation that says ROTFL instead of actually laughing out loud, woken up by my favourite song instead of the crow of a rooster and I take an uber everywhere I go instead of riding a bicycle. Thanks to my good friend Google I have the power to know everyone, everything and every place I could ever need to. Television and YouTube have taught me all the need-to-know life hacks and social media has made me an instafamous celeb. I can no longer be confined to one culture, language or society. I am now part of the global community that personifies diversity.

Lerato, 2017

6

Enacting the Critical Imagination

*From the beginning of the dialogue Baba Mkhize, the landlord, just starts
screaming as he knocks on the door of the woman's flat. The language
he uses is demeaning and even suggests that the woman cannot rear
children on her own. The fact that in the entire dialogue not even once
does he address the lady (who has two kids) correctly but choses to use
ntombazana, which means little girl is also an indication of how much of
a bully he really is. The dialogue is thus one directional, when the man is
barking orders and the women is expected to oblige. Language terrorism is
also used when she is scolded for interrupting him while she speaks when
she tries to explain herself.*

Excerpt from Zama's critical commentary on her dialogue, 2015

Introduction

Imagination and narrative are key conceptual and pedagogic elements of the
sociolinguistics course. We have consistently challenged the binaries between
narrative and traditional academic writing genres, arguing that narrative
pedagogy can enable students to (re)tell their stories creatively and reflexively by
applying a 'critical narrative gaze' (Gill 2014: 76). However, it was only in 2017
(Mendelowitz 2017) that we began to work explicitly to synthesize imagination,
narrative writing and criticality, theoretically and empirically.

As discussed in Chapter 2, imagination is a key aspect of narrative pedagogy.
Writing a narrative is a creative process drawing on both memory and
imagination (Hampl 1999). Narratives can take many different forms, and, in
each iteration, they can do different things and draw on different imaginative
processes. This chapter builds on Chapter 5, which focuses on the dialogue
and critical commentary assignment. The 'storyness' of self plays a key role in
both the language narratives and dialogue assignments, but the dialogues offer

some specific critical imaginative affordances for self-representations, multi-voicedness and expression of the dialogic relationship between self and other. While the language narrative entails movement between past, present and future selves, the dialogue offers students the freedom to write about others and/or to write about themselves from an outsider perspective. They may choose to write from a fly-on-the-wall perspective or insert themselves as active participants in the dialogue and then shift perspective in the critical commentary. This process offers powerful possibilities for students to enact and imagine multiple worlds, and to play with multiple voices. Sometimes this is about enacting the world as it is and then problematizing or explaining it in the critical commentary, other times it is about inventing alternative realities.

This chapter begins with an outline of our conceptualization of the critical imagination and its relationship to narrative, which is followed by examples of students' enactment of the critical imagination. We argue that dialogues offer particularly strong opportunities for embodied narrative work. The juxtaposition of the dialogue and critical commentary facilitates the critical imagination by enabling students to enact, perform and immerse themselves in different discourses. These fluid moves enable students to inhabit and imagine a range of subjectivities and discourses and generate new insights when they step out of role into reflective/analytic mode (Misson and Morgan 2006).

We engage with Lewis's (2014: 189) definition of embodied critical literacy work which 'locates the body as central to both the experience of marginalization and to the enactment of counter-narratives'. These forms of embodied knowing emerge through critical enactments of lived experiences. They are not restricted to dramatic performances but can emerge in any mode where 'students use their bodies to communicate their critical perspectives' (Johnson and Vasuvedan 2014: 98). In the dialogues students create characters who use their bodies to convey critical perspectives.

In this chapter we are particularly interested in embodied enactments of contested gender issues across two contrasting written genres. We analyse two sets of data from the 2015 dialogue and critical commentary assignment.

Framing the critical imagination as theory and praxis

Conceptualizing the critical imagination

We have always considered imagination an integral part of our work as teacher educators and have challenged dichotomies between imagination and rigorous intellectual work. We view imagination as an integrated and interdependent system of thought-feeling, being-knowing which incorporates higher-level thinking, imagination, criticality and emotion (Vygotsky 2004). Viewing imagination in this integrated way is an important step in challenging the prevailing dichotomies, repositioning imagination as a significant element of teaching, learning and literacy research. In addition to Vygotsky's powerful synthesis of key areas of knowing-being, he provides a valuable sociocultural lens for conceptualizing imagination. He banishes the popular image of the lonely genius imagining brilliant new ideas in isolation. Instead, he shows how imagination is developed through social interactions and engagement with available societal resources (Vygotsky 2004).

We now turn to the specific affordances of imagination as an integrated system of thought. Teaching and learning in a space that foregrounds imagination permits playing with ideas in fluid ways, experimenting, taking risks and bringing into being something new. This could take the form of a major invention, a story, a poem or the germ of an idea that has been sitting below the line of consciousness for years and whose time has come. While acknowledging endless possibilities for imaginative inventiveness we focus on the play of ideas that emerge in narrative genres. From our sociocultural position, we understand new ideas to emerge from a dialogic interaction between ideas in one's mind and ideas and resources in society (Vygotsky 2004). Vygotsky refers to this process as 'creative reworking', which, he argues, is essential for human adaptation to change and new experiences. However, what he does not explicitly address is the role of criticality in imagination.

For Vygotsky, creative reworking is about the merging of ideas and experiences so that the texts, ideas or behaviours produced are substantially different to the original. There are some similarities between his notion of 'creative reworking' and the critical literacy notion of redesign, though the ultimate purposes differ: redesign has an ideological underpinning, entailing creative reworking of a text or idea with the intention of challenging the assumptions implicit in the original text. Critical literacy scholars foreground ideological shifts and are mostly silent about the role of the imagination in reconfiguring texts. In our view it is not possible to redesign a text without imaginative play. Rationalist, cognitive ways of thinking are not sufficient to make the redesigning a meaningful and productive process (Janks 2002). We argue that it is important to foreground critical-creative moves when discussing textual redesign and counter-storying.

We regard creativity and criticality as intertwined concepts, which together can enable students to move fluidly between creative and academic genres. As educators with a social justice agenda, we are interested in how retelling a story can entail the repositioning of the writer, challenging dominant discourses and power relations and the (re)construction of identities. Hence, throughout this chapter we consciously use the term 'critical-creative moves' to highlight the interrelatedness of these concepts.

For Greene (1995), a key aspect of imaginative thinking is the capacity to envisage new possibilities, 'visions of what should be and what might be' (1995: 5), possibilities for something better and different from what is, with art in its multifaceted forms providing new perspectives on lived experience and opportunities for 'defamiliarisation of the ordinary' (1995: 4). She differentiates between two types of imagination: the poetic and the social. The former is mobilized when we respond to a story, music, painting and in the act of writing. Poetic imagination enables

> the carnival of possibilities where everything is permitted, nothing censored. It is the willingness to imagine oneself in the other persons' skin, to see things as if one were, momentarily at least, another, to experience how the other half lives. (Kearney 1988: 368–9)

The poetic imagination mobilizes play and empathy while the social imagination involves inventing alternative realities and engages more directly with discursive shifts. The two types of imagination are interdependent, and both are necessary for critical engagement with the world. Kearney (1988: 370) argues that they are two different but complementary ways 'in which imagination can open us to the otherness of the other'. In the data analysis section of this chapter, we show how they can be brought together.

Affordances for pedagogy

In Chapter 3, we discussed our pedagogy in motion – a pedagogy that constantly evolves and is responsive to the changing needs of our students. However, a further aspect of this pedagogy in motion is relevant to our discussion of the critical imagination: working with the narrative imagination enables students to make multiple critical-creative moves. Unsurprisingly, the literature on imagination is replete with images about mental travel, crossing spaces and creating new spaces for re-imagining our world. Greene writes about imagination as a facility that enables empathy and the capacity 'to cross the empty spaces between ourselves and others' (1995: 3), and 'to bring into being an in-between' (1995: 59). For Enciso imagination is 'both a portal and an action' (2017: 31) through which we can re-imagine our worlds. Imagination as portal can take us to unfamiliar worlds and can also facilitate social action. Darvin (2019) explores the interrelationship between creativity and criticality, foregrounding criticality as the element that enables boundary breaking. All these scholars explore the connections between imagination, criticality and social justice, and the key role that narrative plays in creating classroom spaces that facilitate critical-creative moves.

In discussing imagination as critical social practice, Enciso poses an important question: 'With what linguistic, semiotic, and material resources might it be possible to speak and be heard?' (Enciso 2017: 35). There is much discussion in contemporary scholarship about creating the kinds of spaces that Enciso refers to – spaces that enable students to disrupt dominant narratives, spaces for silenced voices and stories to be heard; spaces that encourage our students to have freedom to imagine the possible and the alternative. But there are limited specific examples of how this can be achieved in contexts of multiple institutional constraints.

The narrative dialogue task opens possibilities for students to use their multifaceted resources to mobilize the poetic and social imagination and to critically re-imagine a range of social issues, sometimes creating counter-stories and sometimes not. What does this mean in practice? While the dialogue writing foregrounds the poetic imagination, and the critical commentary the social imagination, they work together. In order to write a strong critical commentary, students needed to select their topic carefully, and to write in ways that are generative for critical discussion. In addition, their analysis draws on the transformational capacity of their imaginations to enable them to engage in 'possibility thinking, questioning and challenging taken-for-granted assumptions' (Greene 1995: 3).

With the decolonial turn some scholars are taking a renewed interest in imagination and the process of re-imagining. In reflecting on their postgraduate module 're-imagining multilingualism', Bock and Stroud (2019, 2021) make several arguments about the centrality of imagination for a decolonial pedagogy. Their module, with its focus on language and identity, draws on students' lived experiences of multilingualism and has much in common with our work (Mendelowitz and Ferreira 2007; Ferreira and Mendelowitz 2009a). The main connections we highlight here are their centring of imagination as a decolonial strategy to provide students with access to knowledge and the agency to become constructers of knowledge.

In reflecting on the relationship between decolonial pedagogies, multilingualism and the key role of imagination in re-imagining multilingualism, De Souza (2019) argues that we need to break out of the constraining and disembodied mould of academic discourse and acknowledge the centrality of imagination in enabling us to find new ways of seeing. This argument resonates with our conceptualization of imagination. However, what is of particular interest in De Souza's work is his focus on embodiment – the imperative to move beyond the artificial western mind/body divide and to re-embody teaching and learning by re-imagining multilingualism and using creativity as a pedagogical tool. The data in this chapter illustrates what embodiment means in practice, particularly in Nombini's counter-narrative 'Fighting back'.

Analysis of assignment data: Critical-creative narrative writing

As discussed in Chapter 5, the assignment, from which the data for this chapter is drawn, juxtaposed a creative text (a dialogue) with an academic text (a critical commentary). The data section of this chapter has two components: a macro analysis of nineteen dialogues and critical commentaries (see Table 6.1) and a micro analysis of two assignments. We analysed 30 per cent of the assignments from the 2015 cohort of 100 students. After a first reading, the assignments were coded in terms of the topics students wrote about and organized into six themes. For the purposes of this chapter, we selected the following three themes for micro and macro analysis. See Mendelowitz (2017) for details about the full dataset.

- Talking about sex
- Constructions of masculinity and femininity
- Sexual harassment and gender-based violence (GBV)

A close critical reading was done to trace how issues were conceptualized and problematized in the critical commentaries. Finally, the reading established whether there had been a critical-creative move from the dialogue to the critical commentaries in the three themes. Two assignments were purposively selected from the sample dataset for a fine-grained analysis in order to illustrate the possible enactments of the critical imagination in a narrative pedagogy where students exhibit a range of critical-creative moves.

As Table 6.1 illustrates, the students' dialogues covered a wide range of topics. Although they have been categorized into three themes, language and gender cuts across all of them and there are many overlaps across categories. Perhaps this focus on gender is not surprising, given the 'deep-seated and cross-cutting nature' of patriarchy in South Africa across formal and informal institutions

Table 6.1 Overview of dialogues

Categories	Topics	Place and participants	Language varieties
Talking about sex	Gossip about pregnant friend.	Hair salon, East Rand township (three young women)	English, isiZulu, Kasitaal, Sesotho
	Parental and religious constraints on one's identity.	Coffee shop, Gauteng (Hindu female and Muslim male)	English, Arabic (sprinklings)
	Supporting a friend going through a relationship break up.	Taxi rank (two young women)	English, isiZulu, siSwati
	The advantages of having a sugar daddy vs. a boyfriend their age.	Home, Orlando (two young women)	English, isiZulu, township slang, Tsotsitaal
	Should a pregnant university student drop out?	Wits University lawn (young woman and man)	Tsotsitaal and standard English
	Tough choices about unwanted pregnancy and abortion.	Public clinic (two young women)	English, isiZulu, Iscamtho
Constructions of masculinity and femininity	The challenges of finding a partner.	Home (two young men)	English, Gayla (gay slang)
	Making plans for a fun night out.	At home (two young men)	English, Afrikaans, slang
	Discussion of anger about being rejected by a girlfriend.	Park (three young men)	Tsotsitaal
	Two friends are having a sexist conversation about women as they prepare for a date.	University residence room (two young men)	English, Afrikaans, isiZulu, Sesotho, social media discourse
	Decisions about marriage and cultural expectations.	At home (young man and woman)	English, Setswana
	Marriage and the shortage of suitable girls.	Backyard (two young men)	English, Afrikaans. Lenasia slang
	Discussion of cultural stereotypes.	School playground (three boys)	Deep/ rural IsiZulu, English
	Discussion of anger towards a female teacher.	School playground (three boys)	Street Sesotho, Afrikaans
	The importance of initiation rites. (CASE STUDY 1)	University residence room (two young men)	English, Tsotsitaal
Sexual harassment and GBV	Caretaker confronts tenant about overdue rent.	Block of flats (female tenant, male caretaker)	English, isiZulu
	A taxi driver harasses a female passenger.	Taxi (male driver and female passenger)	English, Tsotsitaal, isiZulu, Sesotho
	Two boys compete for the affection of the same girl.	Township soccer field (two boys, one girl)	Tsotsitaal, isiZulu, Sesotho
	Discussion of domestic abuse and the victim's retaliation (CASE STUDY 2)	Informal settlement, yard outside house (three women)	isiZulu, Sesotho, isiXhosa, English

(Gender Links 2015: 1) and the role of language in both constituting and resisting this reality.

Students wrote about a range of taboo topics, usually excluded from academic assignments. For example, the informal discussion between three young men in their residence room, while sharing a 'joint'(marijuana), becomes an exploration of Xhosa initiation rites. There is an intimate discussion between two close friends at a clinic about the decision to have an abortion or not. The assignment created opportunities for students to explore how language, sexuality, gender and power operate in their lives and, in the strongest assignments, to re-imagine new possibilities.

Having explained the data selection and analysis procedure, the data description and analysis that follows begins with a macro analysis of the most striking patterns that emerged in the assignments.

Data analysis

Reading each student's assignment has always been akin to unwrapping a gift with multiple layers of wrapping paper and feeling utterly surprised at what one finds as one unwraps each layer. The wide-ranging explorations of topics, characters and issues are extraordinary as are the twists and turns of each assignment. The assignments challenge our assumptions as readers. Dialogues that we assumed to be written by males often turn out to be written by females. Frequently, another surprise awaits as we move to the critical commentaries and realize that the purpose of a dialogue is not what we thought it was. In the analysis that follows, we focus on the three overarching themes with the aim of capturing the most striking aspects of this dataset and the range of critical-creative moves made by the student writers.

Characters, languages and place

One striking aspect of the dialogues is the combinations of male and female characters that feature in them. For example, the talking about sex theme was dominated by female writers and female characters. Only one dialogue was written by a male and featured two male characters. In contrast, the construction of masculinity and femininity theme was dominated by male characters. Four of these eight dialogues were written by female students who raised critical questions about gender dynamics. Only one of these eight dialogues featured a male and female. Although female characters were mostly absent, they were the subject of many of the conversations. Thus, they are constructed in the dialogues in their absence. Most of these constructions are derogatory, highlighting the many negative labels available to refer to girls, particularly with regards to sexual behaviour. This was particularly the case in the dialogues written by females on this theme, which were written in a hard-hitting way in order to enact typically sexist discourses and then to unpack them.

Another striking aspect of the dialogues is the range of language and language varieties, places and spaces evident in them. Most of the spaces are away from authority figures and external pressures, facilitating relaxed and intimate exchanges in which student writers use language varieties that suit the expression of participants' identities and relationships in specific locations. It is not surprising that Tsotsitaal, Kasitaal and Iscamtho are used frequently as these are all urban codes associated with the expression of youth identities. The dialogue performances create powerfully embodied texts in which the writers explore a range of discourses in highly engaged ways.

Critical-creative moves

Finally, there are differences in the extent to which the critical commentaries illustrate a critical-creative move in terms of problematizing the issues raised in the dialogues. While the macro analysis so far has focused on broad patterns, critical-creative moves are discussed in more detail. Two patterns emerge in the constructing masculinity/femininity theme. Four of the eight critical commentaries (three written by males, one female) explore masculinity and cultural issues. Of these four, two writers make critical moves. Thando,[1] the only female writer in this category, presents an informal conversation between two males about initiation rites while Gift, a Zulu male, enacts linguistic power imbalances between isiZulu and Sesotho males in his dialogue. In the critical commentary Thando reflects on the discrimination against Xhosa males who have chosen not to undergo initiation while Sipho reflects on the othering of a Sotho male by two Zulu males, opening a conversation about linguistic and cultural hierarchies and masculinity among friends. In his critical commentary Sipho explains that 'the dialogue highlights how even in different groups of friends, some languages and cultures are viewed to have more power and status than others'.

The remaining four dialogues, all featuring male characters, were written by females and explore contemporary gender issues. Two of these are particularly nuanced in their representation of simultaneous power, rage and vulnerability. In one of these, the female writer shows Thabo expressing his rage at being rejected by his girlfriend and planning aggressive retaliations. But alongside the rage, there is a moment where the writer shows him acknowledging that 'my heart is broken'. The critical imaginative affordances of writing masculinity as an outsider are powerfully evident in these texts, but as Sipho's text shows, it is possible, though more challenging, to make the critically imaginative move while writing as a cultural and gender insider.

The four sexual harassment/GBV dialogues were all written by females and feature female characters interacting with males in a range of spaces: a taxi rank, an informal settlement, a soccer field and a block of flats. In all four dialogues, language and power is enacted and explored, sometimes in nuanced detail, in the interactions between a taxi driver and a foreign female character who rejects his advances and threatens to call the police; a single mother and her landlord, who demands his overdue rent with sexist and xenophobic undertones; a young girl and the dynamics between her two suitors on a soccer field; a discussion of domestic abuse in the yard, outside MaNkosi's home. Patriarchal and misogynistic discourses abound but the female characters assert themselves and challenge the forms of sexual harassment along a continuum of resistance with all four dialogues offering elements of counter-stories. The critical commentaries interrogate the dialogues and what they show about language, gender and power.

In reflecting on how this task enables students to take many different directions, to explore a rich range of topics and to make critical-creative moves, we are struck by the elasticity of narrative and how it can create a space to explore embodied issues that are usually excluded from classrooms. The dialogues illustrate the affordances of the poetic imagination, 'the carnival of possibilities where everything is permitted, nothing censored' (Kearney 1988: 368). Furthermore, play with the poetic imagination facilitates 'defamiliarization of the ordinary' (Greene 1995). Everyday experiences are denaturalized, and in conjunction with disciplinary lenses, the students' analysis generates new insights about self and other. The dexterous moves between different roles (the creative playwright and academic) enable the interplay between criticality and imagination.

While the discussion so far has provided an overview of key themes and critical moves that surfaced in the dataset, the section that follows offers a fine-grained analysis of two assignments in order to illustrate student enactments of the critical imagination along a continuum of critical engagement.

Thando's assignment: Interrogating language, masculinity and culture from an outsider perspective

Thando identifies herself as an urban Tswana. Her dialogue explores the intersection between language, masculinity and culture. It features a conversation between two males, Jama and Mxolisi, about Xhosa initiation rites and their views on young Xhosa males who have not been initiated. Xhosa initiation, which facilitates the transition from boyhood to manhood (Ngumbela 2021), entails a period of seclusion in a hut where the initiate is circumcised. The dialogue takes place at Jama's residence room, a relaxing space where they share a 'joint' and exchange news. Both participants are Xhosa males from the Eastern Cape, far away from family for the first time, and they find comfort in their friendship and shared histories. Their thoughts and feelings can be understood with minimal explanation. Things can be left unsaid.

The dialogue begins with a short, sharp greeting in Tsotsitaal and a ritual of sharing a 'joint' that shows their closeness, indicating that their meeting is a regular occurrence. There is a playfulness in their interaction as they negotiate the availability of cigarettes and rizla. Jama's response to Mxolisi's question underlines their close, comfortable relationship (with Thando's accompanying translations).

Mxolisi: Do you have some joint *ntwana*? (dude)

Jama: Sure, *ntwana ungithatha kanjani?* (Of course, dude, what do you take me for?)

This sets the scene and the mood. Mxolisi tells Jama that he wants to befriend a Xhosa boy in his class called Sthembiso, who is an academically strong student. He is hoping that Sthembiso can assist him with his studies. However, as with most of these dialogues there is a twist in the tale! Jama informs Mxolisi that this friendship is not feasible and proceeds to explain why in the following dialogue extract.

Jama: So *wena unbhayela isekelem?* (So, you want to make him your friend?)

Mxolisi: Exactly *ntwana* (Exactly dude.)

Jama: *Hayi* boy *yinkwenkewe lentwana, asithethi nayo njena!* (No friend, he is just a boy and not a man. We do not associate with people like him.)

Mxolisi: *Hayi ndoda?* (No man!)

Jama: *Struu* (It's true)

Mxolisi: Why *angayi?* (Why doesn't he go?)

Jama: *Uweak uthanda islungu.* (He is weak, he likes English.)

Mxolisi: *Leslungu simoshile.* (This English thing though! It has messed up everything.)

Jama: *Ja ntwana dlalela ver van dae een.* (Yes dude, don't go anywhere close to him or else you will lose your dignity.)

Although the participants are in a private space, they use culturally coded language to discuss the fact that Sthembiso has not undergone the initiation rite that would confer on him the status of Xhosa man (i.e. he is still considered 'just a boy'). Initiation is not explicitly mentioned but Jama's point that Sthembiso is 'not a man' is immediately understood by Mxolisi to mean that Sthembiso has not been initiated. Jama's revelation has the desired effect, as Mxolisi is shocked and easily persuaded not to pursue this friendship. There is no debate about whether this information should prevent a friendship. However, Mxolisi tries to gain insights into why Sthembiso has made this choice.

The sparseness of the dialogue suits Thando's purpose and intention. The coded use of language in the dialogue points towards its taboo content and broader issues around initiation and language. Xhosa initiation rites are shrouded in secrecy and Xhosa women, even the mothers of initiates, are on the periphery and given limited information about the process. Women are also forbidden from talking about initiation (Venter 2011). To add to the code of silence and secrecy, initiates learn a secret language during their seclusion and are not allowed to discuss the details of their experience on their return home. Despite measures being put in place to decrease the health risks associated with this practice, deaths among initiates continue to be reported in the press (Ngumbela 2021). The health risks of initiation and the social pressure placed on young Xhosa males are the central concerns that motivated Thando to write this assignment.

Thando, writing about this as a Tswana female, is breaking multiple taboos and making dexterous critical-creative moves in creating this dialogue from the imagined perspective of the two male participants. Even though she is not part of the Xhosa culture, this would still be seen as taboo as discussing this ritual is reserved for Xhosa men. Her own perspective is embedded in both parts of the assignment, though more explicitly in the critical commentary. Given the level of taboo surrounding initiation, we were surprised that it surfaced as a topic in this assignment, particularly when we realized that a female student wrote it. Amidst the debates about cultural insiders and outsiders, our own positionality, as three white women writing about this taboo topic as outsiders on multiple levels, also needs to be acknowledged.

Thando's assignment illustrates what happens when we break out of the disembodied mould of academic discourses and acknowledge the centrality of imagination (De Souza 2019). More importantly, it shows that when we foreground the students' lived experiences, students draw on a much bigger range of resources than usual, creating conditions of possibility 'to speak and be heard' (Enciso 2017: 35). They bring their embodied selves into the classroom and into the assignments: past selves, present selves, imagined selves of others, as in the case of Thando. Strathern and Steward's (2011) definition of embodiment is helpful in the context of this discussion. They define embodiment as not being about the body per se but rather about focusing on 'culture and experience insofar as these can be understood from the standpoint of bodily being-in-the-world' (2011: 389). Furthermore, they argue that embodiment involves both 'the body as a source of perception' and as the source of 'agency, practice, feeling, custom . . . and in the case of rituals performativity' (2011: 389). This dialogue is strongly focused on embodiment in terms of perceptions of culture, rituals and performativity, although without ever explicitly mentioning the body.

The last four lines of the dialogue raise an interesting issue about constructions of Xhosa masculinity and the participants' perceptions of the role of English. In her critical commentary, Thando describes Sthembiso as 'a brilliant Xhosa boy who speaks English like a white man'. The participants, working with a traditional view of masculinity as being associated with physical and mental strength (endurance), make a connection between Sthembiso's weakness, his failure to undergo the traditional rite of passage and his embracing of English. English serves as proxy for whiteness and western values in the context of initiation, as well as being feminized in its association with weakness and lack of endurance. This positioning of Sthembiso contrasts with Mxolisi's initial linking of Sthembiso's academic strength to his capacity to speak English like a white man.

These contradictory strands resonate strongly with Botsis's argument (2017) that South African youth regard English as an asset in some contexts and a liability in others. Through juxtaposing these contrasting views of English, Thando foregrounds the slippery role of English in the identity construction of the two characters across cultural and institutional contexts. It is associated with success in the university context, but in relation to Sthembiso's refusal to be initiated, Mxolisi comments that it has 'messed up everything'. By the end of the dialogue, not only has Mxolisi agreed not to befriend Sthembiso, but he also accepts Jama's advice that it would be harmful to have any contact with Sthembiso as this could result in a loss of dignity. However, while the characters highlight the dangers of contact with an uninitiated Xhosa male, the dangers of initiation are alluded to in the characters' discussion of weakness (i.e. suggesting one needs courage to undergo this process). And this is something that Thando highlights in her critical commentary:

> It is unfair to enforce something to someone in the name of culture. It is very risky to go to initiation schools because more and more young men are announced dead or critically injured every year because of what happens there.

It is also significant that the dialogue is conducted mostly in Tsotsitaal, an urban, street variety that draws on urban vernaculars from African languages, Afrikaans and English. As discussed in Chapter 5, Tsotsitaal is spoken predominantly by men and can be used to enact displays of forceful masculinity (Bembe and Beukes 2007; Hurst 2009; Deumert 2018). The participants' discussion enacts their hybrid masculine identities: they express traditional Xhosa values and beliefs alongside belief in the value of English for modern, urban aspects of their identities. Thando explains in her critical commentary that Tsotsitaal is commonly spoken by young boys. She reinforces the theme of initiation, language and secrecy in her comment: 'It shows that you know each other and sometimes it is even used to deceive someone who might be listening to your conversation.' Even though the two participants are in a private space, there is still some concern about possible eavesdroppers, and Tsotsitaal offers another potential layer of privacy (depending, of course, on who their neighbours are).

The dialogue illustrates the way language intersects with masculinity in specific cultural contexts and how group membership is contingent on certain performances of masculinity and cultural practices. In the critical commentary Thando also explains that in Xhosa culture, 'if a male has not undergone the process of initiation, he is not allowed to take part in any male activities in the community like tribal meetings.' Hence, Thando raises broader questions about the right to personal choices and what is valued or not valued in specific cultural contexts (i.e. why Sthembiso's academic capacity is valued less than traditional practices). Kumalo and Gama (2018: 4), in their discussion of Xhosa initiation rites, masculinity and cultural identity, provide further insight in its use of masculinist language in the process of initiation, (mis)conceptions of the custom produce manhood, which is then inculcated in initiands while bodies existing outside of these masculine demarcations are disallowed from that cultural space.

In the critical commentary it becomes clear that Thando wrote the dialogue in order to problematize traditional cultural notions of masculinity as the following extract illustrates:

> This dialogue is written for young African men who are still ill-treated because they didn't go to initiation school. These young men are disrespected because they are not yet men according to their culture. They are called silly names just to discredit their manhood. . . . It is okay for young boys to be afraid of going there and it is unfair for Jama to discourage Mxolisi from befriending him only because he is still regarded as 'inkwenkwe' (insulting term to refer to a Xhosa male who has not undergone initiation as a boy, regardless of age).

Thando works implicitly to explore the relationships between key concepts such as language, identity, gender and culture. She captures the way language can be used to police cultural practices that enforce masculinity. She explains that a Xhosa male labelled as an '*inkwenkwe*' will be excluded from participation in any male activities in the community. Thando's critical-creative move would be strengthened by using more precise sociolinguistic terminology. For example, she refers to the labelling of some males as '*inkwenkwe*' as 'silly names' while later showing how devastating this label is. There is scope for more explicit discussion of the relationship between language, power and group membership. However, her assignment is multi-voiced, juxtaposing different discourses about initiation through her role as creative playwright and academic commentator, from an outsider perspective. The narrative space enables her to insert herself and her voice into a discussion from which she would usually be excluded, and to disrupt discourses that she usually has no power to disrupt. In addition, because she does not belong to this group of Xhosa males, she is able to see things differently from insiders. Her dialogue demonstrates 'the willingness to imagine oneself in the other persons' skin' (Kearney 1988: 368) but she goes even further. She seizes patriarchal voices that usually control her, inhabiting their voices and bodies.

These moves between different discourses and roles facilitate the release of the critical imagination by opening a conversation about the possibilities of fluid ways of viewing masculinity. She achieves this through playing with both the poetic and social imagination (Greene 1995; Kearney 1988) by projecting herself into the minds and feelings of Jama and Mxolisi, and then creating an alternative discursive space where many critical questions are asked, and different voices can be heard. From a pedagogical perspective, Thando's assignment illustrates Greene's (1995: 6) vision of classroom environments which open spaces for students to ask, 'in all tones of voice *why*?' .

Nombini's assignment: Fighting back

Nombini identifies herself as being an urban Zulu. Her dialogue is one of four that enacts patriarchal and misogynist discourses, highlighting how these discourses shape lived experience. While Thando enacts discursive shifts in her move from the dialogue to critical commentary, Nombini's dialogue enacts multiple discourses in both parts of her assignment.

The dialogue is set in an informal settlement located in the East Rand of Johannesburg. Home (a temporary abode in a crowded urban area) frequently consists of a single room, typically the size of a garden shed. Inhabitants of informal settlements have limited access to running water, electricity and food.

The participants in the dialogue are three women, all residents of the same neighbourhood. It begins with a conversation between MaNkosi and Nomaswazi, later joined by MaNkosi's friend, MaMpho. Nomaswazi expresses shock at the sight of MaNkosi's black eye. MaNkosi explains that her husband beat her up because she spent the day drinking and didn't prepare a meal for him. While the subject matter is extremely serious, the women joke about it, particularly when MaNkosi confesses that she fought back and exaggerates the injuries she inflicted on her husband. MaNkosi's difficult feelings about a serious issue are juxtaposed with humour, playfulness and linguistic deviance. Humour as a 'two-edged sword' (Golden 1996: 5) helps create this juxtaposition between seriousness and humour, as the laughter shared by the women is both pleasurable and a way of processing a painful experience. But at the same time, MaNkosi has altered the rules of the game in her marriage by fighting back. There is also a significant contrast between the setting and the content of the conversation. Nombini describes the setting as follows:

> The dialogue takes place at MaNkosi's house, outside in the yard, under the tree. It is during the day on a sunny Saturday and these women feel free to talk about what happened last night in MaNkosi's house. The environment provides comfort and relaxation as the husbands are at work and the children are off to play in the street. The area allows the women to talk in the language of their choice.

Hence, the dialogue occurs in a free space, and the women enjoy the pleasure of intimate sharing between two close friends and neighbours without external pressures of husbands and children.

The opening lines of the dialogue, accompanied by Nombini's translations, are significant in what they reveal about prevailing attitudes towards gender-based violence both in what is said and in the silences. The silences are later broken open in Nombini's critical commentary.

> Nomaswazi: *Yho! Mfazi* (sister), what happened to your eye?
>
> MaNkosi: *It is lesisidididi sendola* (this stupid man) who beat me up yesterday after coming back from the *imbibe.* (tavern)
>
> Nomaswazi: *Yho! Aji njani? (No ways, what did you do?)*
>
> MaNkosi: He found out that I was drinking the whole day yesterday and did not cook. *Sase siba nenxabano.* (Then we had an argument.)
>
> Nomaswazi: *Mara why nawe ungaohekanga?* (But why didn't you cook?)
>
> MaNkosi: *Hha, ngipheka njalo kodwa angitholi ndondo.* (I always cook but he is never grateful.)

Nomaswazi's response to MaNkosi indicates that wife-beating is commonplace in their community. She does not focus on the fact that MaNkosi has been a victim of abuse. There is also no mention of reporting the attack to the police. Instead, she focuses her attention on what MaNkosi might have done to provoke her husband. This is consistent with research findings that a high proportion of men and women believe that a man has a right to beat his wife (Gender Links 2015). Such beliefs create an environment where it is difficult for women to claim their rights as conservative views are prevalent. Nombini has written the dialogue skilfully to enact these issues through the questions raised by Nomaswazi and the silences in the text.

While MaNkosi is not the recipient of any empathy from her friend – and is treated more like perpetrator than victim – as a reader of the text one is primed to expect a victim narrative. However, the dialogue contains a counter-narrative which becomes evident when MaNkosi explains that she retaliated. In this moment, MaNkosi is repositioned as a woman with agency, who challenges her husband's expectations and refuses the role of passive victim. Multiple voices, in a Bakhtinian sense (1981), are evident in the dialogue with Nomaswazi echoing the dominant view of gender relations while MaNkosi represents a counter-voice and position. She tells Nomaswazi that she is tired of cooking for her ungrateful husband and of his endless expectations of servitude.

MaNkosi: *Ngingaphela* (I could not stand it anymore)*, name ngimmurile* (I fought back). You should check out his neck and the right middle finger is no more.

Nomaswazi: *Ungitshelani (What?) Bengingazi* (I did not know) that you eat human flesh.

(They both laugh.)

The foregoing extracts are examples of critical-creative enactments which utilize amplification and humour and generate opportunities for 'student-initiated critical literacy' (Lewis 2014: 189). MaNkosi's body is both a casualty of gender-based violence and a weapon she employs to retaliate. As a character in the dialogue, she thus interrupts dominant discourses about gender in specific socio-material conditions.

Verbal play, creativity and inventiveness are on display at a number of levels in the dialogue. The women code switch between isiZulu, Sesotho, isiXhosa and English. However, unsurprisingly, the most emotional responses are expressed in an African language. MaNkosi plays with possible meanings when she tells Nomaswazi that her husband's finger is 'no more', a phallic image that adds sexual innuendo to the multiple layers of meaning. Nomaswazi jokingly takes this to mean that MaNkosi ate her husband's finger. Their 'loud screams and laughs' attract the attention of the third participant, MaMpho, who joins then to investigate the cause of the hilarity. She becomes the butt of their extended joke as Nomaswazi informs her that MaNkosi ate her husband's finger.

MaMpho: How can you be laughing about such matters, *unjan' yena* (How is he?)

MaNkosi: *Mxm, yaz' wena ubeliever yonke intoy'zwayo.* (You know you believe everything you hear.)

MaMpho: *Hawu kganthi le nketsa stlatla* (Oh, so I am just being made an idiot). MaNkosi, you are used to making people idiots because I remember you did this with the matter about your son.

MaNkosi: *Uthin' lo* (What is this one saying now?) Hey, don't you dare involve my son in this.

MaMpho expresses concern about MaNkosi's husband and disgust that her two friends are laughing about this serious matter. When she realizes that she has been tricked, she becomes angry and raises an old gripe with MaNkosi. This adds new emotional currents to a dialogue that is already a complex cocktail of conflicting and shifting emotions including shock, resentment, anger, amusement and pleasure, illustrating the argument that 'affective relationships to embodied texts take complicated, conflicted forms absent in many logical, rational rubrics for critical literacy practice' (Johnson and Vasudevan 2014: 100).

Ultimately though, the two women are reconciled after MaMpho apologizes, and the dialogue ends with the women acknowledging their friendship ('you know we are one') and laughing and singing songs that usually play on the jukebox in the nearby tavern. The dialogue is an example of the way aesthetic texts 'allow us to know the world' (Misson and Morgan 2006: 121) in unique ways for both readers and writers. The performative, imaginative and embodied nature of the text facilitates deep engagement with social and emotional issues. Like a poem, and many other works of art, the dialogue is compressed yet intense. A world is created on the page, and we are invited to imagine this world and 'to travel mentally through time and space at extraordinary speed and in surprising depth' (Ricoeur cited in Kostopoulos 2016). Hence, the dialogue calls on both the poetic and social imagination, though it is in the critical commentary that the social imagination is unpacked more explicitly.

Although critical social issues are embedded in the dialogue, the critical commentary is an important and necessary aspect of a narrative pedagogy that foregrounds the critical imagination. Nombini effectively enacts and embodies pressing gender issues in her dialogue. How does her critical commentary extend and deepen her assignment as a whole? What is her critical-creative move in the recontextualized text?

Nombini explains her motivation as follows:

> When I was writing this dialogue, I was hoping to demonstrate the lives that other South Africans live (specifically women) daily, being beaten and treated horribly by men they call husbands and how women don't respect themselves in the society they live in. This is not only happening in the squatter camps but even in the suburbs. This demonstrates how men show their masculinity by abusing women in search of authority.

Although her main aim is to raise concerns about abuse of women, she refuses to set up a complete victim/perpetrator binary. She refers here to MaNkosi's alcoholism as being an indicator of a lack of self-respect. This makes the dialogue and critical commentary a more nuanced, possibly ambivalent read, which includes an important comment about the prevalence of gender-based violence across all social classes. She works productively with sociolinguistic concepts such as language, power, masculinity and identity in ways that illustrate how disciplinary metalanguage can strengthen and deepen the social imagination.

While the dialogue contains multiple voices, discourses and positions on gender-based violence, in the critical commentary Nombini repositions herself with an academic, authoritative voice, moving from the poetic to the social. She makes it clear that she rejects the discourse of blaming women (represented by Nomaswazi) for their oppression as follows:

> MaNkosi lacks self-respect because as a married woman she should respect her husband and cook for her children but instead she drinks the whole day. However, this does not give her husband the right to beat her up. In this case MaNkosi is not like many women who take the beating. She fought back; hence this is not the first time she is being beaten.

Nombini also interrogates the power relations and double standards enacted in the dialogue. She questions why the scenario would be different if the roles were reversed and a man came home late. She also explores how and why the socio-material environment enables these double standards:

> The protecting services against women abuse are not near and even if they were they wouldn't pay much attention to what she says judging from her dress-code to the alcohol she will be breathing. This imposes a certain identity to these kinds of women by society. They are viewed as people who ask to be beaten because they don't behave or abide by the rules placed by their husbands.

In this extract, Nombini addresses a silence in the dialogue text: the fact that neither MaNkosi nor her friends raise the option of reporting the abuse to police, thus reinforcing the sense of entrapment created by the broader social context. Nombini underlines how social class exacerbates the situation as women like MaNkosi have access to few resources and are unlikely to elicit empathy. This analysis, to some extent, exemplifies Lewis's point that 'environments can alienate bodies or draw them in, and students can design spaces that will effect positive change and create a sense of belonging and joy' (Lewis 2014: 189). It is beyond the scope of Nombini's assignment to 'design spaces that will effect positive change' (Lewis 2014: 189). But her writing is a starting point for the development of criticality and social awareness. What is striking is that Nombini, through the process of writing the dialogue and the critical commentary, has used her imagination as a springboard 'to cross the empty spaces between ourselves and others and to challenge taken-for-granted assumptions' (Greene 1995: 3).

Conclusion

> I hope we can ponder the openings of wider and wider spaces of dialogue, in which diverse students and teachers, empowered to speak in their own voices, reflect together as they try to bring into being an in-between. (Greene 1995: 59)

Our intention in this chapter has been to highlight the importance and the power of the critical imagination as a way of knowing and to demonstrate how the imagination, criticality and narrative can be brought together in a teacher education class. What has emerged from the theoretical overview and empirical data is that a crucial aspect of the critical imagination entails creating pedagogical spaces that mobilize affect and empathy alongside criticality. Embodied literacy work across different genres and modes can play a significant role in facilitating the critical imagination (both the poetic and the social) by enabling students to enact, perform and immerse themselves in different discourses, ultimately generating new ways of seeing.

In thinking about practical implications of this research for teachers and teacher educators, we argue that the juxtapositioning of critical and creative texts across different modes both in class activities and assignments enables fluid movements between imagination and criticality, and immersion and critical distancing. Reflection should play a significant role in unpacking the layers of meaning generated by their creative texts. Finally, if preservice teachers are to engage coherently with imagination and criticality in their classrooms, they need to experience pedagogies that enable this work, in their professional education.

English and/in the Colonial Matrix of Power

I can divide my academic career into two parts: before #fmf and after #fmf – it was a moment when theory walked off the page and marched into the classroom as students' lived reality. And we have been compelled to sit up and take notice.

Extract from Ana's journal, 2020

Introduction

The #FeesMustFall student protests were the defining feature of the period from which the final set of student data is drawn. Perhaps because of our own lived experience as academics during this time, we were hoping to see evidence of this moment of massive social change writ large on the pages of these students' language narratives. But what the data reveals is, not surprisingly, far more subtle and has been the result of a fine-grained analysis of the student narratives. In this chapter we use extracts from five narratives written in 2017 and 2018 to present an analysis of how students are (re)positioning themselves in relation to English, paying particular attention to how these (re)positionings may be disruptive of – or show continuities with – the hegemony of English. We argue that while few narratives refer explicitly to the protests, the ways in which students position themselves and the discourses they draw on index broader social discourses circulating during that time. In this way, this chapter, like Chapter 4, also centres student identities. Taken together these two chapters bookend the data analysis chapters, presenting language narratives from the early years (2005–7) and from the most recent years (2017–18) respectively.

The chapter is structured as follows: we begin with a brief and imperfect account of the #FeesMustFall movement framed by our perspective as privileged, white, middle-class academics at an elite, urban university. This is followed by a decolonial 're-description' of how students are positioned within the racialized structural inequalities of the university and the impact of this on voice and agency (Luckett 2016). We then consider the complex position of English in this post-colonial, multilingual context where it can be seen both as a colonial language and as asset to be appropriated and owned (Rudwick 2022). The analysis which follows demonstrates how ownership of English can be uncritically assimilationist or lean towards critical appropriation and how the relationship between language and race can shape students' experiences of inclusion or exclusion in institutional spaces.

#FeesMustFall

Maldonado-Torres (2017: 14) describes the #FeesMustFall movement as 'a major earthquake that moved the foundations of South African consciousness and society [and] brought back the idea of decolonization as an incomplete project'. The narrative of this time is a contested one and our view is, of course, a partial one. This extended moment changed higher education spaces and irrevocably changed us as lecturers. In March 2015, a student at the University of Cape Town threw faeces at a statue of Cecil John Rhodes, 'literally covering the white colonial statue at the centre of campus in black shit' (Gillespie and Naidoo 2019: 235). This symbolic act drew attention to the ways in which the very fabric of our universities continued to be imbued with coloniality and structured by Eurocentric curricula. It kickstarted the hashtag #RhodesMustFall (#RMF) and placed these long-standing issues in the public domain. Even though black students were now in the majority at all South African universities, the assimilationist ethos operating in institutions of higher education meant that white, western culture was normative and was being experienced as alienating for the majority of students. Thus for young black South African students 'the experience of assimilating into the educational institutions designed overtly to create elite white colonial subjectivities and professions has been one of epistemic and ontological violence' (Gillespie and Naidoo 2019: 233).

Against this heightened awareness around untransformed university spaces, when a nationwide university fee increase was announced in October 2015, the first wave of student protests began. Similarly themed fees protests had occurred in previous years at historically black institutions of higher learning (Godsell and Chikane 2016). But only when the elite, historically white universities took up the fight did the ideas gain traction in the public sphere and the broader #FeesMustFall movement took off. Starting at Wits

University, protests rapidly spread to other universities across the country, gaining momentum and leading to a mass movement not seen since the days of the anti-apartheid struggle.

In the 2015 protests, students collectively managed to shut down universities, bring the academic programme to a halt and ultimately succeeded in securing an agreement from the state of a 0% fee increase for 2016. Additional gains continued to be made, for example, students successfully campaigned to end the outsourcing of the university's cleaning and maintenance staff whom they viewed as mothers and fathers economically exploited by neoliberal and capitalist structures of the university (Chinguno et al. 2017: 26). But it was a fraught time. While we experienced the first round of protests as students speaking truth to power, there were also times when protests seemed to be shaped by students' party-political alignments. While initial protests had been disruptive but largely peaceful, Wits management's controversial decision to bring private security/ police onto campus to prevent the disruption of classes led to violent clashes between students and police, resulting in a number of student arrests and many accusations of police brutality. Malabela (2017: 137), a postgraduate student at Wits, writes that when the student movement eventually employed violence, this 'tended to alienate non-protesting students and lost the movement public sympathy'.

Because the Education campus is a satellite campus, we did not initially witness the clashes or experience the high levels of disruption that occurred on the central campus. This changed as the movement regained momentum in 2016, and in 2017 the School of Education experienced its own wave of protests specifically related to the funding of the Bachelor of Education degree. Eventually all three of us, at one time or another, experienced having our classes disrupted and shut down by protesting students, or were involved in student stand-offs with the police. As academics, we often felt torn between our ideological sympathies with the foundational principles of the student movement; our commitment to the academic programme; our own discomfort with our location as privileged, middle-class, white academics; and our sense of being caught between two opposing forces: university management and protesting students. The protests provoked strong emotions and beliefs (Constandius et al. 2018), as evident in the multiple accounts of this period written by student activists (Chikane 2018; Ngcaweni and Ngcaweni 2018; Langa 2017; Chinguno 2017), university vice chancellors (Jansen 2017; Habib 2019) and others, in a plethora of publications interpreting the movement through various disciplinary lenses.

The matrix of power in the post-colonial university

The #FeesMustFall protests were an extended moment of confluence of issues of identity, experience, curriculum and pedagogy. They required – and continue to require – critical reflection for us to better understand who we are, who our students are and what kinds of relational dispositions are embedded in the institutional fabric of our curriculum and pedagogy.

As a starting point for understanding how our students are positioned within elite institutions, Luckett's (2016) work on the post-colonial university has proven useful. Drawing on Archer's morphogenetic cycle, Luckett adopts a decolonial gaze to 're-describe' the post-colonial university. She identifies three categories of students who are differently positioned in relation to the curriculum by virtue of their racial, cultural and class positions. Poor black students, the first category, are both materially and culturally marginalized and thus function as *subjects* with constrained agency. Middle-class black students, the second category, are not materially marginalized but they are culturally marginalized; they thus function as *new citizens* whose agency is both emerging and constrained. White students, the third category, align with the university's normative western culture, they are neither materially nor culturally marginalized. They function as *full citizens* whose agency is more developed than that of students in the other two categories. Luckett's set of categories is further overlain with unequally distributed access to linguistic proficiency in the dominant language, English. The symbolic linguistic capital of English is tied to race (whiteness) and to class, as a function of a schooling system in which 'the procurement of English as a linguistic asset' (Botsis 2017: 92) is available to middle-class learners. Luckett further argues that the hegemonic position of English in the institution does not recognize African languages and thereby withholds a cultural resource for agency. She writes that 'all black students . . . will invariably experience a cultural system and curriculum that devalues and negates home languages, cultures, histories and identities – thus positioning them as culturally deficient' (Luckett 2016: 421).

Luckett's framework is useful for showing how students are differently positioned within the power structures of the university according to their raced, classed and cultural identity locations. While these categories may appear somewhat reductionist, Luckett maintains that they are not determined because these positions are 'always mediated by human agency and reflexivity' (Luckett 2016: 418). We agree with Botsis when she reminds us that what it means to be black or white or middle class, of from a particular cultural group is not easily articulated. The undoing of apartheid was the beginning of the undoing of these ideologically loaded categories. The instability of these ideological signifiers is readily visible in the linguistic habitus of [university students]. (2017: 91)

Thus our analysis in this chapter is informed by Luckett's categories but works with a more fluid, intersectional approach to identity, albeit one that foregrounds race. This is in keeping with the 'move away from the reconciliation and non-racialist approach of the Rainbow Nation towards a re-racialised debate, in which racial particularity is at the forefront of the argumentation' (Nielsen 2021: 405). We also remain mindful of the ways in which students can disrupt hegemonic relations even from positions associated with limited agency.

Decolonizing the language curriculum: The position of English

Throughout this time we were acutely aware of the uncomfortable position of English in the conversation on decolonizing the curriculum – as an imperial language (Mignolo 2007b) that, given its current global position, continues to be entangled in the colonial matrix of power (Quijano 2000). The Rhodes Must Fall Mission Statement (UCT, March 2015: n.p.) identified one of its long-term goals as centring Africa in the curriculum 'through addressing *not only content, but languages* and methodologies of education and learning' (our italics). Although the need to valorize indigenous languages was implicit in the call to decolonize the university curriculum, the challenge to the hegemonic position of English as a colonial language was not visibly taken up in the public domain. When protesting students at the Afrikaans-medium universities demanded that #AfrikaansMustFall and be replaced by English, a number of commentators pointed out the irony. They asked 'why protesting black students, knowing well that English is also a language of colonisation, still choose it as a language of tuition over and above their own indigenous languages?' (Dube 2017: 14), and pointed out the danger of constructing 'an artificially depoliticised English' (Painter 2015). While such comments point out the ongoing valuing of English over indigenous languages in the higher education terrain, they elide the oppressive ways in which Afrikaans was used by the apartheid government.

A closer look at protesting students' personal narratives and commentaries does, however, show that the problematic position of English was not overlooked.

Chikane (2018) writes that at meetings, students often shifted between English and indigenous languages. However, he contends that eloquence in English was a form of power and that 'English was often inadvertently used by the elite as a means of gaining authority in the protest, but, simultaneously, English as the dominant language was also pushed against' (2018: 239). A further symbolic challenge to English can also be seen in the fallist version of the South African national anthem which was sung at the beginning and end of student meetings and excluded English and Afrikaans found in the official anthem (Moloi 2017: 67).

In the academic arena, Mbembe (2015: n.p.) made his position clear:

> A decolonized university in Africa should put African languages at the centre of its teaching and learning project. Colonialism rhymes with monolingualism. The African university of tomorrow will be multilingual.

Makalela (2018a: 5) subsequently argued for the value of 'translanguaging as a decolonising agent given the historical association of monolingualism with colonisation'. And others pointed to the slow pace at which multilingual policies were being implemented by universities as well as 'lack of clarity on the positioning of African languages as languages of learning and teaching' (Mayaba et al. 2018: 1).

Appropriation and ownership of English

In keeping with the dual gaze of the access paradox, however, we argue that it is not sufficient to see English purely as a colonial language. In her work on the localization and appropriation of English, Higgins (2009: 11) 'explores the many ways that users of English index their *ownership* of the language' (original italics). Using the notion of heteroglossia, she theorizes English usage in multilingual contexts as an intersection of 'linguistic imperialism (a centripetal force) and theories of appropriation and transcultural flows (centrifugal forces)' (2009: 15). This aligns with the ambivalence towards English that is well documented in the literature. See for example McKinney (2007) and Parmegiani (2014). Similarly, in her work on the complex position of English as a lingua franca in South Africa, Rudwick (2022) points out that

> The binary views of English as a non-African, 'colonial', and 'alien' language, on the one hand, and English as local, hybrid, and 'Africanized', on the other hand, play out in complex ways in everyday South African reality. (11)

Added to this is the growing acceptance by some scholars (Jeyifo 2020; Kamwangamalu 2019) of English as an African language. It therefore feels fitting to devote some attention not only to the ways in which students are (re) positioning themselves in relation to English but to the ways in which they are (re)positioning English itself and how a sense of ownership of English is at play in these positionings.

Ideas about the ownership of English emerge in students' language narratives. In analysing these narratives, we align ourselves with Parmegiani's (2010) rejection of the 'birthright paradigm' (i.e. the common-sense approach of viewing only the mother tongue as legitimate language ownership), and support his proposal of a more 'fluid, open, and decentred' model of language ownership, where additional languages can be fully and legitimately appropriated. To determine whether a student's narrative demonstrates ownership of English, we apply the model proposed by Seilhamer (2015, drawing on Parks 2011) in which three dimensions of language ownership are identified: *prevalent usage* (i.e. quantity of use), *affective belonging* (i.e. emotional attachment) and *legitimate knowledge* (i.e. expertise and authority over the language/right to speak). In a multilingual society such as South Africa, what constitutes knowledge of or expertise in English must be flexible enough to decentre prestige varieties of English associated with Anglonormative (McKinney 2017) ideologies so as to make space for multiple local varieties of English and 'hybrid codes'. This approach facilitates access for speakers of marginalized languages (Parmegiani 2010: 363).

Nevertheless language ownership in South Africa is constrained by the 'perceived correlation between race and ascribed native language' (Parmegiani 2010: 366). A common – though increasingly unreliable – expectation is that, with regard to 'mother tongue', black South Africans speak one of the indigenous African languages, coloured South Africans speak either English or Afrikaans, Indian South Africans speak English and white South Africans speak English or Afrikaans. Language is written on the body, or in the words of Rosa (2018: 2) 'languages are perceived as racially embodied and race is perceived as linguistically intelligible'. Thus there is a colonial logic at work at the intersection of the birthright paradigm of language ownership and assumptions about the correlation between language and race. However, Botsis (2017), in her discussion of language use, takes a more nuanced view. While she recognizes that 'Apartheid created the framework for language, race and culture to be mapped onto each other, which has created ideologically loaded expectations about what certain bodies should speak, and how they should sound' (2018: 95), she believes that these once clear-cut organizing principles are 'in a state of flux' (2018: 106). This framework is being undone and, to use Rosa's terms, the racial body is no longer 'linguistically intelligible', and instead a more open and fluid model of language ownership is emerging. However, what we can infer from some student narratives is that, while their linguistic practices are contributing to the dismantling of this language/race/culture paradigm, they are often subjected to the linguistic prejudices associated with the old paradigm, even from family or community members. As Rudwick (2022: 150) states, English in South Africa occupies a contested position, 'engender[ing] multiple powers and disempowerments, inclusion and exclusion, and complex racialisation processes'. Our analysis of students' language narratives is an attempt to provide some insight into how students position and reposition themselves in these processes.

Analysis of students' language narratives

After coding a total of thirty-eight narratives from 2017 to 2018 (twenty-two from 2017 and sixteen from 2018) in relation to ways in which students positioned themselves with regard to English, we selected five narratives which spoke to the following issues:

- Ownership of English
- Language and race in institutional spaces

In addition to the language narratives, the data analysis in this chapter also draws on transcripts of four focus group discussions held with a total of fourteen of the thirty-eight students from the 2017 to 2018 cohorts whose narratives constitute the full set of data. As these focus group discussions took place in February and March 2020, students were talking about their experiences of the course and the writing of their narratives two to three years after completing the sociolinguistics course. Where we use data from this retrospective reflection on the course, it adds an additional layer to the analysis.

Ownership of English

In this section the two language narratives demonstrate two different orientations to the ownership of English: the first shows ownership of English as a form of assimilation into Englishness and Anglonormativity and the second one shows a more critical appropriation of English.

Ownership as assimilation

The first language narrative is written by Kefuwe, a young black female for whom English is the dominant language. Kefuwe introduces herself as 'a Sotho woman with a English tongue'. While she states that she holds Sesotho 'to such high esteem' and views it as her 'default language', as her narrative unfolds it becomes clear that she hardly ever speaks it.

Kefuwe: A little more than just 'urban black' (2018)

Unlike a lot of black children growing up in the township, English has been quite dominant in my life from an early age. It probably helped that my mother went to a multiracial school (yes, this was during the apartheid era) so she speaks the language fluently. My two older sisters also went to multiracial schools and they speak fluent English as well. Therefore, I cannot possibly be blamed for having learnt the language approximately around the same time that I learnt how to speak. The variety of television shows in English and English reading books were a great starting point in developing my fluency. After that came attending multiracial schools in which English was the language of instruction. My background with the language served as a great advantage at school because it was easy for me to understand instructions and grasp information. However, living in Pimville in Soweto, speaking English more than vernacular can be problematic.

A very clear reminder of this is the one time in my life, between the ages of 10 and 12, when I decided to make friends in my neighbourhood. It did not help that all of them went to local township schools so the type of English that they spoke was different from mine. Furthermore, they deliberately avoided speaking in English as much as possible and communicated primarily in Sesotho. Generally, one would not expect that there would be a communication barrier of any sort because I grew up in the same place as them so I should be able to communicate effectively in Sesotho. No. Not this girl. My Sesotho is mediocre to the extent that would bring shame to me if I cared enough. This created a bigger rift than I had anticipated. I was officially the township snob and the exclusion intensified by the day. I was like Candace. A coconut. Treated differently because 'I'm smart and I speak perfect English' (Matlwa 2007 as cited in Candace 2009). The number of inside jokes among the rest of the group increased rapidly. I was excluded from conversations as they spoke about everything that went on at their schools. My presence went unnoticed and my comments unheard. Or maybe they were just misunderstood. Even when I spoke my kasi [township] *Sesotho, it was just never enough. There were times when my twelve-year-old self thought that maybe I had to put in a little more effort when speaking Sesotho and try not to be so obvious when I did not understand what they were saying. I thought that perhaps I had to stop correcting them when they made mistakes in English.*

Perhaps that offended them and there I was thinking I was being a good friend and lending a helping hand. Eventually I gave up. It truly was not my fault that I spoke fluent English and they did not. It was just a matter of people having different opportunities in life and I was not going to apologise that I spent my childhood reading instead of playing diketo [Sesotho: childhood game played with stones].

I no longer socialise with the locals here. I have chosen to make my own preferences a priority and I have never been happier. Honestly, trying to please and accommodate people ke spani [Sesotho slang, too much work] *and I just do not have the energy for it. Besides, my fluency in English is more relevant to my life than Sesotho will ever be. I went to an English high school and I am attending an English university where I am majoring in English. I plan on being one of the best English teachers this country has to offer. And just to add a little spice, I passed my language competency in Sesotho so I cannot possibly be that bad, right?*

A dominant feature of this extract from Kefuwe's narrative is the dissonance caused by living in the township and attending a 'multiracial school', that is a historically white school outside the township in a historically white suburb. These two places are associated with different ethnolinguistic profiles and different socioeconomic class positions. Although Kefuwe initially presents herself as proud of her Sesotho language, it turns out that her Sesotho is 'mediocre to the extent that would bring shame to me if I cared enough'. This, coupled with the fact that she and other neighbourhood youngsters spoke different varieties of English, apparently creates a 'rift' between her and them. In addition, various discursive markers, such as 'township snob' and the multiracial schools that her family has always attended, suggest that Kefuwe occupies a middle-class position. This is reinforced by her mastery of English, a classed linguistic asset (Botsis 2017). We can infer that the neighbourhood youngsters' insistence on speaking Sesotho may be a deliberate form of exclusion in retaliation for Kefuwe's sense of superiority, particularly with regard to her correction of their spoken English. Her narrative style hints at this awareness when she wonders if she might be offending them by constantly correcting then, adding (perhaps with ironic intent): 'there I was thinking I was being a good friend and lending a helping hand.'

Being labelled a 'coconut' seals this alienation. When used in a derogatory manner, this act of labelling polices the borders of blackness, punishing someone for transgressing these boundaries:

It confers outsider status to an individual who is purportedly no longer an 'authentic' black [. . .] person by virtue of their perceived attempt to take up behaviour associated with another racial category – in this case, to 'act white'. (Ferreira 2016: 1258)

Linguistically, it is also associated with 'African people who speak Standard and/or excessive English' (Rudwick 2022: 3). While the term 'coconut' has more recently been taken up in more agentic and self-determining ways (discussed later in this chapter), it is clear that here the neighbourhood youngsters use it pejoratively. Kefuwe herself, however, seems ambivalent about this characterization. While she recognizes that it is intended to index exclusion, she associates the term with being 'smart' and speaking 'perfect English' (quoting a student language narrative from a previous year), alluding to processes of assimilation. Although Kefuwe is defensive about how English came to be her dominant language, she wields her English like a sword. With regard to ownership of English, she subscribes to all the criteria (Park 2011): as her dominant language, it has prevalent use; her mastery of the language is evident, as is her projection of herself as a legitimate speaker – in her ease with correcting others and her intention to be 'one of the best English teachers this country has to offer'; the latter further suggests her emotional attachment to the language.

But she is in thrall to Anglonormative ideologies (McKinney 2017) and her ownership of English is uncritical. In a focus group discussion (3 March 2020), Kefuwe talked about how she became excited at the thought of being able to incorporate her languages into her English-language narrative assignment but then realized that actually the only language she really knows is English. So she wrote it in English and had to get help from people to translate bits into Sesotho and isiZulu. This, she explains, helped her to 'see and understand the coconut that everyone else was seeing'. This is a fascinating behind-the-scenes comment both on how the process of narrativizing one's language identity offers a way of standing back and looking at oneself with new eyes, as well as the performance of multilingualism that she enacts in order to meet the expectations of the assignment.

Critical ownership of English

The next narrative, written by Refilwe, demonstrates critical ownership of the English language and an awareness that it has come at a cost. Refilwe retains a strong attachment to her African identity, and expresses a deep sense of loss over not speaking her mother tongue fluently, showing critical awareness of issues of power and race.

Refilwe: My Native Tongue Matters (2017)

My L1 is Sesotho, but I have never been to Lesotho. I'd like to refer to myself as a proudly Mosotho woman, but that would be a blatant lie. My identity is a cocktail of almost all the languages that are spoken in Johannesburg. I was born and grew up in Soweto. Soweto is my home, my roots are in Jozi (Moya 2005). I am a modern black child who is shaped by the city she lives in.

I went to a very good school. My township friends used to tease me by saying I attend a private school in the township. Yes, it was a private school, and yes, it was in the heart of Soweto. The school was known for how strict it was, I remember we were not allowed to wear earrings or have chemically treated hair. The head mistress insisted that we wear our k-- hare ['k--', a deeply offensive term for an African person; 'hare', hair in Afrikaans] *as it is. The only tool we were allowed to use was an afro comb* [comb with handle and long teeth used to detangle hair]. *I'm not sure if this was to teach us to embrace our blackness or to help our parents save money since most of it was going towards our school fees.*

K-- hare *is a term I still use to this day, I find no offence in it. I took the term and I owned it soon as I hit high school, just when I was trying to find my identity. I wouldn't let just a word define me. My hair is thick, coarse and that of a black person – my gorgeous* k-- hare. *I'd have to agree with Naylor when she says 'Words themselves are innocuous; it is the consensus that gives them true power'* (2000: 475).

All was well in school, until one cold morning in May 1999. The intercom went on, and the stern voice of the head mistress came on: 'Good morning learners. Please make your way to the assembly. Thank you.' We got to the assembly and the head mistress announced that as from that moment on, we were all required to communicate in Standard English. She said she acknowledges our blackness but we must leave our mother tongues outside the gate. She emphasised 'Sesotho or IsiZulu will not take you anywhere in the world. If you plan on succeeding in life, English will take you there.' We were told that any students heard speaking a native language will be punished. 'Zkhiphan' manje la?!' [What's going on here!] I exclaimed to Dudu, my friend from Mzimhlophe, a predominantly Zulu section in Soweto. Dudu and I communicated in a mixture of nonstandard versions of Sesotho, isiZulu, English and broken Afrikaans. Afrikaans is a language that reminded us of the struggle, thus we refused to acknowledge it. Afrikaans was forced on our grandfathers now it's English on us. Why is our language not good enough? Yes English was the language of instruction, but how on earth would I be able to hold an entire conversation in English? English was going to show me my mother struu [kasitaal, English is really going to be a struggle]. *I had always viewed English as the language of authority. The language of power and privilege. Things that were not mine by virtue of the fact that I am black. English frightened me. Every time the phone rang at home and my father spoke in English, I knew it was authority on the other side of the line, giving him orders. Am I now supposed to turn my back on my blackness so doors could open for me? Are these people trying to strip me of my identity? I was in a state of confusion. I had no idea how I was going to speak* is'ngamla [English] *to my friends who are not* bo ngamla [white people]. *I will definitely be shunned by my friends at home for this. I felt oppressed. So much for a rainbow nation. I felt like I was carrying a heavy burden on my shoulders. Standard English had a hold on me, and it was not about to let go. Not in this generation.*

As the year went on I started feeling angry. In actual fact I was furious! Mainly because I felt like I was in prison, I felt like I were a slave to a certain variety of English. I was also angry at myself because that is the year I decided it would be best if I surrender. I waved my white flag and declared peace. I was going to learn how to speak Standard English. I needed to. 'It's their world, alright? They own it, and we in it' (Obama 2007: 83).

I now realise how English made me angry, how I didn't want to associate with a language that had already declared its power over my native languages. But it has nothing to do with me, I'm a victim of colonialization. That year shaped my linguistic identity. Today I speak Standard English as if it were my own and my dialect changes depending on where I am and to whom I am speaking. This makes me sad because I am an African who speaks English more fluently than any native language. '[H]ere I am with English and I'm not white, definitely not white' (Pamela in Tusini 2016b). I still speak nonstandard isiZulu, Sesotho, isiXhosa and Setswana, but English has forcefully declared itself as numero uno [number one, Italian]

I've come to accept my linguistic identity. I now I understand that my languages changed with my needs. I was moving into a world that is dominated and controlled by English and I had to adapt. I take pride in being a modern black child. An African child who moves easily between dialects and varieties of language. I hardly feel excluded when it comes to language. I pride myself in how naturally code switching occurs to me. My base is English, however I'm still firmly grounded in the languages I grew up with.

I still dislike how English and Afrikaans were imposed on the African child, as if our native languages were inferior. English is still regarded as the 'powerful' language. The language of the well-educated, those of a certain standard of living. English is used to judge and place people in certain social categories. How? Because of the power it has attached to it. While our mother tongues, the languages of the nation are viewed as useless and to be used when addressing the illiterate. I refuse to be a slave to English. It doesn't own me, I own it. I've found my balance, and my power lies in the ability to switch back and forth between the world that I grew up in and the world that I am told will opens doors for me (Obama 2007). In conclusion, I realise that my responsibility as a future teacher is a great one.

Future generations need to know that linguistically English or any other European
language is not in any way superior to any African language.

Refilwe presents herself as multilingual, urban, modern and the product of a private school in Soweto. She describes how her school suddenly made it mandatory to communicate exclusively in English and to 'leave [their] mother tongues at the gate'. (This was in 1999.) Refilwe resists in no uncertain terms what she sees as the colonial imposition of English, comparing it to the imposition of Afrikaans on her grandparents' generation. A key aspect of her narrative, however, is her shifting attitude to English. Initially she regards it with fear, dislike and anger, experiencing it as a burden, a prison or slavery. Eventually she 'surrenders' to it, invoking Obama (2007) when he capitulates to English. Paradoxically, her surrender to English enables her to own this powerful language and bend it to her needs: 'today I speak standard English as if it were my own'; 'I refuse to be a slave to English. It doesn't own me, I own it.' This is language ownership on her own terms. She demonstrates prevalent usage and legitimate knowledge but her attachment seems strategic and critical rather than emotional, and she retains a strong attachment to her African identity.

A powerful way in which Refilwe claims her African identity is through her relationship with her hair. When she refers to 'my gorgeous k-- hare', the phrase is dense with signification. The k-word that Refilwe uses is a deeply offensive, racially derogatory South African label for a black person (on par with the n-word in the United States). By choosing to voice this term in Afrikaans, 'k-- hare', Refilwe is invoking the racist history under the Afrikaans nationalist apartheid regime. But she destabilizes the negativity of this meaning by placing the word 'gorgeous' alongside it. She explicitly states that she 'owns' this term and consciously strips it of its power to oppress by refusing to concede to its negative meaning, directly referring to Naylor's (2000) discussion of the n-word in doing so. Although she does not make direct mention of it, her stance echoes an incident around school rules governing hair that took place in 2016 at Pretoria High School for Girls, an elite, historically white school. Drawing inspiration from the #FeesMustFall movement, a number of black students took a stand against entrenched school policies which saw white students' hair as the 'unmarked' norm and black students' hair, especially natural and untreated, as 'marked' and in need of domestication (Menezes de Souza 2021). Here Refilwe is foregrounding the bio-politics of speaking as a black woman and powerfully embracing her blackness in a way similar to that employed by the schoolgirls.

Refilwe's narrative demonstrates a strong critical ownership of English and there is no sense of either conscious or unconscious assimilation into Englishness or whiteness. Drawing on the Tusini (2016b) newspaper article which is provided as one of the course readings, Refilwe quotes Pamela, a student interviewed by Tusini, 'here I am with English and I'm not white, definitely not white'. The teaching of English can be seen as 'an enforcement of whiteness' (Bomer 2017: 12), but what Refilwe does is suggest that from a conscientized position, such as the one she embodies, it is possible for her to take up English, take ownership of this language *on her own terms*, and delink (Mignolo 2007a) it from whiteness. This delinking seems to be effected in two key ways. First, she wields English in various self-determined, non-standard and empowering ways, for example 'my dialect changes depending on where I am and to who I am speaking'; 'I take pride in being a modern black child . . . who moves easily between dialects and varieties of language'; and 'my power lies in the ability to switch back and forth between the world that I grew up in and the world that I am told will open doors for me'. Second, she retains a strong sense of her own African identity, which includes an emotional attachment for her African languages even if this comes with a deep sense of loss at not being fluent in 'any native language'. We see this as a pivotal move which counters Anglonormative ideologies – demonstrating a very different linguistic position from Kefuwe's assimilationist one. Refilwe's voice is strong, her conclusion is powerful and there is a sense that her eyes are wide open to challenges of navigating her relationship with a hegemonic language.

Language and race in institutional spaces

In this category we look at two different institutional spaces, juxtaposing two white students' descriptions of incidents at university with an Indian student's discussion of events at an elite, historically white English school in Johannesburg.

The persistence and insufficiency of English 'monolingualism'

Here we present two short extracts from the language narratives written by Jacques and Mary: two white students who self-identify as monolingual speakers of English. These extracts index broader contextual factors that simultaneously both enable the persistence of English monolingualism and demonstrate its insufficiency within the multilingual South African landscape.

Jacques is a white male who describes himself as being born into a traditional white, English-speaking South African family. In the extract, he describes his sense of exclusion during his first few days at Wits.

An extract from Jacques's language narrative (2018)

During Orientation week at Wits I began to feel exclusion because of my lack of ability to speak a black South African language such as Zulu or Xhosa. For the first time in my life I longed so hard that I had just made the conscious decision to have taken the chances I had been given to have actively learnt Zulu or Xhosa. I knew that if I were able to have spoken one of these two languages I would've been able to fit in a lot easier and make friends a lot quicker (Zodwa, student 2009). I recall feeling particularly left out when we were given our introductory talks about the different courses and the one lecturer stood up and spoke about Zulu and she said that the one lecturer who took [taught] Zulu was white and then proceeded to say, 'To all you white kids, if he can do it so can you.' I didn't like the feeling of being categorized and stereotyped because of my skin and I didn't like the fact that I was proving her stereotypes right by not being able to speak the language she presumed I couldn't speak just because of the colour of my skin. I felt a sense of rage take over my body and I loathed the fact that I was in that situation.

Jacques conveys strongly his sense of being an outsider and the discomfort and anger that this provokes. His regret at not having taken up past opportunities to learn an African language suggests both his awareness of the social value of speaking a dominant African language and his desire to achieve greater social integration with the multilingual student body than is possible as a monolingual English speaker. Additionally, he responds with acute sensitivity to the lecturer's assumption that he and the other white students present, are examples of the South African stereotype of the white person who cannot speak an African language. In the case of Jacques, this is in fact an accurate assumption yet he appears to be disproportionately enraged by it. The target of his rage, however, is not clear. Himself for not having learnt an African language? Others for imposing upon him the expectation that he should? The lecturer for reminding him of this personal failing? Or possibly a complex mix of these. His insistence on the role of his 'skin' suggests that he experiences discomfort at having his skin, and thus his whiteness, rendered visible *and* having the power of his whiteness come under attack. The notion of 'white fragility' (Diangelo 2018) has been coined to describe white people's defensive responses to 'being seen racially' (Diangelo 2018: 1). Jacques's defensive rage speaks to the discomfort of having his racial body made linguistically intelligible (Rosa 2018) as a white person accustomed to benefitting from the invisibility of whiteness.

Mary is a white female from an English-speaking family who describes her upbringing as 'linguistically sheltered' (drawing on Michelle, student 2009) and sees her arrival at Wits as a step into the 'big' world and a 'reality check'. The extract from her narrative describes a moment when she was attending a lecture that was disrupted by protesting students. The extract begins when, after much noise and shouting is heard outside, the protesting students enter the lecture theatre.

An extract from Mary's language narrative (2018)

They entered like ants at the sight of a delicious, chocolate cake, ready to devour it in a matter of seconds. It must have been quite a sight, a whole lecture hall filled with petrified first years facing their worst nightmare. The crowd was so excited I could literally hear and feel the high voltage of energy zinging through the hall and people. It got students who were sitting next to me up on their feet joining in the chant. There were people standing on the desks shouting with raised fists in the air. I was so scared and had no idea what was happening, as all of the chanting and singing was in Zulu (I think). I was confused and scared, annoyed and frustrated I had absolutely no idea what was going on? This was when I wished I could speak an African language, my language had deserted me, it felt like it had been torn right out of my throat and I was left sitting speechless. I turned to one of the girls next to me who had joined in the chanting and singing, and asked her, 'What are they saying? What's happening?' 'Asi khoni ukufunda. Siyabasaba na? Hayi asibasabi siyaba funa.'[1] 'This was the first time I found myself wishing I could speak and understand another language' (Michelle, student 2009). I turned to face my friend and my eyes met a rather frightened face. My friend and I snatched our bags and quickly retreated the hall and headed for my silver Ford.

Mary captures her fear, her confusion and the intensity of the atmosphere in vivid sensory detail. She begins by constructing a self/other binary between the students in class (the frightened 'us') and the protesting students (the frightening 'them'). Her initial simile – 'they entered like ants' – echoes racist, colonial tropes used to portray black people in animalistic forms, and here it underscores her sense of fear. However, this binary starts dissolving when it becomes clear that many of her peers soon join in the chanting and singing. In the end, the 'us' is reduced to Mary and her equally frightened (presumably also white and monolingual English-speaking) friend who beat a hasty retreat to her 'silver Ford' – ironically an image indexing the kind of race and class privilege that is at the centre of the protests which she cannot understand.

In this moment, in this formal institutional space, English carries no symbolic or material power – indeed, English monolingualism becomes a liability and is associated with vulnerability and fear. Mary feels unable to speak, understand or even recognize any of the languages now dominating this usually-English space. Her metaphor for her sudden voicelessness – 'my language had deserted me, it felt as if it had been torn right out of my throat' – is graphic and violent. The fragment of isiZulu chanting that Mary quotes (and translates, incompletely, in a footnote) is from a South African struggle song (i.e. anti-apartheid, liberation songs). This is interesting in that it is an embodied form of indigenous knowledge that does not subscribe to western notions of identification or authorship (i.e. like most struggle songs it does not have a title or author and, at the time of writing, has no internet presence). Mary could only have accessed this information by consulting her black peers. Like Kefuwe, she too – from a different positionality – reached out for assistance with translations for her language narrative.

In a focus group discussion, three years later, Mary returns to her feelings of exclusion, this time making the racial dynamic explicit when she says:

> Like everyone knew what was happening and like all the white people were like, what's going on? . . . that's when I wish I knew how to speak isiZulu or Xhosa so I could partake in that. Like I felt like a spectator, not even like a participant . . . like if we could understand then we'd be like, yes, we agree, but we were like, what's happening?

Her description of being a 'spectator' and not a 'participant' conveys both her imagined voicelessness (she can only see, not speak) and her inability to act or to be agentic. In this situation her position is thus raced, languaged and rendered marginal. Like Jacques, Mary's discomfort seems to be at least partially tied to having her racialized monolingual habitus rendered visible. Botsis (2017: 99), drawing on Steyn's (2012) notion of 'the ignorance contract', makes links between what she refers to as 'ignorant whiteness' and language in the following way:

> The white linguistic habitus in South Africa is structured by the objectively dominant position of white South Africans historically, and reproduced through *an active* (generative and structuring) *ignorance of other languages* (our italics).

We know from the two extracts that neither Jacques nor Mary can speak an African language but over and above this, they seem to lack knowledge *about* African languages. Jacques, for example, does not seem to know that isiXhosa is not a dominant language in Gauteng and thus very unlikely to be offered at school level here, especially alongside isiZulu since they are mutually intelligible Nguni languages; and Mary indicates that she could not tell what language students were chanting in. Over the years, a majority of white, middle-class, English-speaking students have self-identified as monolingual. By virtue of its ongoing linguistic privilege, English enables a new, post-apartheid generation of white, English-speaking students to have a trouble-free language experience, moving seamlessly between home, school and university as virtually monolingual English students. This is so despite the fact that the national curriculum makes it compulsory for all students to study a second language throughout their schooling. Most white, English-speaking students continue to take Afrikaans as their second language – either through choice (as alluded to by Jacques) or because that is the only second language a school offers – and thus leave school without having learnt an indigenous African language. Their inability to speak an African language and their surprise at the complex, multilingual lives of their black peers can be seen as features of 'ignorant whiteness' (Botsis 2017). By referring to themselves as monolingual in English, they are disavowing their competence in Afrikaans, however partial that may be, and quite pointedly delimiting their own linguistic horizons.

The course thus functions pedagogically to raise awareness of linguistic diversity and of how the dominance of English can be experienced as oppressive for students who navigate this linguistic terrain without default access to English. What they do with this awareness, however, differs from student to student. For example, the vignette quoted at the start of Chapter 3 was written by Ariela, a white, English-speaking student from the 2017 cohort who also self-identifies as monolingual. She expresses the realization that 'All this time [she] had been wrong, most people did not communicate the same way [she] did'. But she then proceeds to enumerate the insights she has gained about the often fraught relationship between language and identity from being exposed to her peers' language histories in class, undertaking to learn more about her peers.

Given that the course valorizes multilingualism, it is unsurprising that both of these students view their inability to speak an African language as a limitation. However, for Jacques and Mary the experiences of discomfort which they narrate do not appear to prompt them to reflect on their own positionalities and the privileges that English confers on them. Instead they remain locked in their affective responses and respond to their perceived vulnerability by retreating further into whiteness. The absence of critical self-awareness in these extracts (and their respective full narratives) is disappointing. We have previously analysed narratives by white English-speaking students in early student cohorts (see John in Mendelowitz and Ferreira 2007; and Michelle in Ferreira and Mendelowitz 2009b) that showed greater levels of criticality. Perhaps it was easier to be self-reflective and magnanimous about whiteness in the early years; Jacques's and Mary's racialized discomfort and inability to do this points to a possible backlash to a perceived threat to whiteness.

A question that needs to be asked is: Why, after more than twenty-five years of democracy, supported by a raft of language policies aimed at redress and the protection of language rights and linguistic diversity, is it still possible for young people in South Africa to be monolingual? Or, more specifically, for young people not to speak – however imperfectly – an African language? What are the social and systemic conditions prevailing in South Africa that continue to enable this? Can this situation be ascribed simply to the gap between policy and its implementation? Or are the situations in which Jacques and Mary find themselves indicative of the ongoing boundaried nature of whiteness and its linguistic accomplice, English? The widening of access to English needs to happen in tandem with a widening of access to African languages. As Janks has stated:

> Only when desire runs in both directions – when those of us who have English desire other languages alongside those who desire ours; only when all of our identities are informed by linguistic diversity and cultural hybridity; only when power is not reserved for one global language, only then can we reverse the history of linguistic and cultural imperialism. (2004: 40)

More needs to be done at school level not only to provide the opportunities for English-speaking learners to study and use an African language proficiently but to stimulate in them the appetite to do so.

Finally, according to Luckett's (2016) race/class/culture categories, as white students in the post-colonial university space, Jacques and Mary function as full citizens vis-à-vis black students whose various degrees of marginalization constrain their agency. Yet, their narratives suggest that not *all* institutional spaces function in this way *all* the time. The incidents they narrate are disruptive of 'the power of the monolingual English habitus in elite university spaces' and radically circumscribe the 'ubiquitous power of whiteness in the university space' (Botsis 2017: 94), if only temporarily. While these experiences do not suggest that English is in danger of losing its dominant institutional position, they do suggest that African languages are increasingly being seen as carriers of linguistic capital, even if it is – in this case – largely in the social or interstitial (or unofficial) spaces of university life.

Language, oppression and race

The final narrative presented is written by Akeem, an Indian male student who attended an elite, historically white, all boys' school. The focus of this extract is on his experiences of language and race at school during the time when the #FeesMustFall protests were unfolding in the universities.

Akeem: My language and my politics are inextricable (2017)

'Fuck blacks. Fuck n--. They're stupid. They're illiterate. They smell. They never shower.'

The words filled me with a rage that I couldn't fully understand. Scribbled untidily on the door of a bathroom stall at my school, I kept going back to photos of the racist graffiti, taken by my friend Thato, to make sure that I was reading them correctly. It wasn't long before they were circulated around the school.

Inspired by the wave of anti-colonial student protests that had erupted around the country, a WhatsApp group was formed between a number of senior black [school name] students. It served as a platform for voicing frustrations at both implicit and explicit experiences of racism at the school, for debating views regarding how to go about addressing institutional racism, and for sharing experiences related to the notion that there are 'different ways to be black' (Tusini 2016b). The fact that I had been added to the group suggested a recognition that both black African students and Indian students shared common struggles; against 'micro-aggressions', misunderstood sensitivities, and conflicts that arose out of being at a white institution, with English, and not being white, 'definitely not [being] white' (Tusini 2016b). It was on this group that the photos were first shared, and I knew then that I wasn't alone in my rage.

My experience of the school taught me to look at this incident not as an isolated one, but as one in a long line of instances in which language had been used to oppress, to dehumanize, to insult and to assert aggression against black bodies. Just as Gloria Naylor (2000) came to 'hear' the word 'n-- r' as a means of humiliation, I would argue that many black students at the school (myself included, in some instances) came to hear backhanded compliments such as 'You're so eloquent' and questions such as 'Can I call you Danny?'[2] as being reflective of far more sinister, deeply rooted attitudes.

These experiences of racism, regardless of whether or not they impacted me directly, had a profound effect on the development of my linguistic identity. The struggle to make sense of the discomfort I felt at times, while I was at the school, motivated me to deepen my understanding of concepts such as racism, social justice, colonialism etc. This was achieved through listening to and engaging in conversations with anti-Apartheid activists, reading books such as 'The Autobiography of Malcolm X' and 'Black Skin, White Masks' by Frantz

Fanon, and learning from the experiences of individuals like my brother, who had attended the school and had dealt with many of the struggles that I faced. Through this process, not only was my identity shaped as far as my language use was concerned, with words like 'coloniality' and 'tokenism' finding their way into my idiolect for instance, but it was also shaped in terms of my understanding of the world and the issues facing it. On more than one occasion, issues like 'institutional racism' found their way into my speeches as school public speaking competitions.

The racist graffiti incident can be used to highlight a number of points relating to the relationship between language, context and identity, and the relationship between language and power. Tusini's 'Language Matters' article (2016b) is particularly relevant in this regard, as it focuses on some of the struggles that arise when trying to negotiate black identities in predominantly white institutions.

That a (presumably) white student felt comfortable while writing these words on a bathroom stall door, with little to no fear of consequence, is quite revealing of the power dynamics that existed (or were assumed) in this situation. While the origin of these power dynamics may be left for another discussion, it could be argued that the incident serves to illustrate how language can be used/manipulated as a tool for domination over others (Kaschula and Anthonissen, 1995). In many ways, it highlights the point made by Kaschula and Anthonissen that in order to oppose the manipulation of language for the sake of domination, and in order for us to engage in 'enlightened language practices', the relationship between language, context, identity and variety needs to be understood. [. . .]

In conclusion, as far as my linguistic biography is concerned, I have seen that just as language can be used to oppress and discriminate against individuals on the basis of race/gender/national identity etc., my experiences of language have taught me that it can also be used to stand up against oppression and discrimination.

Akeem's language narrative moves beyond the tensions and negotiations among different languages that most of the student narratives deal with and looks at language as a tool that can be used both to oppress and discriminate and to stand up against oppression and discrimination. In his focus group discussion (27 February 2020), Akeem spoke about having used the writing of his language narrative as a form of 'therapeutic catharsis' to reflect on experiences that had built up over time at school. It is the most overtly politicized narrative of this student cohort and is steeped in the kinds of discourses that have emerged during the #FeesMustFall movement. It is significant that Akeem's schooling context is one of historical whiteness and privilege. His school, like that where the protests against school rules for black hair took place, forms part of the elite schools where students took up fallist discourses in various ways. Akeem makes this connection explicit in the focus group, saying that the #fmf protests 'found resonance' at his school. He points out that '2016 was a year in which black students had sort of expressed that enough is enough and that they'd started to experience the frustration using some of the discourse that was coming out of the universities'. Chikane (2018) would argue that these are precisely the schools that give rise to the 'coconuts' who have the agentive resources to 'lead the revolution'. In an argument that resonates with that of Luckett (2016), he contends that students from these elite schools, like himself, 'carry both the economic and social capital to create new forms of discourses within the mainstream narrative of South Africa' (Chikane 2018: 7). Or, as Chigumadzi (2015) has argued, where black students, rather than becoming 'agents of whiteness', can leverage their 'proximity to whiteness' to effect change from within white institutional spaces. But it is a precarious and fraught position, as can be seen in the questions Chikane (2018: 15) asks:

> Can coconuts be trusted with a revolution? Can they undergo a process of rejection that involves the removal of their complicity within a system that offers them opportunities for advancement, while simultaneously explicitly denouncing it, using the privileges the same system has vested in them?

A key focus of Akeem's narrative is how to deal with the problem of institutional racism, specifically the need to negotiate black identities in white spaces. Like Refilwe, he too references the interviewee who talks of taking up English but 'definitely' not being white (Tusini 2016b). In fact, the short media article by Tusini that the students were given to read draws on her own work (Tusini 2016a) on black students in the 1980s who, as a result of the early racial desegregation of private schools, were the first to inhabit white spaces. At that point, such spaces were unchartered territory and Tusini argues that the 'first guinea pig black bodies' to have access to these previously forbidden spaces – and the ability to succeed in them – experienced this as a victory at the time; but in retrospect it is possible to discern the dual process of assimilation and alienation that played itself out in that generation of black students. Akeem and his school peers of colour can thus be seen as the next generation of black students navigating white spaces. They are Chikane's empowered but complicit, revolutionary coconuts. And 'to be young, black and conscious in South Africa is to be in a state of constant and uncertain liberty' (Chikane 2018: 20).

What is interesting is that despite his politically engaged stance, in his language narrative Akeem does not raise issues around the position of English as a colonial language in South Africa. He is also silent about his own relationship with English and other languages in his life. However, a poem which he wrote in response to the language metaphor task in the earlier part of the course gives some insight into his thoughts on this.

Shipwrecked

I've washed up on the shores of English
and set up shelter on its sands.
I've lost my ship,
and behind me are the oceans,
    of Arabic
    and Urdu.
I let their waters pass over my feet, in the spaces between my toes.
Amir Sulaiman says that, 'Anyone can imagine a sea without shore.
It's harder to imagine a shore without sea.'
Holding a handful of sand in my hand,
    I let the remnants of the Anglo-Saxon
    fly off into the wind.
The beach is beautiful,
    but I cannot help but look out longingly,
into the ocean.

Akeem's poem is resonant with meaning, capturing both loss and ambivalence. While the 'shores of English' on which he stands are beautiful, he longs for the languages of his past. But perhaps the most poignant irony is that he has captured his feelings for Arabic and Urdu so evocatively in English, the language on which he has 'washed up'. In the focus group, he spoke briefly about his insecurities about his language identity, arising in part from the intergenerational language loss of Urdu and Gujarati. Given the political engagement he demonstrated as a first-year student, it was not surprising to hear that his political education was ongoing when he talked about critical Muslim studies and decoloniality, as well as his desire to begin 'carving out niches where we can develop new ways of thinking'.

Conclusion

The language narratives analysed in this chapter bear out the comment that South Africa can be seen as 'an ontological laboratory for the doing and undoing of linguistic and racial identity politics' (Rudwick 2022: 131). Looking at these narratives alongside the earliest ones, analysed in Chapter 4, we find them raising familiar issues that play themselves out in new ways, as well as bringing new issues to the fore. Students' voices are assertive, and sometimes politicized, and there is a new focus on racialized linguistic identities. Jacques's and Mary's narratives demonstrate their awareness of how their white, English monolingualism places them in a deficit position in the shifting racio-linguistic dynamics of university spaces, and indexing forms of 'ignorant whiteness' that, in this case, continue to support the hegemony of English. For Kefuwe, her mastery of English has ensured access to ongoing social mobility but, owing to her uncritical ownership of and assimilation into English, she too contributes to the growing power of English. Akeem and Refilwe, however, both demonstrate a self-reflexive awareness of their raced language identities, explicitly positioning themselves as English-dominant speakers but 'definitely not white' (Tusini 2016b). And it is this move that introduces the possibility of delinking English from whiteness, something that we believe must become the guiding principle of our developing pedagogy.

So we now reach the point where the question we are asking is: What could delinking English from whiteness look like in a course that aims to teach English? And how could we develop a pedagogic approach that facilitates that in classrooms of the Global South? Refilwe herself provides insight into the kind of *disposition* that would facilitate this process. But we need to explore what this might look like in practice in the classroom. We need to work collaboratively with school teachers and our respective students to experiment with ways of teaching English that strip it of intimidating veneer, encourage in students a sense of agency and ownership over English and value innovative, playful, even irreverent English usage while also providing access to standard English. Drawing inspiration from Milani (2019: 24), we propose the idea of using 'undisciplined practices' to teach the discipline of English. By 'undisciplined practices' we mean those ways of teaching and learning that facilitate epistemic disobedience (Mignolo 2007b) and can thus be used to delink (Mignolo 2007a) English from its construction as white, standard and Anglonormative. To do so constitutes a precarious balancing act between access and critique, between standardization and creative appropriation. Thus far we have caught only glimpses of what this might look like in practice in the English classroom but if there is any chance that work of this nature could further challenge the linguistic inequalities in society, then we have the responsibility to investigate it.

Conclusion: Final Voices

Given that the inspiration for our teaching and research on the sociolinguistics course has always come from student voices and we have made a case for how important these are, it seems appropriate to end this book with a selection of them. Thus, we have chosen not to write a conventional conclusion, but rather to end with a metalogue in which students are in conversation with the course. A metalogue is 'a form of reflective dialogue where the mode of conversation reflects the topic being explored' (Coghlan 2018: 386). The 'topic' in this case emerged from a provocative question asked by a reviewer of the book proposal. They wanted to know whether there was evidence of the impact of the sociolinguistics course on students. We do not believe that the reviewer wanted this question answered in a narrow instrumentalist way with impact and learning reduced to numbers. We have chosen to use a metalogue as a discursive continuation of the challenge our work poses to monoglossic forms of language education. This choice, we argue, can be harnessed as a southern methodology for representing our data (Heugh et al. 2022), because the genre lends itself to expressions of multiple ways of knowing through the individual and idiosyncratic voices (Staller 2007) of our students. It also shows the ways in which all of our learnings on the course are co-constructed and relational. In describing the relational nature of the metalogue, Bateson and Bateson (1988: 4) see relationality as 'the conversation . . . always moving between intellect and emotion, always dealing with relationship and communication, within and between systems'. The emphasis on movement encourages a creative and expansive narrative style that conventional endings are likely to constrain.

The data for this metalogue comes from student focus groups. At the beginning of 2020, we invited third- and fourth-year students, who had completed the course in their first or second year of study, to participate in focus group conversations. We sent students questions to think about and asked them to read through their language narratives and bring them to the focus group. Interestingly, many of them had kept their narratives. We completed four focus group conversations with a total of fourteen students. In two focus groups a part-time assistant lecturer who had taken the course in her undergraduate degree joined the conversations, adding her insights. We asked the students to reflect on their experiences of the course: what they had learnt about linguistic identities, their thoughts on narrative as a form of assessment and whether this course had affected how they thought about themselves as language teachers or their practice as language teachers. The focus groups were strongly dialogic as students reflected on the course and their learning. They built on each other's answers, returned to ideas, shared common experiences, laughed and articulated a range of strong opinions. While the transcript of each conversation is fascinating reading in itself, we have interwoven all four.

The chapter is divided into the following themes that were striking for us: the influence of narrative as a pedagogical tool; the value of metalanguage for developing a critically reflexive stance; how interactions with diversity reshape the self; and how past, present and future come together as students reveal their developing practice as teachers and in some instances show an awareness of being able to take action. Reconstituting the focus group transcripts to create a metalogue is a way of working at a new metalevel (Tobin and Roth 2002) that provides insights about student engagement. We use this new dialogic reconfiguration to contemplate past learnings and possibilities for a multilingual pedagogy.

The influence of narrative as a pedagogical tool

There are three elements to this theme. The first deals with narrative ways of knowing, the second reveals the stark contrasts that students draw between academic writing and narrative writing and the third presents other perspectives on the experience of narrative writing and the challenges associated with this genre.

Narrative ways of knowing

Shakira: What stood out for me in this course was the fact that it wasn't completely academic, so I could get in touch with myself. So, in writing I realised there were certain parts of myself that I had never questioned or understood, and this helped me to explore those . . . things such as my culture or heritage, I've never really thought so far about those things, and this helped me to dig deeper into who I am as a person.

Zanele: So, I feel like the narrative allows you to explore yourself, it allows you to get to know yourself in ways that you wouldn't have, had you not been given the chance. Because till now, even though you write so many things, you get to develop your mind-set, and everything, but then this sort of assessment makes you look into yourself deeper. It makes you consider so many things that you wouldn't have, had you been confined to just an essay in which, 'Okay, read this extract and a few things and then assess yourself in a sentence or two.' So . . . ja, I prefer it, because it even makes you get to know how diverse people are. Things that you wouldn't think if it was just you and the readings.

Shakira: Doing a narrative . . . it becomes more personal, and I'd rather write about something that is personal because then I have personal knowledge on that, whereas if I'm writing about something that's new to me, I can't really think deeply about it because I lack that knowledge. I can't engage as much as I would like to because it's something so foreign to me that I have to force myself to actually pick a side. Whereas with the narrative you know, okay, this is how I feel about something.

Thulisile: [It] made me kind of reflect on my own life and how I've been with language since then. But now all of a sudden, it made me be like, 'English is not the same for everyone, so how do we then look at that in the classroom?' In first year already I was like, that is something I need to look into. And then from that, I started having more questions, I started engaging more with other people in class. I feel as if, before this, I would have been a person who would have stuck to themselves, attend and leave, attend and leave, but all of a sudden, I was interested in other people, because now I had my story, and this was my story, and I want to know, 'What's your story?'

The academic essay versus narrative writing

Tracy: And in that first year, we got that awful education essay (*laughs*) that everyone hated, that everyone probably did really badly and I did really badly in. And it was very formal. It was strict and you have to mention certain things, you have to show certain things, and it never allowed for you to think outside the box. And then to get this English assignment, it was very different to what we had experienced . . . where we're allowed to give our own opinions, our own voice, our own story.

Thulisile: So how did I feel about being assessed through narrative? That was the best thing to ever happen in my entire existence probably at Wits . . . because after all these academic essays, where it's not about you, it's about who said what and how and when, and that's just you putting all those pieces together to submit. I feel as if academic essays don't do justice. So, in a way writing a narrative was great and that made me think about how we might be having options to actually further [our] studies or assess people . . . Because looking at the narratives that we did, we could even use our own languages, we just had to put in little things there at the bottom [footnotes]; that was something new that I actually learnt in first year.

Kefuwe: It helped me do introspection. And I think for me, with introspection comes critical thinking, because, like, you are thinking on a much deeper level. Because honestly, with the standard academic essay, you are not really thinking, you are taking the content from the reading and you're taking the content from the lecture and the content from the tutorial and you're putting it in new words. And you are referencing. There's not really much thought that goes into it. It's a parrot thing. So, this narrative allows for introspection, it allows for critical thinking, it allows room for creativity. Because at the end of the day, I feel like, I don't know why, but like on the part of the marker, I think it was more interesting to mark these than it is to mark your regular academic essays. . . . So ja . . . I think it was good in that it encouraged thinking in a different way, and in a different way for everyone. Everyone could think in their own direction and there was no . . . there was very little limits. And even the quotes we had to use, the references we had to use, weren't your traditional references. It was things written by normal everyday people in normal everyday language. So those are also readings that are easy to work with. Because you're not stuck on every sentence trying to figure out the meaning of a word.

Narrative as an uncomfortable writing experience

Mary: I remember grappling with this assignment. Yoh! It was like a fight, I was like, oh, I don't know what I'm going to write, I would type and then delete. But I actually really enjoyed it because it's something that I'd never really thought about. And I think it was so important to do, like going to university in such a big institution when there's so many different people from different backgrounds and languages and cultures, like it really makes you think.

Maria: I think I also had a pretty similar experience. It was kind of like a more stressful thing for me, I was just like, I'd rather it just be an academic essay, it's actually easier for me just to write academic because . . . I struggle more to be a reflective person and to write about myself and all of that type of stuff. But . . . it really did force me to think deeply on a lot of these issues because if it was an academic essay, I probably wouldn't have assessed a whole bunch of things around my surname and around how people talk, you know? So, it did probably solidify the concepts a lot better, but at first it was difficult because I was like, I don't have anything to write about, I don't want to write about myself.

Nonhlanhla: So, I had to be okay with exposing some parts of my life that were very personal and very difficult to go back to and actually think about. So, it was very emotional to a certain degree. It was also letting go of something, this was just part of my journey, so let me share it with some people. So it was not about language, but talk about our whole life, centred around all languages. But once I was okay with that, it was like, 'I'm going to share my language experiences and I'm going to get it out there, and I'm going to be okay with being exposed' (*laughs*) . . . ja, so it was about me letting go of that and saying, 'Let me just let this go, this is actually a thing to share, an experience to share.' Ja, so it was like that . . . it was therapeutic.

(Meta)language and critically reflexive stances

We are interested in how everyday ways of knowing that are embodied and shaped by time, place and disciplinary knowledge can work together productively. As the students' comments in the previous section indicate, their immersion into academic disciplines is often thwarted by the reading and writing they are required to do, and the acquisition of disciplinary language, rather than being useful, is alienating. Working with narrative enables the personal and academic to rub up against each other in ways that provide new insights and challenge orthodoxies. In this section students talk about the ways in which the disciplinary language of sociolinguistics enabled insights into the relationships between language, identity and power.

Zanele: The impact that the course had is that more than anything you've made me aware of parts of language, or how language is used, previously I wouldn't have thought about it at all, it was just, 'Okay, you just talk, you write, whatever', like it means nothing. But now it allowed me to be conscious about the way I use language and how language can either be used to elevate you or just bring you down, because that was the heart of my languages.

Velaphi: Okay. So same as Zanele said, I had only focused on language as a tool to communicate. But this course forced me in a way to think much more deeply about language. That it's not only about using it to communicate but it taught me about different languages like dialects. And I'd never been forced to think about languages having their own dialect. So that's what stood out for me mostly, that's my biggest impact, ja.

Zanele: Yes. And even in the African languages, because like with me I just knew like Xitsonga as okay, there's just Xitsonga. I don't speak the right version of this. Someone else speaks the right version. Only to find out that, okay, depending on which part of Limpopo you're in, that also affects the way we speak, and then I was able to also locate my dialect and actually see that it was not my doing but also like the place that I was in.

Akeem: The thing that stood out for me about this particular course was having to think more consciously about my linguistic identity. And then having some sort of theoretical framework that would allow me to deepen my thinking.

Shakira: I just want to say, I think the course also helped me to give terms to things that I couldn't explain or feel . . . the way I was feeling. So, for instance, in my essay I compared myself to other types of coloureds, and I used the idea of standard and non-standard English. Before that I wouldn't have associated it with that term, so the course just gave a term to something that I was feeling or ways that I would act and things like that. There was an article in the course that I could relate to a lot because . . . I think it was Candice . . . she went through similar things, and it was just this idea of us versus them and 'Who's right, who's wrong?' So you start to challenge yourself as a person and 'Why am I a certain way? How do I make other people understand who I am as an individual?' And you come to varsity, and you expect everybody to sort of be open-minded and academic, you know, in terms of the way they think, because we're all here doing the same thing. But it's not the reality of it. So, when people see you, they expect certain whatever-it-is from you, but if you speak differently then it's sort of 'Why do you speak that way?' And even when people don't see you, it's sort of like they have this idea of how you should look, how you sound, and that's a stereotype that we need to eradicate because that's labelling people. We can't label each other based on how we sound without seeing each other, or even seeing each other, now you're labelling me because of what you see. And that's a problem in society because now it's excluding others, marginalising, you know, there's a lot to it.

Akeem: Ja, so I mean there's also labelling in this context of xenophobia and the sort of discourse around people who are immigrants, right, and how the language that's used to talk about it. Like people use words without thinking more critically about the effect that that language is having on entire communities of people who are being labelled one thing and reduced to a particular idea. I think . . . it does show how language influences our actions and it influences the steps that people will then take, like the conversations that we have. And when people don't speak up and people don't challenge the xenophobic language it just breeds, right, and continues to be normalised. Which is why I feel it's necessary to challenge it when you see it.

Diversity and the reshaping of self

How to engage productively with diverse student cohorts is an important question in teacher education particularly in light of the ways in which so many international educational policies and practices are assimilationist, exclusionary, racist and work to vilify difference (van Avermaek et al. 2018). We see our narrative heteroglossic pedagogy as more than just a pedagogy for diversity, or a pedagogy for working in a multilingual context. In our work as teacher educators, we also need to think about how the pedagogical and content choices we make present alternative ways of knowing, doing and being in classrooms so that student teachers are able to deal with diversity (Conteh 2018). Encouragement of critical reflexivity is a key element in the course design as we want students to develop an awareness of self and others in relation to the language practices and pedagogies that they will take into the classroom. Students' 'encounters across difference' (Stroud 2018: 18) disrupt taken-for-granted assumptions and have the potential to change how we all are and can be in the world.

> Velaphi: I didn't think much about how people are sometimes forced to adapt to an area because of language. Some people learn language out of interest but there's one student in my class who shared her story, saying her family had to move to different places, each and every year, and so they were forced to become a chameleon. So, she was always adapting to the area. When they speak English, she had to learn English; if the area [was one] where Afrikaans was dominating, she had to learn Afrikaans. So that's how she interacted and learnt these languages so far. So, I didn't think about any of that. I thought language was about your mother tongue or the tongue that is spoken in your family and that's it.

Zanele: So for me, also with the linguistic identities of people, I feel like there's another language narrative in the context where this writer was talking about – how you look at someone and then you assume that sometimes they might identify with you, just by looking at them, and then you assume that, 'Okay, because you look like this, this is how you're supposed to be.' So, with the language identities it gave me something that I wouldn't have gotten had you not been exposed to those linguistic identities. I would have continued assuming so many things about people without actually getting to know them. The whole linguistic identity allowed me to actually look into people or just wait to be told or know more about people without just assuming so many things that you just assume about a person just by looking at them and making your own conclusions.

Akeem: When I reflect on it, I realise that I had a few insecurities about my linguistic identity before I actually went through the process of unpacking it a bit more critically and consciously. So that may have been a source of insecurity, like 'What language should I be accustomed to and familiar with?' The other came in the form of accent and dialect. So, now going through this white school, it changes your accent, right, and you adapt obviously to be understood within that kind of space, but there's also a degree of these expectations that are created about what a good accent sounds like, or how do you speak well in a certain context. And I remember meeting somebody and they asked me where I'm from, and I said, 'I'm from Mayfair.' And they said, 'Oh, okay, but you don't sound like you're from Mayfair.' And even though it wasn't a malicious kind of thing that they were saying, I remember being quite taken aback by the comment because obviously Mayfair is an area that's very close to my heart and it's very much a big part of my identity. And yet, because of the way that I speak it's become a way of differentiating. So, it's a question like, so what do people from Mayfair actually sound like, right?

Past, present and future: New ways of knowing and being

While it is impossible to know what students take into their practice as teachers once they graduate, especially what they take from a first-year course that is one of many in a four-year degree programme, students talked about how their experience in the course fed into their experiences on their teaching practical and what this means for them as future teachers. In addition to developing identities as language teachers, it is clear that for some students the past, present and future operate together so that their learning from this course and their engagement with decolonial thinking has become part of taking action in classrooms and other social contexts.

Becoming teachers

Akila: So, I went to a school where most of the children spoke English, it was just kind of, for me, everyone spoke English, in my mind. And after this course and at university I realised that it's difficult to speak English, it's not an easy language, some words make absolutely no sense, the spellings make no sense, and some children might not understand and it's okay to let other languages into the classroom and for people to be able to express themselves in other languages so that we can help them further their education.

Thulisile: In my first year for teaching experience, I was in a very location-like [township] school . . . and I've never schooled at one of those schools. So, if it wasn't for sociolinguistics, I think I would have approached it in a very different manner. I would never have had an understanding with any of the learners in the classroom. But because of what I already did and already looking into other people's experiences and so on, I was able to take that into account when I actually was in the classroom, to know that, okay, not everyone is going to be speaking English at home. Not everyone is going to pronounce this in this manner and so on and whatnot.

Nonhlanhla: I'm always, always aware and conscious of how the kids that I teach relate to English, because . . . well, I've gone to township schools, so English is seen as a whip, if I may be that graphic. It's seen like something to punish the kids with, as something that they hate, an imposition on them. So, what I've tried to do now is, open up the communication 'Let's talk about English, what is it about this English that scares you so much? What are your insecurities about this English?' And we draw a monster on the board, 'Let's say this is the English monster. So what features could you add?' So they make English look very scary, and I say, 'Do you realise that you can actually own English and make English your own? You've always done that.' I give them examples that, for example, when you speak in a way, you speak to each other you actually change some English words to make them relevant to you, that is you speaking English, that is your own that you've made. But now once you do that, find out what the standard word for that is so that you can know about your own creation and the standardised. And in that way then they are able to get more excited about any English, they will throw those words around . . . we actually terrorise English, we take it down, we call it words, we give it names, and then we bring it up today and we make it our own. I say, 'Okay, now English, you can be our friend.' That's what the sociolinguistic module made me more conscious about, how we present English and how we can get the kids to actually own English and let's think about what English should be.

Thulisile: English was never interesting for me, to be honest, it was just one of those things that I had to get done. It was never interesting for me. But all of a sudden, I realised with this that, 'You know what, actually in our first year already we're having something very different from English, in the module, so maybe in classrooms as well we might be able to find grounds of making English interesting the way I was finding the course interesting.' So, in a way, that kind of changed a lot for me, because now I'm here, I want to be an English teacher, I want to be a really good English teacher.

Tracy: And as the course has gone on, I've started to realize that it's not really about what you teach the kids, but what you're trying to teach us as teachers. It's how we look at the kids, it's not just a bunch of thirty or so kids learning a language. It's learning who they are, it's learning their identities through this language and it's finding out different things about people. And I think that one of the beautiful things about English is that it can bring us together and help people learn more about each other, rather than this barrier that a lot of people see it as. It can be a barrier but opened in the correct way it can be a very useful tool, especially as a teacher, to learn more about your kids and in that way learn how to teach them better . . . not just in English but in everything.

Taking action

Velaphi: Right now, I'm learning about the history behind all the languages so that I can understand them better. So now that we've learnt about things like decolonisation, we have to go back to understanding . . . if one wants to understand what language should be used to teach the learners, then which one would we choose? So, I'm going back to history to just try to understand what could we do currently.

Akeem: In terms of where I'm now . . . I think being immersed in the academic space for the last few years has given me an opportunity to broaden that language of resistance in many ways. . . . So if I had to compare where I am now compared to first year, I would say that language base has expanded, and I've been able to articulate my thoughts a little bit more deeply now because now I understand how to tap into theory, how to substantiate my viewpoints a little.

Zanele: Now that *we're* looking at this, I feel like we're still at the same place because even when you talk about decolonisation, even of language itself, I feel like some languages are always put in the forefront and then some are always side-lined. . . . Early this year, there was that thing they were saying that all Tsonga people must go back to wherever they came from. And I'm like, wait, 'What do you mean, where must we go?' . . . And even now I feel like we're still at the same point, at the same place, instead of us talking about, 'Okay, how do you learn each other's languages?' Most people will just be like, 'Oh well, if this is the dominant language, stop complaining, just get on with the programme'. So, for me it's still really a problem. I still feel that way. But then more than anything to be quite honest, like this course has made me . . . if you go around, if there's anyone who's like the most Tsonga-tested on this campus, I'm that person (*laughter*). No, honestly, you know, and you will find people and they'll be like, 'You know I wish I was as proud as you are'. Because like I will just rant on, in the bus, you see like the bus is full, so when I say something, I'll say it in Tsonga. And then if someone says, 'I don't hear you', I'm like, '*Nami angikutwa*, I also don't hear you'. (*laughter*) And people are like, 'How do you do it? How do you stand your ground?' Because it's really hard if you're going to speak a language and everyone else is telling you that, no, no one is hearing you.

As we reach the end of this chapter, we are aware that readers may want an accounting of the ways in which the interviewer effect affected this data set. They may also want an acknowledgement that this data may be skewed by the small number of students who chose to participate in the focus groups. The voices of students who disliked this course or who have consigned it to hazy first-year memories are absent. The intention of this final chapter was not to go in search of an unchanging or fixed 'truth'. Rather we take up Walsh's (2020: 606) suggestion that a decolonial praxis entails 'thought-analysis-reflection-action'. The metalogue provides an entry point into student learning that comes into being through conversation that, while always partial and incomplete, enabled reflexive returns as we and the students engaged in a process of re-storying the course. As the three of us return to the transcripts, they enable us to see new aspects of student learning, which in turn provoke new questions and possibilities for action.

We have argued in this book that the power of narrative lies in its provisional nature, which enables the retelling and reconfiguring of knowing and being. We are struck by the memories and experiences students carry with them and how they've worked with them in generative ways. While we are not surprised that the act of telling stories about their histories or events has been a part of deepening what student teachers know about themselves (or as Shakira puts it, 'dig deeper into who I am as a person'), we are interested in what this storytelling means for teacher education. We aimed to show how validating the personal through narrative can be leveraged as a valuable pedagogical tool for students and what this means for practice. We've done this with a singular focus on the sociolinguistics course with the aim of cracking open the workings of its design, pedagogy, content and theory to meet our students' needs. However, in our reflection and discussions about this metalogue, we have realized that this focus needs to be opened up by considering this course in relation to the other English courses that students take as part of the degree programme. There is a need for dialogic engagement with this course and the others we teach in order to consider how its decolonial potential can be used productively to decolonize a curriculum in ways that are not tokenistic. There is an important lesson about the ways in which courses on 'diversity', 'inclusion' or 'multiculturalism' in teacher education programmes may have less impact on student classroom practice than desired. The sociolinguistics course was never designed to be a course about teaching methodologies. But it is clear from the examples in the metalogue that students can extrapolate implications for pedagogy from what they have learnt and implement these in their classrooms. There is power in multiple narratives, and as Thulisile reminds us, we all have stories. The possibilities of working collaboratively with students like Nonhlanhla, who have found ways to 'make friends with English', offer less hierarchical and more relational ways of working that are more responsive to the realities student teachers face in schools. It points to the potential of southern perspectives that offer productive ways of working to make the world better.

These student conversations are also a reminder that our own positionality as academics is different from that of first-year students. While this is an obvious point, it is worth unpacking what is behind the obvious. The sociolinguistics course is often one of the first that students take as they adjust to university life. We are comfortable in this space and in our discipline. Our academic habitus is steeped in the field of language education and fundamentally shapes how we think about and interpret the world. As Velaphi reminds us, some students have not thought about language other than as a form of communication and, as Akila points out, are unaware of the multilingual reality of the society they live in. One of our aims is to raise students' consciousness, in the Freirean sense, of the workings of language and of the ways in which we are all implicated in the workings of power. We are interested in how new ways of knowing emerge when students write their textual selves into being and reread their experiences at the university, in school classrooms, in their communities and across their social networks. The sociolinguistics course is a space in which to consider how the imposition of languages, entrenched views about which languages should be spoken, and how they should be spoken are shaped by a colonial history which continues to perpetuate acts of symbolic violence that have lasting material consequences on communities. In reflecting on the focus group conversations, we are reminded again that what we ask our students to share involves a form of emotional labour. They take risks in revealing aspects of themselves. While our hope has always been that adding their voice to the multitude of voices that constitute the course is generative and enables them to find points of contact and difference with which to tell their stories, it is easy after all these years to focus on the multi-voiced tapestry and forget the risks first-year students take in exposing themselves. Working with these metalogues is a reminder for us that our pedagogical practice is about explicitly acknowledging the collective trauma captured in these language histories and the courage with which students navigate their lives. It is what Stroud and Bock (2021) would refer to as a humanizing pedagogy.

We began this book by considering how the past, present and future are entangled. It is the multi-voicedness and linguistic diversity of students' pasts that are captured in evocative stories and creative turns of phrase that live on, as both we and the students carry them with us into the future. We've shown how students make critical and creative moves by using disciplinary language to name their worlds. We ask that students pull against centripetal forces that entrench monoglossic orientations and reinforce inequity. But this requires more than following prescribed lesson plans or following activities in textbooks. Students' accounts over the years, and the burgeoning activism of students in the metalogue, remind us that there is more work to be done. This educational project is not bound by classroom walls. Their 'language of resistance' may be different to ours as will be the actions they take in their different contexts. But when a young woman stands up on a bus to make herself heard, we all bear a collective responsibility to say with the power of our multiple voices, 'We hear you'.

Appendix 1 Published Language Narratives Used 2005–2020

Writer	Title	Publication	Text type	Context	Language issues emerging
Anzaldúa, Gloria	How to Tame a Wild Tongue	Anzaldúa, G. (2000a). *Borderlands/La Frontera: The New Mestiza.* 2nd edn, 75–86. San Francisco: Aunt Lute Books.	Memoir, poetry and historical analysis	1980s Texas, USA	The connection between home language, dialects and identity; linguistic persecution and linguistic terrorism from the perspective of a Chicana writer.
Botha, Elizabeth	Umntu Ngumntu Ngabantu	Botha, E. (1994). 'Umntu ngumntu ngabantu'. *BUA!* August: 30.	Magazine article	1950s and 1960s A multilingual township community in Johannesburg, South Africa	A personal exploration of the acquisition of African language varieties that co-exist in townships.
Cisneros, Sandra	*My Name*	Cisneros, S. (1984). *The House on Mango Street.* Houston, TX: Arte Público Press.	Semi-autobiographical novel	1950s and 1960s Hispanic area of Chicago, USA	A reflection on the different sounds and associations of a name in Spanish versus English; name and identity.
Fiona	Fiona's Story	Bird, C. (1998). *The Stolen Children.* Australia: Random House.	From a book of testimonies from Aboriginal children	1930s Australia	Language loss and trauma experienced by Aboriginal children who were forcibly removed from their parents by the Australian authorities.

(Continued)

Appendix 1 (Continued)

Writer	Title	Publication	Text type	Context	Language issues emerging
Harris, Rainier	This is the casual racism that I face at my elite high school	Harris, R. (2020). 'This is the causal racism that I face at my elite high school'. *The New York Times*, September 24.[a]	Newspaper article	Contemporary New York, USA	A New York high school student reflects on how his school dealt with racism through dialogue and restorative justice. Raises questions about whether language awareness helps bring about changes in attitudes.
Hong Kingston, Maxine	The Woman Warrior	Hong Kingston, M. (1967). *The Woman Warrior: Memoirs of a Girlhood among Ghosts*, 150–1. London: Picador.	Memoir	Setting alternates between China and California, USA	Childhood reflections on voice and identity in different languages and different school settings from the perspective of a Chinese-American author.
Johnston, Nicole	A Cocktail of Cultures	Johnston, N. (2006). 'A cocktail of cultures'. *Mail and Guardian*, 5 January: 20–1.	Newspaper article	2006 Johannesburg, South Africa	Explores different perspectives of identities among South African youth from minority ethnic communities.
Lyiscott, Jamila	Three Ways to Speak English	Lyiscott, J. (2014). 'Three ways to speak English'. TED Conferences.[b]	TED talk	Contemporary New York, USA	Explores the distinct flavours of the three different varieties of English she speaks with friends, parents and in the classroom; challenges negative attitudes towards non-standard varieties of English.

Matlwa, Kopano	*Coconut*	Matlwa, K. (2007). *Coconut*. Johannesburg: Jacana.	Novel	Contemporary South Africa	A young woman grapples with the relationship between language, culture and identity; explores the roles of English and Sepedi in her life; concerns about assimilation into whiteness.
Muzondiwe, Takunda	Yesterday I was African, Today I am Lost	Muzondiwe, T. (2019). Speaking for Justice: Working for Unity. Race Unity Speech Awards 2019.[c]	Spoken word poetry on YouTube	Contemporary New Zealand and Zimbabwe	Reflection on being an immigrant and ethnic minority living in New Zealand; the power of language and the relationship between language, home and identity.
Moya, Fikile-Ntsikelelo	Ekasi is My Roots	Moya, F.N. (2006). 'Ekasi is my roots'. *Mail and Guardian*, 5 January: 20.	Newspaper article	2006 Johannesburg, South Africa	Challenges assumptions about language heritage and identity from the perspective of an urban Black male.
Muleya, S.A.	The True African	Muleya, S. (2003). 'The true African'. *Y Mag*, December–January: 24.	Magazine article	2000s Johannesburg, South Africa	Navigating global culture without losing one's African identity; especially in relation to indigenous languages and African stories.

(Continued)

Appendix 1 (Continued)

Writer	Title	Publication	Text type	Context	Language issues emerging
Naylor, Gloria	A Question of Language	Naylor, G. (2000). 'A question of language', in D. McQuade and R. Atwan (eds), *The Writer's Presence: A Pool of Readings*, 474–7. Boston and New York: Bedford and St Martin's.	Essay	1950s Harlem, New York, USA	The shifting meanings of language and naming in different domains traversed by a working class African-American community.
Noah, Trevor	Son of Patricia	Noah, T. (2018). *Son of Patricia* (Comedy Show).	Stand-up comedy	Contemporary Chicago, USA	Explores the reappropriation of racist words and the way the meanings of words shift across contexts.
Obama, Barak	*Dreams from My Father*	Obama, B. (2007). *Dreams from My Father*. Edinburgh: Canongate.	Autobiography	1970s and 1980s Honolulu and Chicago, USA	Reflections on racial identity, language usage and group membership of a biracial young man.
Poplak, Richard	Ja, No, Man	Poplak, R. (2007). *Ja, No, Man: Growing up White in Apartheid Era South Africa*. Toronto: Penguin Canada.	Memoir	1970s and 1980s Johannesburg, South Africa	English/Afrikaans slang use by young white boys growing up in apartheid South Africa.
Rabinowitz, Nik	Languages in the New South Africa	Rabinowitz, N. (2008). *Languages in the new South Africa*. The South African Comedy Awards.[d]	Stand-up comedy on YouTube	Contemporary South Africa	The limits of self-expression in English and how different South African languages offer a range of ways to express oneself.

Rodriguez, Richard	*Aria: Memoir of a Bilingual Childhood*	Rodriguez, R. (1982). *The Hunger of Memory: The Education of Richard Rodriguez*. New York: Bantam Books.	Autobiography	1960s California, USA	Rodriguez, the son of Mexican immigrants, mounts a counter argument to the idea that Mexican/Spanish-speaking children in the United States should be educated in their mother tongue.
Selepe, Magoleng Wa	My Name	Selepe, M. (1981). 'My Name', in M. Chapman (ed.), *A Century of South African Poetry*, 350. Cape Town: Jonathan Ball.	Poem	Apartheid South Africa	Naming and identity; highlighting emotional impact of mispronunciation of name and of oppressive naming practices.
Smith, Zadie	Speaking in Tongues	Smith, Z. (2009). 'Speaking in Tongues'. *The New York Review of Books*.[e]	Public lecture at the NY Public Library in December 2008	1990s London and Cambridge University	An exploration of shifts in voice, accent and language variety across identities, especially biracial ones.
Soyinka, Wole	Telephone Conversation	Soyinka, W. (1963). 'Telephone Conversation', in R. Malan (ed.), *Worldscapes*, 146. Oxford: Oxford University Press.	Poem	London in the post-war decade	A satirical commentary on the racial prejudice encountered when attempting to rent an apartment.

(Continued)

Appendix 1 (Continued)

Writer	Title	Publication	Text type	Context	Language issues emerging
Swain, Martyn	The Single Language Polyglot	Swain, M. (1994). 'The single language polyglot'. *BUA!* August: 24.	Magazine article	1990s South Africa	An argument for a multilingual South African society in which people need not *speak* one anothers' languages in order to *understand* these languages, written from the perspective of a simultaneous translator.
Tusini, Nolwazi	Language Matters	Tusini, N. (2016b). 'Language Matters'. *City Press*, August: 2 and 6.	Newspaper article on the 2016 Ruth First Memorial Lecture	1990s Johannesburg, South Africa	Explores language loss and attitudes to English through interviews with Black students who attended historically white schools in the early 1990s.
wa Thiong'o, Ngũgĩ	*Decolonising the Mind*	Wa Thiong'o, N. (1986). *Decolonising the Mind: The Politics of Language in African Literature.* Oxford: James Currey.	Academic book	1950s Rural Kenya	The problems caused by studying in an alien language; language, identity and culture; language and colonization.
Wolfe, Tom	*I am Charlotte Simmons*	Wolfe, T. (2004.) *I am Charlotte Simmons.* London: Jonathan Cape.	Novel	Contemporary USA college setting	Race and youth language varieties; inclusion and exclusion.

[a]https://www.nytimes.com/2020/09/24/nyregion/regis-catholic-school-racism.html.

[b]https://www.ted.com/talks/jamila_lyiscott_3_ways_to_speak_english?utm_campaign=tedspread&utm_medium=referral&utm_source=tedcomshare

[c]https://www.youtube.com/watch?v=2jirm3x5waU

[d]https://www.youtube.com/watch?v=Ab8R4TBmmmM.

[e]https://www.nybooks.com/articles/2009/02/26/speaking-in-tongues-2/

Appendix 2 The Original Language Diary Activity

DIARY OF YOU AND YOUR LANGUAGES

Below is an example of Dimakatso's language diary. She sees herself as Tswana but she grew up in a Sotho environment. She is from Phomolong near Kroonstad in the Orange Free State.

Now make your own language diary in a similar way to Dimakatso's above. Then look at your diagram and think about who or what determines which language you speak in each context. Who has the power to choose which language you speak? Give reasons.

We all use different languages in different situations. We always try to use a language which will allow us to communicate effectively in a particular situation. Sometimes we can choose which language to use and at other times the choice is made for us – by other people or by the situation. There are also times when some people cannot choose the language that would allow them to communicate most effectively in a particular situation. Can you think of some examples?

Figure A2.1 Reproduced with permission from the Orlek estate.

Notes

Chapter 1

1   Only the first three weeks of the course are dealt with in this book because the focus is on language and identity. See Ferreira and Mendelowitz (2009a) for some discussion of the full six-week course.
2   It should be noted that 2009 is an anomalous year in that there was a group of over 200 in-service teachers from Limpopo province who were in first year. This accounts for the significant rise in the number of Sepedi, Tshivenda and Xitsongo speakers that year.
3   When it is capitalized, Home Language refers to the level of language subject in the official school curriculum. Uncapitalized term refers to the language spoken in the home.

Chapter 4

1   In an earlier article (Mendelowitz and Ferreira 2007) we indicated that Mashudu was from Venda (a rural area) and attended a rural school. While writing this chapter, we obtained new information that he was from Tembisa (an urban township) and attended an urban township school until he moved to a boarding school.
2   Tsotsitaal is a township variety of street speech that draws on urban vernaculars from African languages and Afrikaans. See Chapter 5 page 121 for further explanation.

Chapter 6

1   In an earlier version of this chapter (Mendelowitz 2017), Thando was categorized as a male. Subsequently, we obtained new information that confirmed that Thando is a female.

Chapter 7

1   We can't learn. We want them. [The student's translation as captured in this footnote is incomplete. It would be more accurate to transliterate the isiZulu speech as: 'We can't learn. Are we afraid of them? No, we aren't afraid of them, we want them.']
2   When the student's name is Endani, for instance.

References

Abdulatief, S., Guzula, X., and McKinney, C. (2021), 'Delinking from Colonial Language Ideologies: Creating Third Spaces in Teacher Education', in Z. Bock and C. Stroud (eds), *Language and Decoloniality in Higher Education: Reclaiming Voices from the South*, 135–58, London: Bloomsbury.

Achebe, C. (1976), *Morning Yet on Creation Day*, New York: Anchor Press.

Adams, M., Bell, L.A., with Goodman, D. and Joshi, K. (2016), *Teaching for Diversity and Social Justice*, London and New York: Routledge.

Adhikari, M. (2005), 'Contending Approaches to Coloured Identity and the History of the Coloured People of South Africa', *History Compass*, 3 (1): 1–16.

Adikhari, M. (2006), 'Hope, Fear, Shame, Frustration: Continuity and Change in the Expression of Coloured Identity in White Supremacist South Africa, 1910–1994', *Journal of Southern African Studies*, 32 (3): 467–87.

Alexander, N. (1997), 'Language Policy and Planning in the New South Africa', *African Sociological Review/Revue Africaine de Sociologie*, 1 (1): 82–92.

Alexander, N. (2009), 'Afrikaans as a Language of Reconciliation, Restitution and Nation Building', in *Roots-Conference Held at the University of the Western Cape*, 22–3. Available online: https://marxists.architexturez.net/archive/alexander/alexand erafrreconciliation.pdf (accessed 28 December 2021).

Amnesty International (2020), *Broken and Unequal: The State of Education in South Africa*. London: Amnesty International Ltd.

Antia, B.E. and Dyers, C. (2016), 'Epistemological Access through Lecture Materials in Multiple Modes and Language Varieties: The Role of Ideologies and Multilingual Literacy Practices in Student Evaluations of Such Materials at a South African University', *Language Policy*, 15 (4): 525–45.

Antia, B.E., Weldemichael, T., and Dyers, C. (2021), 'Multilingual Assessment: Levelling the Cognition–Emotion Playing Field at the University of the Western Cape', *Language Matters*, 52 (1): 50–70.

Anzaldúa, G. (2000a), *Borderlands/La Frontera: The New Mestiza*, 2nd edn, San Francisco: Aunt Lute Books.

Anzaldúa, G. (2000b), 'How to Tame a Wild Tongue', in D. McQuade and R. Atwan (eds), *The Writer's Presence: A Pool of Readings*, 311–21, Boston/New York: Bedford/ St. Martin's.

Arao, B. and Clemens, K. (2013), 'From Safe Spaces to Brave Spaces', in L.M. Landreman (ed.), *The Art of Effective Facilitation: Reflections from Social Justice Educators*, 135–50, Virginia: Stylus Publishing.

Armitage, J. (2022), 'Desert Participants Guide the Research in Central Australia', in K. Heugh, C. Stroud, K. Taylor-Leech, and P. De Costa. (eds), *A Sociolinguistics of the South*, 215–32, New York and London: Routledge.

Bailey, B. (2012), 'Heteroglossia', in M. Martin-Jones, A. Blackledge, and A. Creese (eds), *The Routledge Handbook of Multilingualism*, 499–507, New York and London: Routledge.

Bakhtin, M. (1981), *The Dialogic Imagination: Four Essays,* trans. C. Emerson and M. Holquist, Austin, TX: University of Texas Press.

Bateson, G. and Bateson, M. (1988), *Angels Fear: Toward an Epistemology of the Sacred*, New York: Bantam Books.

Baudot Morcillo, A. (2016), 'David Crystal: A Language Changes to Reflect Society', Terminology Coordination European Parliament, 20 October. Available online: https://termcoord.eu/2016/10/david-crystal-a-language-changes-to-reflect-society/ (accessed 24 December 2021).

Bauman, R. (1977), *Verbal Art as Performance*, Prospect Heights, IL: Waveland Press.

Bauman, R. (2004), *A World of Other's Worlds: Cross Cultural Perspectives on Intertextuality*, Malden, MA: Blackwell Publishing.

Bembe, P. and Beukes, A. (2007), 'The Use of Slang by Black Youth in Gauteng', *Southern African Linguistics and Applied Language Studies*, 25 (4): 463–72.

Bentley, K. and Habib, A. (2008), 'Racial Redress, National Identity and Citizenship in Post-Apartheid South Africa', in A. Habib and K. Bentley (eds), *Racial Redress and Citizenship in South Africa*, 3–32, Cape Town: HSRC Press.

Blackledge, A. and Creese, A., eds (2014), *Heteroglossia as Practice and Pedagogy*, Dordrecht: Springer.

Blommaert, J. (2010), *The Sociolinguistics of Globalisation*, Cambridge: Cambridge University Press.

Blommaert, J., Collins, J., and Slembrouck, S. (2005), 'Spaces of Multilingualism', *Language & Communication*, 25 (3): 197–216.

Bock, Z. and Stroud, C. (2019), 'Introduction', *Multilingual Margins*, 6 (1): 1–4.

Bock, Z and Stroud, C., eds (2021), *Language and Decoloniality in Higher Education: Reclaiming Voices from the South*, London.

Boler, M. and Zembylas, M. (2003), 'Discomforting Truths: The Emotional Terrain of Understanding Difference', in P.P. Trifonas (ed.), *Pedagogies of Difference*, 115–38, New York and London: Routledge.

Bomer, R. (2017), 'What Would it Mean for English Language Arts to Become More Culturally Responsive and Sustaining?', *Voices from the Middle*, 24 (3): 11.

Botsis, H. (2017), *Subjectivity, Language and the Postcolonial: Beyond Bourdieu in South Africa*, New York: Routledge.

Bradbury, J. (2020), *Narrative Psychology and Vygotsky in Dialogue: Changing Subjects.* London/New York: Routledge.

Bradbury, J. and Clark, J. (2012), 'Echoes of the Past in Imaginings of the Future: The Problems and Possibilities of Working with Young People in Contemporary South Africa', *Global Studies of Childhood*, 2 (3): 176–89.

Brooks, H. (2020), 'Youth Language in South Africa: The Role of English in South African Tsotsitaals' in R. Hickey (ed.), *English in Multilingual South Africa: The Linguistics of Contact and Change*, 176–95, Cambridge: Cambridge University Press.

Bruner, J. (1986), *Actual Minds, Possible Worlds*, Cambridge, MA: Harvard University Press.

Bucholtz, M. and Hall, K. (2005), 'Identity and Interaction: A Sociocultural Linguistic Approach', *Discourse Studies*, 7 (4–5): 518–614.

Bucholtz, M. and Hall, K. (2010), 'Locating Identity in Language', in C. Llamas and D. Watt (eds), *Language and Identities*, 18–28, Edinburgh: Edinburgh University Press.

Bundy, C. (2014), *Short-Changed? South Africa since Apartheid*, Auckland Park: Jacana Media.

Busch, B. (2014), 'Building on Heteroglossia and Heterogeneity: The Experience of a Multilingual Classroom', in A. Blackledge and A. Creese (eds), *Heteroglossia as Practice and Pedagogy*, 21–40, Dordrecht: Springer.

Busch, B. and Schick, J. (2007), 'Educational Materials Reflecting Heteroglossia: Disinventing Ethnolinguistic Differences in Bosnia-Herzegovina', in S. Makoni and A. Pennycook (eds), *Disinventing and Reconstituting Languages*, Clevedon: Multilingual Matters.

Canagarajah, S. (2006), 'TESOL at Forty: What are the Issues?', *Tesol Quarterly*, 40 (1): 9–34.

Casino, M. (2014), *Staff Riding*. VImeo. [Online Video]. Available online: https://vimeo .com/83486021. (accessed 1 May 2022).

Chadwick, R. (2017), 'Thinking Intersectionally with/through Narrative Methodologies', *Agenda*, 31 (1): 5–16.

Chigumadzi, P. (2015), 'Why I Call Myself a "coconut" to Claim My Place in Post-Apartheid South Africa', *Ruth First Lecture*. Available online: http://wits.journalism .co.za/wp-content/uploads/2019/03/Ruth-First-Lecture-by-Panashe-Chigumadzi -2015.pdf

Chikane, R. (2018), *Breaking a Rainbow, Building a Nation: The Politics behind #MustFall Movements*, Johannesburg: Picador Africa.

Chinguno, C., Kgoroba, M., Mashibini, S., Masilela, B., Maubane, B., Moyo, N., Mthombeni, A., and Ndlovu, H. (2017), 'Introduction: Reflexivity: Decolonising the Process', in C. Chinguno (ed.), *Rioting and Writing: Diaries of Wits Fallists*, 16–28, Johannesburg: Society, Work and Development Institute.

Clark, R., Fairclough, N., Ivanič, R., and Martin-Jones, M. (1990), 'Critical Language Awareness Part I: A Critical Review of Three Current Approaches to Language Awareness', *Language and Education*, 4 (4): 249–60.

Clark, R., Fairclough, N., Ivanič, R., and Martin-Jones, M. (1991), 'Critical Language Awareness Part II: Towards Critical Alternatives', *Language and Education*, 5 (1): 41–54.

Coghlan, D. (2018), 'Edgar Schein at 90: A Celebratory and Exploratory Metalogue', *The Journal of Applied Behavioral Science*, 54 (4): 385–98.

Comaroff, J. and Comaroff, J.L. (2012), *Theory from the South: Or, How Euro-America is Evolving Toward Africa*, 1st edn, London and New York: Routledge.

Conteh, J. (2018), 'From the Margins to the Centre: Multilingual Teachers in a Monolingual System: Professional Identities, Skills and Knowledge', in P. Van Avermaet, S. Slembrouck, K. Van Gorp, S. Sierens, and K. Maryns, (eds), *The Multilingual Edge of Education*, 211–33, London: Palgrave Macmillan.

Cook, S.E. (2009), 'Street Setswana vs. School Setswana: Language Policies and the Forging of Identities in South African Classrooms', in J.A. Kleifgen and G.C. Bond (eds), *The Language of Africa and the Diaspora: Educating for Language Awareness*, 96–116, Bristol: Multilingual Matters.

Costandius, E., Nell, I., Alexander, N., Mckay, M., Blackie, M., Malgas, R., and Setati, E. (2018), '#FeesMustFall and Decolonising the Curriculum: Stellenbosch University Students' and Lecturers' Reactions', *South African Journal of Higher Education*, 32 (2): 65–85.

Crystal, D. (1994), 'What is Standard English?' Available online: https://davidcrystal .com/Files/BooksAndArticles/-5308.pdf (accessed 24 December 2021).

Crystal, D. (2013), 'World Englishes', *British Council Serbia*. Available online: https:// www.youtube.com/watch?v=2_q9b9YqGRY (accessed 24 December 2021).

Daniels, B., Sterzuk, A., Turner, P., Cook, W., Thunder, D., and Morin, R. (2022), "ē-ka-pimohteyāhk nīkānehk ōte nīkān: nēhiyawēwin (Cree Language) Revitalization and Indigenous Knowledge (Re)generation', in K. Heugh, C. Stroud, K. Taylor-Leech, and P. De Costa. (eds), *A Sociolinguistics of the South*, 199–214, New York and London: Routledge.

Darvin, R. (2019), 'Creativity and Criticality: Reimagining Narratives Through Translanguaging and Transmediation', *Applied Linguistics Review*, 2019: 1–26.

Darvin, R. and Norton, B. (2017), 'Language, Identity, and Investment in the Twenty-First Century', in T.L McCarty and S. May (eds), *Language Policy and Political Issues in Education, Encyclopedia of Language and Education*, 1–15, Cham: Springer International Publishing.

Deleuze, G. (1994), *Difference and Repetition*, New York: Columbia University Press.

De Souza, L.M.T.M. (2019), 'Decolonial Pedagogies, Multilingualism and Literacies', *Multilingual Margins*, 6 (1): 9–13.

Deumert, A. (2010), 'Tracking the Demographics of (Urban) Language Shift–An Analysis of South African Census Data', *Journal of Multilingual and Multicultural Development*, 31 (1): 13–35.

Deumert, A. (2018), 'Tsotsitaal Online- the Creativity of Tradition', in C. Cutler and U. Røyneland (eds), *Analyzing Multilingual Youth Practices in Computer Mediated Communication (CMC)*, 109–26, Cambridge: Cambridge University Press, doi:10.1017/9781316135570.007.

DiAngelo, R. (2018), *White Fragility: Why it's so Hard for White People to Talk About Racism*, Great Britain: Allen Lane.

Dixon, K. and Mendelowitz, B. (2016), 'Giving Voice to the Citizen Scholar: Generating Critical Thinking by Combining Traditional and Non-Traditional Genres in a First-

Year English Course', in J. Arvanitakis and D. Hornsby (eds), *Universities, Citizen Scholars and the Future of Higher Education*, 85–101, London: Palgrave Macmillan.

Dube, B. (2017), 'Afrikaans Must Fall and English Must Rise – Ironies and Contradictions in Protests by South African University Students', *Africa Insight*, 47 (2): 13–27.

Dyers, C. and Antia, B.E. (2019), 'Multilingual and Multimodal Mediation in One University Module: The People and Processes Involved', *Southern African Linguistics and Applied Language Studies*, 37 (1): 62–76.

ELTIC (1997), *Multilingual Learning: Working in multilingual classrooms, Johannesburg*: Maskew Miller Longman.

Enciso, P. (2017), 'Stories Lost and Found: Mobilizing Imagination in Literacy Research and Practice', *Literacy Research: Theory, Method and Practice*, 66: 29–52.

Erasmus, Z. (2017), *Race Otherwise: Forging a New Humanism for South Africa*, Johannesburg: Wits University Press.

Fairclough, N. (ed.), (1992), *Critical Language Awareness*, London and New York: Longman.

Falkof, N., and Van Staden, C., eds (2020), *Anxious Joburg: The Inner Lives of a Global South City*, Johannesburg: Wits University Press.

Ferreira, A. (2016), '"A Sort of Black and White Past and Present Thing": High School Students' Subject Positions on South Africa's Recent Past', *Race Ethnicity and Education*, 19 (6): 1247–61. doi:10.1080/13613324.2015.1095175.

Ferreira, A. and Mendelowitz, B. (2009a), 'Diversity, Double Talk and (mis)alignment: Pedagogic Moves for Epistemological Access', *Southern African Linguistics and Applied Language Studies*, 27 (1): 77–92.

Ferreira, A. and Mendelowitz, B. (2009b), 'Creating a Dynamic Contact Zone: An Undergraduate English Course as Multilingual Pedagogic Space', *English Teaching: Practice and Critique*, 8 (2): 54–79.

Fleisch, B. (2008), *Primary Education in Crisis: Why South African Schoolchildren Underachieve in Reading and Mathematics*, Cape Town: Juta and Company Ltd.

Foucault, M. (1981), 'The Order of Discourse', in R. Young (ed.), *Untying the Text: A Post-Structuralist Reader*, 48–78, Boston, London and Henley: Routledge & Kegan Paul.

Freire, P. (1972), *Pedagogy of the Oppressed*, Harmondsworth: Penguin.

Freire, P. (1996), *Pedagogy of the Oppressed*, 2nd edn, New York: Continuum.

Fricker, M. (2007), *Epistemic Injustice: Power and the Ethics of Knowing*, Oxford: Oxford University Press.

Fricker, M. (2017), 'Evolving Concepts of Epistemic Injustice', in I.J. Kidd, J. Medina, and G. Pohlhaus Jr (eds), *Routledge Handbook of Epistemic Injustice*, 53–60, London and New York: Routledge.

García, O. and Wei, L. (2014), *Translanguaging: Language, Bilingualism and Education*, London: Palgrave Pivot.

Gender Links for Equality and Justice (2015), 'Policy Brief: Gender Links' Theory of Change', Johannesburg. Available online: https://genderlinks.org.za/wp-content/uploads/2016/03/21226_gltoc_2015.pdf (accessed 24 December 2021).

Gill, S. (2014a), 'Mapping the Field of Critical Narrative', in I. Goodson and S. Gill, *Critical Narrative as Pedagogy*, 13–37, London/New York: Bloomsbury.

Gill, S. (2014b), 'Critical Narrative as Pedagogy', in I. Goodson and S. Gill, *Critical Narrative as Pedagogy*, 67–99, London/New York: Bloomsbury.

Gillespie, K. and Naidoo, L.A. (2019), 'Between the Cold War and the Fire: The Student Movement, Antiassimilation, and the Question of the Future in South Africa', *South Atlantic Quarterly*, 118 (1): 226–39.

Glaser, C. (2000), *Bo-Tsotsis: The Youth Gangs of Soweto, 1935–1976*, Oxford and Cape Town: Heinemann.

Godsell, G. and Chikane, R. (2016), 'The Roots of the Revolution', in S. Booysen, G. Godsell, R. Chikane, S. Mpofu-Walsh, O. Ntshingila, and R. Lepere (eds), *Fees Must Fall: Student Revolt, Decolonisation and Governance in South Africa*, 54–73, Johannesburg: Wits University Press.

Golden, J. (1996), 'Critical Imagination: Serious Play with Narrative and Gender', *Gender and Education*, 8 (3): 323–36.

Goodson, I. and Gill, S. (2014), *Critical Narrative as Pedagogy*, London/New York: Bloomsbury.

Grainger, T., Goouch, K., and Lambirth, A. (2005), *Creativity and Writing: Developing Voice and Verve in the Classroom*, London and New York: Routledge.

Green, B. and Reid, J.A. (2008), 'Method (s) in Our Madness? Poststructuralism, Pedagogy and Teacher Education', in A. Phelan and J. Sumsion (eds), *Provoking Absences: Critical Readings in Teacher Education*, 17–31, Rotterdam: Sense Publishers.

Greene, M. (1995), *Releasing the Imagination: Essays on Education, the Arts and Social Change*, San Francisco: Jossey-Bass.

Grosfoguel, R. (2007), 'The Epistemic Decolonial Turn', *Cultural Studies*, 21 (2–3): 211–23.

Guzula, X., McKinney, C., and Tyler, R. (2016), 'Languaging-For-Learning: Legitimising Translanguaging and Enabling Multimodal Practices in Third Spaces', *Southern African Linguistics and Applied Language Studies*, 34 (3): 211–26.

Habib, A. (2019), *Rebels and Rage: Reflecting on #FeesMustFall*, Johannesburg and Cape Town: Jonathan Ball.

Hampl, P. (1999), *I Could Tell You Stories*, New York and London: W.W. Norton & Company.

Harris, R. (2020), 'This is the Casual Racism I Face at My Elite High School', *New York Times*, 24 September: 4.

Heugh, K. (2018), 'Conclusion: Multilingualism, Diversity and Equitable Learning: Towards Crossing the "Abyss"', in P. Van Avermaet, S. Slembrouck, K. Van Gorp, S. Sierens, and K. Marijns (eds), *The Multilingual Edge of Education*, 341–67, London: Palgrave Macmillan.

Heugh, K. and Stroud, C. (2019), 'Multilingualism in South African Education: A Southern Perspective', in R. Hickey (ed.), *English in Multilingual South Africa: The*

Linguistics of Contact and Change. Studies in English Language, 216–38, Cambridge: Cambridge University Press.

Heugh, K., Stroud, C., Taylor-Leech, K., and De Costa, P. (eds). (2022), *A Sociolinguistics of the South*, New York and London: Routledge.

Hibbert, L. (2016), *The Linguistic Landscape of Post-Apartheid South Africa*, Bristol: Multilingual Matters.

Higgins, C. (2009), *English as a Local Language*, Bristol: Multilingual Matters.

Horner, K. and Dailey-O'Cain, J., eds (2019), *Multilingualism, (Im)mobilities and Spaces of Belonging*, Bristol: Multilingual Matters.

Hoss, J. and Blokland, L. (2018), 'Sugar Daddies and Blessers: A Contextual Study of Transactional Sexual Interactions among Young Girls and Older Men', *Journal of Community & Applied Social Psychology*, 28 (5): 306–17.

Huberman, M. (1995), 'Working with Life-History Narratives', in H. McEwan and K. Egan (eds), *Narrative in Teaching, Learning, and Research*, 127–65, New York: Teachers College Press.

Hurst, E. (2009), 'Tsotsitaal, Global Culture and Local Style: Identity and Recontextualisation in Twenty-First Century South African Townships', *Social Dynamics*, 35(2): 44–257.

Janks, H. (2002), 'Critical Literacy: Beyond Reason', *Australian Educational Researcher*, 29 (1): 7–27.

Janks, H. (2004), 'The Access Paradox', *Literacy Learning: The Middle Years/English in Australia*, 12 (1): 33–42.

Janks, H. and Ivanic, R. (1992), 'CLA and Emancipatory Discourse', in N. Fairclough (ed.), *Critical Language Awareness*, 305–31, London and New York: Longman.

Jansen, J. (2017), *As by Fire: The End of the South African University*, Cape Town: Tafelberg.

Jeyifo, B. (2020), 'English is an African Language–Ka Dupe!: For and Against Ngũgĩ', in E. Fischer-Lichte, T. Jost, and S. Jain (eds), *Theatrical Speech Acts: Performing Language*, 31–47, Oxon and New York: Routledge.

Johnson, E. and Vasudevan, L. (2014), 'Looking and Listening for Critical Literacy', in J.Z. Pandya and J. Avila (eds), *Moving Critical Literacy Forward: A New Look at Praxis Across Contexts*, 98–112, New York and London: Routledge.

Johnston, N. (2006), 'A Cocktail of Cultures', *Mail & Guardian*, 5 January: 20–1.

Kamwangamalu, N.M. (2003a), 'Social Change and Language Shift: South Africa', *Annual Review of Applied Linguistics*, 23: 225–42.

Kamwangamalu, N.M. (2003b), 'When 2+ 9= 1: English and the Politics of Language Planning in a Multilingual Society', *The Politics of English as a World Language: New Horizons in Postcolonial Cultural Studies*, 7: 235.

Kamwangamalu, N.M. (2019), 'English as a Naturalized African Language', *World Englishes*, 38 (1–2): 114–27.

Kaschula, R.H. (2022), *Languages, Identities and Intercultural Communication in South Africa and Beyond*, London and New York: Routledge.

Kaschula, R.H. and Anthonissen, C. (1995), *Communicating Across Cultures in South Africa: Toward a Critical Language Awareness*, Johannesburg: Hodder & Stoughton and Wits University Press.

Kearney, R. (1988), *The Wake of Imagination*, London: Hutchinson.

Kostopoulos, C. (2016), 'South Africa's EFF: Excellent Politics of Props and Imagination', *The Conversation Africa*, 2 June, https://theconversation.com/south-africas-eff -excellent-politics-of-props-and-imagination-59918 (accessed 5 June 2016).

Kumalo, S.H. and Gama, L. (2018), 'Interrogating Conceptions of Man-Hood, Sexuality and Cultural Identity', *Image & Text*, 32: 1–19.

Ladson-Billings, G. (1995), 'Towards a Theory of Culturally Relevant Pedagogy', *American Educational Research Journal*, 32 (3): 465–91.

Langa, M., Ndelu, S., Edwin, Y., and Vilakazi, M. (2017), *# Hashtag: An Analysis of the #FeesMustFall Movement at South African Universities*, Johannesburg: Centre for the Study of Violence and Reconciliation.

Leclerc-Madlala, S. (2003), 'Transactional Sex and the Pursuit of Modernity', *Social Dynamics*, 29 (2): 213–33.

Leibowitz, B. (2017), 'The Significance of SOTL in the South', *Scholarship of Teaching and Learning in the South*, 1 (1): 1–3.

Leibowitz, B. and Bozalek, V. (2018), 'Towards a Slow Scholarship of Teaching and Learning in the South', *Teaching in Higher Education*, 23 (8): 981–94.

Lewis, C. (2014), 'Affective and Global Ecologies: New Directions for Critical Literacy', in J.Z. Pandya and J. Avila (eds), *Moving Critical Literacies Forward: A New Look at Praxis Across Contexts*, 187–93, New York and London: Routledge.

Little, D. and Kirwan, D. (2020), *Engaging with Linguistic Diversity: A Study of Educational Inclusion in an Irish Primary School*, London: Bloomsbury Publishing.

Long, W. (2021), *Nation on the Couch: Inside South Africa's Mind*, Cape Town: Melinda Ferguson Books.

Looker, P. (2018), 'Contextualising Contexts–Scholarship of Teaching and Learning and Cultural Difference', *Scholarship of Teaching and Learning in the South*, 2 (1): 112–28.

Luckett, K. (2016), 'Curriculum Contestation in a Post-Colonial Context: A View from the South', *Teaching in Higher Education*, 21 (4): 415–28.

Luckett, K. (2019), 'A Critical Self-Reflection on Theorising Educational Development as "Epistemological Access" to "Powerful Knowledge"', *Alternation*, 26 (2): 36–61.

Makalela, L. (2015), 'Moving out of Linguistic Boxes: The Effects of Translanguaging Strategies for Multilingual Classrooms', *Language and Education*, 29 (3): 200–17.

Makalela, L. (2017), 'Bilingualism in South Africa: Reconnecting with Ubuntu Translanguaging', in O. Garcia, A. Lin, and S. May (eds), *Bilingual and Multilingual Education*, 297–309, New York: Springer.

Makalela, L. (2018a). 'Our Academics are Intellectually Colonised: Multilanguaging and Fees Must Fall', *Southern African Linguistics and Applied Language Studies*, 36 (1): 1–11.

Makalela, L. (2018b), 'Teaching African Languages the Ubuntu Way: The Effects of Translanguaging Among Pre-Service Teachers in South Africa', in P. Van Avermaet, S. Slembrouck, K. Van Gorp, S. Sierens, and K. Maryns (eds), *The Multilingual Edge of Education*, 261–82, London: Palgrave Macmillan.

Makoni, S. and Pennycook, A. (2012), 'Disinventing Multilingualism: From Monological Multilingualism to Multilingual Francas', in M. Martin-Jones, A. Blackledge and A. Creese (eds), *The Routledge Handbook of Multilingualism*, 439–53, London and New York: Routledge.

Malabela, M. (2017), 'We Are Not Violent but Just Demanding Free Decolonized Education: University of the Witwatersrand', in M. Langa, S. Ndelu, Y. Edwin, and M. Vilakazi (eds), *# Hashtag: An Analysis of the #FeesMustFall Movement at South African Universities*, 132–47, Johannesburg and Cape Town: Centre for the Study of Violence and Reconciliation.

Maldonado-Torres, N. (2007), 'On the Coloniality of Being', *Cultural Studies*, 21 (2–3): 240–70.

Maldonado-Torres, N. (2017), 'Foreword', in C. Chinguno (ed.), *Rioting and Writing: Diaries of Wits Fallists*, 14, Johannesburg: Society, Work and Development Institute.

Maldonado-Torres, N. (2018), 'The Decolonial Turn', in J. Poblete (ed.), *New Approaches to Latin American Studies*, 111–27, London and New York: Routledge and Taylor & Francis.

Martin, F. and Pirbhai-Illich, F. (2016), 'Towards Decolonizing Teacher Education: Criticality, Relationality and Intercultural Understanding', *Journal of Intercultural Studies*, 37 (4): 355–72.

Matlwa, K. (2007), *Coconut*, Auckland Park: Jacana.

Mattes, R. (2012), 'The "Born Frees": The Prospects for Generational Change in Post-Apartheid South Africa', *Australian Journal of Political Science*, 47 (1): 133–53.

Mayaba, N.N., Ralarala, M.K., and Angu, P. (2018), 'Student Voice: Perspectives on Language and Critical Pedagogy in South African Higher Education', *Educational Research for Social Change*, 7 (1): 1–12.

Mayher, J.S. (1990), *Uncommon Sense: Theoretical Practice in Language Education*, Portsmouth: Boynton/Cook Publishers.

Mbembe, A. (2015), *Decolonizing Knowledge and the Question of the Archive*, Lecture. Available online: https://wiser.wits.ac.za/sites/default/files/private/Achille%20Mbembe%20-%20Decolonizing%20Knowledge%20and%20the%20Question%20of%20the%20Archive.pdf (accessed 24 December 2021).

Mbembe, A. and Nuttall, S. (2004), 'Writing the World from an African Metropolis', *Public Culture*, 16 (3): 347–72.

McEwan, H. and Egan, K., eds (1995), *Narrative in Teaching, Learning, and Research*, New York: Teachers College Press.

McKinney, C. (2007), 'If I Speak English, Does it Make me Less Black Anyway?' Race and English in South African Desegregated Schools', *English Academy Review*, 24 (2): 6–24.

McKinney, C. (2010), 'Schooling in Black and White: Assimilationist Discourses and Subversive Identity Performances in a Desegregated South African Girl's School', *Race Ethnicity and Education*, 13 (2): 191–207.

McKinney, C. (2017), *Language and Power in Post-Colonial Schooling: Ideologies in Practice*, New York and London: Routledge.

McKinney, C. (2018), 'Literacy in English: Literacies in Englishes', in P. Seargeant, A. Hewings, and S. Pihlaja (eds), *Routledge Handbook of English Language Studies*, 168–82, London and New York: Routledge.

McQuade, D. and Atwan,R., eds, (2000), *The Writers Presence: a pool of readings*, Boston/New York: Bedford/St Martin's.

Mendelowitz, B. (2017), 'Conceptualising and Enacting the Critical Imagination through a Critical Writing Pedagogy', *English Teaching: Practice and Critique*, 16 (2): 178–93.

Mendelowitz, B. and Davies, H. (2011), 'A Circle of Learning: The Impact of Narrative Multilingualism Approach on In-service Teachers' Literacy Pedagogies', *Reading & Writing-Journal of the Reading Association of South Africa*, 2 (1): 41–61.

Mendelowitz, B. and Dixon, K. (2016), 'Risky Writing: Working with a Heteroglossic Pedagogy to Deepen Preservice Teachers' Learning', *Perspectives in Education*, 34 (1): 120–34.

Mendelowitz, B. and Ferreira, A. (2007), 'Engaging Narratives: Using Language Biographies to Facilitate Student Learning', *Southern African Linguistics and Applied Language Studies*, 25 (4): 487–504.

Menezes de Sousa, (2021), 'Foreword: A Decolonial Project', in C. Stroud and Z. Bock (eds), *Language and Decoloniality in Higher Education: Reclaiming Voices from the South*, London, Bloomsbury Publishing.

Mesthrie, R. (2008), "'I've Been Speaking Tsotsitaal all my Life Without Knowing it": Towards A Unified Account of Tsotsitaal in South Africa', in M. Meyerhof and N. Nagy (eds), *Social Lives in Language-Sociolinguistics and Multilingual Speech Communities: Celebrating the Work of Gillian Sankoff*, 95–109, Amsterdam: John Benjamins.

Mgqwashu, E.M. (2019), 'Education for Public Good in the Age of Coloniality: Implications for Pedagogy', *Journal of Decolonising Disciplines*, 1 (1): 64–81.

Mignolo, W.D. (2007a), 'Delinking: The Rhetoric of Modernity, the Logic of Coloniality and the Grammar of De-Coloniality', *Cultural Studies*, 21 (2–3): 449–514.

Mignolo, W.D. (2007b), 'Epistemic Disobedience': The De-Colonial Option and the Meaning of Identity in Politics', *Gragoatá*, 12 (22): 11–41.

Mignolo, W.D. (2009), 'Epistemic Disobedience, Independent Thought and Decolonial Freedom', *Theory, Culture & Society*, 26 (7–8): 159–81.

Milani, T. (2019), 'Southern Perspectives on Race/Gender/Sexuality: Undisciplined Applied Linguistics', *Cadernos Discursivos*, 1 (1): 8–28.

Misson, R. and Morgan, W. (2006), *Critical Literacy and the Aesthetic*, Illinois: National Council of Teachers of English.

Moll, I. (2004), 'Curriculum Responsiveness: The Anatomy of a Concept', in H. Griesel (ed.), *Curriculum Responsiveness in Higher Education*, 1–19, Pretoria: South African Universities Vice-Chancellors Association.

Moloi, N. (2017), 'Organising a Legal Team in Times of Protest', in C. Chinguno (ed.), *Rioting and Writing: Diaries of Wits Fallists*, 16–28, Johannesburg: Society, Work and Development Institute.

Moosavi, L. (2020), 'The Decolonial Bandwagon and the Dangers of Intellectual Decolonisation', *International Review of Sociology*, 30 (2): 332–54.

Moroke, M.S. (2015), 'Train Surfing: The Soweto Pastime', Masters Research Report, University of the Witwatersrand, Johannesburg.

Morreira, S., Luckett, K., Kumalo, S.H., and Ramgotra, M. (2020), 'Confronting the Complexities of Decolonising Curricula and Pedagogy in Higher Education', *Third World Thematics: A TWQ Journal*, 5 (1–2): 1–18.

Morrel, E. (2008), *Critical Literacy and Urban Youth: Pedagogies of Access, Dissent and Liberation*, New York: Routledge.

Moya, F.N. (2006), 'Ekasi is My Roots', *Mail & Guardian*, 5 January: 20.

Muzondiwa, T. (2019), 'Speaking for Justice, Working for Unity', Race Unity Speech Awards. Available online: https://www.youtube.com/watch?v=2jirm3x5waU (accessed 24 December 2021).

Nakata, M., Nakata, V., Keech, S., and Bolt, R. (2012), 'Decolonial Goals and Pedagogies for Indigenous Studies', *Decolonization: Indigeneity, Education & Society*, 1 (1): 120–40.

Naylor, G. (2000), 'A Question of Language', in D. McQuade and R. Atwan (eds), *The Writer's Presence: A Pool of Readings*, 474–7, Boston and New York: Bedford and St. Martin's.

Ndhlovu, F.J. (2016), 'A Decolonial Critique of Diaspora Identity Theories and the Notion of Superdiversity', *Diaspora Studies*, 9 (1): 28–40.

Ndhlovu, F.J. and Makalela, L. (2021), *Decolonising Multilingualism in Africa: Recentering Silenced Voices from the Global South*, Bristol: Multilingual Matters.

Ndlovu-Gatsheni, S.J. (2013), *Empire, Global Coloniality and African Subjectivity*, New York and Oxford: Berghahn Books.

Ngcaweni, W. and Ngcaweni, B. (2018), *We Are no Longer at Ease: The Struggle for #FeesMustFall*, Auckland Park: Jacana.

Ngumbela, X. (2021), 'Troubled Custom, Custom Trouble: Initiation Challenges in the Province of the Eastern Cape, South Africa', *African Journal of Gender, Society and Development*, 10 (1): 197–214.

Nielsen, V. (2021), 'In the Absence of Rhodes: Decolonizing South African Universities', *Ethnic and Racial Studies*, 44 (3): 396–414.

Noah, T. (2018), *Son of Patricia*, [Comedy Show], Netflix.

Norton, B. (1997), 'Language, Identity and the Ownership of English', *TESOL Quarterly*, 31 (3) Autumn: 409–29.

Norton, B. (2000), *Identity and Language Learning: Gender, Ethnicity and Educational Change*, Essex: Longman.

Nuttal, S. (2004), 'City Forms and Writing the "now" in South Africa', *Journal of Southern African Studies*, 30 (4): 743–8.

Nwadeyi, L. (2021), 'The Right to Re-Member Ourselves', *Mail & Guardian*, 4–10 June: 22.

Obama, B. (2007), *Dreams from My Father*, Edinburgh: Canongate.

Odendaal, R.T. (2019), 'Wits Imagined: An Investigation into Wits University's Public Roles and Responsibilities, 1922–1994', Masters diss., University of Cape Town, Cape Town.

Orlek, J. (1993), *Languages in South Africa*, Johannesburg: Hodder & Stoughton and Wits University Press.

Painter, D. (2015), 'Monolingualism, Not Afrikaans, Must Fall', *Litnet*, 2 December. Available online: http://www.litnet.co.za/monolingualism-not-afrikaans-must-fall (accessed December 2021).

Park, J. (2011), 'Ownership of English: Implications for Heritage, Identity, and our Future', Talk presented 31 March at Singapore National Library, Singapore.

Parmegiani, A. (2010), 'Reconceptualizing Language Ownership. A Case Study of Language Practices and Attitudes among Students at the University of KwaZulu-Natal', *Language Learning Journal*, 38 (3): 359–78.

Parmegiani, A. (2014), 'The (dis)ownership of English: Language and Identity Construction among Zulu Students at the University of KwaZulu-Natal', *International Journal of Bilingual Education and Bilingualism*, 17 (6): 683–94, doi:10.1080/13670050.2014.953775.

Pavlenko, A. and Blackledge, A. (2004), 'Introduction', in A. Pavlenko and A. Blackledge (eds), *Negotiation of Identities in Multilingual Contexts*, 1–28, Clevedon: Multilingual Matters.

Paxton, M. (2007), 'Students' Interim Literacies as a Dynamic Resource for Teaching and Transformation', *Southern African Linguistics and Applied Language Studies*, 25 (1): 45–55.

Peirce, B.N. (1995), 'Social Identity, Investment and Language Learning', *TESOL Quarterly*, 29 (1): 9–31.

Pennycook, A. and Makoni, S. (2020), *Innovations and Challenges in Applied Linguistics from the Global South*, Abingdon, Oxon and New York, NY: Routledge.

Petrus, T. and Isaacs-Martin, W. (2012), 'The Multiple Meanings of Coloured Identity in South Africa', *Africa Insight*, 42 (1): 87–102.

Posel, D. and Zeller, J. (2016), 'Language Shift or Increased Bilingualism in South Africa: Evidence from Census Data', *Journal of Multilingual and Multicultural Development*, 37 (4): 357–70.

Posel, D. and Zeller, J. (2019), 'Language Use and Language Shift in Post-Apartheid South Africa', in R. Hickley (ed), *English in Multilingual South Africa: The Linguistics of Contact and Change*, 288–309, Cambridge: Cambridge University Press.

Posel, D., Hunter, M., and Rudwick, S. (2020), 'Revisiting the Prevalence of English: Language Use Outside the Home in South Africa', *Journal of Multilingual and Multicultural Development*, 1–13, doi:10.1080/01434632.2020.1778707.

Pratt, M.L. (1991), 'Arts of the Contact Zone', *Profession*: 33–40.

Quijano, A. (2000), 'Coloniality of Power, Eurocentrism, and Latin America', *Nepantla: Views from South*, 1 (3): 533–80.

Quijano, A. (2007), 'Coloniality and Modernity/Rationality', *Cultural Studies*, 21 (2–3): 168–78.

Ramani, E. and Joseph, M. (2002), 'Breaking New Ground: Introducing an African Language as Medium of Instruction at the University of the North: New Developments and Research', *Perspectives in Education*, 20 (1): 233–40.

Ranganathan, M., Heise, L., MacPhail, C., Stockl, H., Silverwood, R.J., Kahn, K., Selin, A., Gómez-Olivé Watts, C., and Pettifor, A. (2018), '"It's Because I Like Things... It's a Status and he Buys me Airtime": Exploring the Role of Transactional Sex in Young Women's Consumption Patterns in Rural South Africa (Secondary Findings from HPTN 068)', *Reproductive Health*, 15 (102). doi:10.1186/s12978-018-0539-y.

Rodriguez, R. (1982), *The Hunger of Memory: The Education of Richard Rodriguez*, New York: Bantam Books.

Rolón-Dow, R. and Davison, A. (2021), 'Theorizing Racial Microaffirmations: A Critical Race/LatCrit Approach', *Race Ethnicity and Education*, 24 (2): 245–61.

Rosa, J. (2018), *Looking Like a Language, Sounding Like a Race*, New York: Oxford University Press.

Rowe, M. (2008), 'Micro-Affirmations and Micro-Inequities', *Journal of the International Ombudsman Association*, 1 (1): 45–48.

Rudwick, S. (2022), *The Ambiguity of English as a Lingua Franca: Politics of Language and Race in South Africa*, New York and London: Routledge.

Salo, E. (2003), 'Negotiating Gender and Personhood in the New South Africa', *Cultural Studies*, 6 (31): 345–65.

Santos, B. (2012), 'Public Sphere and Epistemologies of the South', *Africa Development*, 37 (1): 43–67.

Scaglione, S. and Caruana, S. (2018), 'Migration and Plurilingualism in Southern European Homes and Schools', in P. Van Avermaet, S. Slembrouck, K. Van Gorp, S. Sierens, and K. Maryns, (eds), *The Multilingual Edge of Education*, 139–64, London: Palgrave Macmillan.

Seilhamer, M.F. (2015), 'The Ownership of English in Taiwan', *World Englishes*, 34 (3): 370–88.

Shalem, Y. and Slonimsky, L. (2006), 'Towards Academic Depth: Managing the Gap', in *SAUVCA National Symposium on Curriculum Responsiveness*, Vol. 26, Johannesburg, March

Shell-Weiss, M. (2020), 'The Power of Narrative: A Practical Guide to Creating Decolonial, Community-Based Projects', in B. Chindila and T. Corrigan (eds), 35–54, IntechOpen. Available online: https://www.intechopen.com/chapters/65976 (accessed 24 December 2021).

Slonimsky, S. and Shalem, Y. (2006), 'Pedagogic Responsiveness for Academic Depth', *Journal of Education*, 40 (1): 35–58.

Soudien, C. (2004), 'Constituting the Class: An Analysis of the Process of "integration" in South African Schools', in L. Chisholm (ed.), *Changing Class: Education and Social Change in Post-Apartheid South Africa*, 89–114, Cape Town: HSRC Press.

Soudien, C (2021), *Narrative and Vygotsky: Changing Subjects*, Webinar, University of the Witwatersrand, Johannesburg.

Staller, K. (2007), 'Metalogue as Methodology: Inquiries into Conversations among Authors, Editors and Referees', *Qualitative Social Work*, 6 (2): 137–57.

Stevens, G. and Lockhat, R. (1997), '"Coca-Cola Kids"-Reflections on Black Adolescent Identity Development in Post-Apartheid South Africa', *South African Journal of Psychology*, 27 (4): 250–5.

Steyn, M. (2012), 'The Ignorance Contract: Recollections of Apartheid Childhoods and the Construction of Epistemologies of Ignorance', *Identities*, 19 (1): 8–25.

Strathern, A.J. and Stewart, P.J. (2011), 'Embodiment and Personhood', in F.E. Mascia-Lees (ed.), *A Companion to the Anthropology of the Body and Embodiment*, 338–402, Oxford: Wiley-Blackwell.

Stroud, C. (2015), 'Linguistic Citizenship as Utopia', *Multilingual Margins*, 2 (2): 20–37.

Stroud, C. (2018), 'Introduction', in L. Lim, C. Stroud, and L. Wee (eds), *The Multilingual Citizen: Towards a Politics of Language for Agency and Change*, 1–14, Bristol: Multilingual Matters.

TELIP (1998), *Organisational Skills Course*, Johannesburg: University of the Witwatersrand.

Thesen, L. (2014), 'Risk as Productive: Working with Dilemmas in the Writing of Research', in L. Thesen and L. Cooper (eds), *Risk in Academic Writing: Postgraduate Students, Their Teachers and the Making of Knowledge*, 1–26, Toronto: Multilingual Matters.

Tobin, K. and Roth, W.M. (2002), 'The Contradictions in Science Education Peer Review and Possibilities for Change', *Research in Science Education*, 32 (2): 269–80.

Tuck, E. and Yang, K.W. (2012), 'Decolonization is Not a Metaphor', *Decolonization: Indigeneity, Education & Society*, 1 (1): 1–40.

Tusini, N. (2016a), 'The 80s Kids: A Story of Collaboration as Disruption'. Available online: http://witsvuvuzela.com/wp-content/uploads/2016/08/Nolwazi-RF-final -draft.pdf?616031 (accessed 24 December 2021).

Tusini, N. (2016b), 'Language Matters', *City Press*, 21 August: 2–6.

UCT Rhodes Must Fall Mission Statement (2015), Cape Town, March. Available online: https://www.lse.ac.uk/sociology/assets/documents/events/UCT-Rhodes-Must-Fall -Statement.pdf.

University of the Witwatersrand (2003), *Admissions Policy*.

University of the Witwatersrand (2006), *Admissions Policy*.

Van Avermaet, P., Slembrouck, S., Van Gorp, K., Sierens, S., and Maryns, K. (eds), (2018), *The Multilingual Edge of Education*, London: Palgrave Macmillan.

Venter, M.A. (2011), 'Some Views of Xhosa Women Regarding the Initiation of Their Sons', *Koers*, 76 (3): 559–75.

Vice, S. (2017), 'Race, Luck, and the Moral Emotions', in P. Taylor, L. Martín Alcoff, and L. Anderson (eds), *The Routledge Companion to Philosophy of Race*, 446–60, New York: Routledge.

Vygotsky, L.S. (1997), *The Collected Works of L.S. Vygotsky. Vol III: Problems of the Theory and History of Psychology*, eds R.W. Rieber and J. Wollock, New York: Plenum Press.

Vygotsky, L.S. (2004), 'Imagination and Creativity in Childhood', *Journal of Russian and East European Psychology*, 42 (1): 7–97.

Walsh, C. (2020), 'Decolonial Learnings, Askings and Musings', *Postcolonial Studies*, 23 (4): 604–11.

wa Thiong'o, N. (1986), *Decolonising the Mind: The Politics of Language in African Literature*, Oxford: James Currey.

Weeden, C. (1987), *Feminist Practice and Poststructuralist Theory*, London: Blackwell.

Wolf, M. (2008), *Proust and the Squid: The Story and Science of the Reading Brain*, New York: Harper Collins.

Zamel, V. (1998), 'Questioning Academic Discourse', in V. Zamel and R. Spack (eds), *Negotiating Academic Literacies: Teaching and Learning across Languages and Cultures*, 187–98, London and New York: Routledge.

Zembylas, M. (2018), 'Affect, Race, and White Discomfort in Schooling: Decolonial Strategies for "Pedagogies of Discomfort"', *Ethics and Education*, 13 (1): 86–104.

Index

Milton Keynes UK
Ingram Content Group UK Ltd.
UKHW022112250124
436710UK00005B/264